PSYCHOLOGY AND EDUCATION FOR SPECIAL NEEDS

Psychology and Education for Special Needs

Recent Developments and Future Directions

Edited by
Ingrid Lunt and Brahm Norwich
with Ved Varma

Published by
Arena
Ashgate Publishing Limited
Gower House
Croft Road
Aldershot
Hants GU11 3HR
England

Ashgate Publishing Company
Old Post Road
Brookfield
Vermont 05036
USA

British Library Cataloguing in Publication Data

Psychology and Education for Special
Needs: Recent Developments and Future
Directions
   I. Lunt, Ingrid
   371.9

Library of Congress Catalog Card Number: 95-79270

ISBN 1 85742 306 2

Printed in Great Britain by Biddles Ltd, Guildford

Contents

vi   *Contents*

List of figures

List of tables

Acknowledgement

We would like to acknowledge the patience and support of Helen Jefferson-Brown who produced the manuscript and who was flexible, good-humoured and tolerant throughout the work.

Notes on contributors

Harry Daniels is a senior lecturer in the Department of Educational Psychology and Special Educational Needs at the Institute of Education, University of London, and was recently appointed to be Professor in the Education Department at Birmingham University.

Jennifer Evans is a lecturer in the Department of Policy Studies at the Institute of Education, University of London, and course tutor for the MA course in Educational Administration and Management.

Peter Evans was a senior lecturer at the Institute of Education until 1989, when he moved to the OECD in Paris to direct studies on children with special educational needs at the OECD Centre for Educational Research and Innovation (CERI).

Peter Farrell is a senior lecturer at the University of Manchester, where he is course director for the professional training course for educational psychologists.

Sheila Henderson is a reader in the Department of Educational Psychology and Special Educational Needs at the Institute of Education, University of London.

Geoff Lindsay is Principal Educational Psychologist for Sheffield Local Educational Authority and Professor Associate at the University of Sheffield.

Ingrid Lunt is a senior lecturer in the Department of Educational Psychology and Special Educational Needs at the Institute of Education, University of London, and course tutor for the professional training course for educational psychologists.

Peter Mittler is Professor of Special Educational Needs at the University of Manchester, where he is currently Dean of the School of Education.

Brahm Norwich, recently appointed to succeed Klaus Wedell as Professor of Special Needs Education, is currently the Chairperson of the Department of Educational Psychology and Special Educational Needs at the Institute of Education, University of London.

Margaret Peter was editor of the *British Journal of Special Education* from 1974 to 1994. She was editorial consultant to the National Curriculum Council in 1989–90, and is now a lay inspector for schools and contributes to *The Times Educational Supplement*.

Peter D. Pumfrey is Professor in the School of Education at Manchester University.

Ved Varma was an educational psychologist with the Institute of Education, University of London, Tavistock Clinic, London, and the London Boroughs of Richmond-upon-Thames and Brent.

Jannet A. Wright is responsible for continuing professional development at the National Hospital's College of Speech Sciences, now University College London Department of Human Communication Sciences.

1 Introduction

Ingrid Lunt and Brahm Norwich

Special needs education is currently undergoing the most significant changes since the implementation of the 1981 Education Act in 1983. The 1988 Education Reform Act and the 1993 Education Act and its Code of Practice (DfE & WD, 1994) have introduced fundamental changes in the way in which special educational provision is made and the context for the development of policy in this area. This changing context has fundamental implications for the place and role of psychology and psychologists in the system. Psychology and psychologists have traditionally held a dominant position in the field; psychological theories have underpinned many of the developments in the special needs area, and psychologists – both educational and clinical – have been at the forefront both of research and practice. This position has changed in recent years, as other disciplines and other professionals have increasingly contributed to developments in this field.

This book aims to provide a perspective on some of these developments over the past ten years and on some of the prospects for the future leading up to the year 2000 in the context of the national changes in the education system.

Klaus Wedell has been a leading light in the field of special educational needs (SENs) for the past twenty years. The book draws on many aspects of Klaus's work and contribution to the field of educational psychology and SENs. The contributors to the book have all worked with Klaus and have been inspired variously by him as colleague, tutor, supervisor, co-lobbyist and friend. His idealism, commitment and his intellectual and human qualities have consistently provided encouragement and inspiration to those who have worked with him. The contributors come from a range of fields and represent contact with different periods of Klaus's working life.

The book is organised in three parts. To an extent, these reflect three major

1

areas of development in Klaus's work in the field of educational psychology and special educational needs.

Part I, 'Provision for special needs', reflects some of Klaus's early concerns with identifying difficulties in children at an early stage and ensuring that appropriate provision is made. His early work both as an educational psychologist and as an educator of educational psychologists provided him with the opportunity to develop frameworks for early identification and special educational provision. Geoff Lindsay (Chapter 2) traces the history both of Klaus's interest in early identification and Geoff's own work in this field, which began with his training as an educational psychologist at Birmingham University with Klaus as tutor. Sheila Henderson (Chapter 3), Peter Pumfrey (Chapter 4) and Jannet Wright (Chapter 5) address some of the difficult issues raised in relation to provision for children with perceptuo-motor difficulties, with specific learning difficulties and with communication difficulties. These three areas of difficulty illustrate some of the tensions between making specialist intervention and modifying the generally available curriculum to meet individual needs.

Part II 'Teaching, assessment and support approaches', reflects Klaus's developing interest in the curriculum and ways in which this may be adapted to meet the needs of pupils with SEN, thus making the learning environment more positive, and helping such pupils to overcome some of their disadvantages. Central here is Klaus's commitment to the notion of 'compensatory interaction' and to the interactive nature of SENs. Many cohorts of educational psychologists who trained at the University of Birmingham while he was there owe Klaus appreciation for the model of curriculum-based assessment and intervention developed on the course. Judith Ireson and Peter Evans (Chapter 6) and Harry Daniels (Chapter 7) draw on a close collaboration with Klaus and his ideas in the area, and reflect some of the fundamental issues with which Klaus has grappled over the years in developing his strategy for investigation and intervention. In Chapter 8, Peter Farrell, another of Klaus's trainees from the University of Birmingham, looks at some aspects of the role of professional educational psychologists and speculates on recent changes and possible future developments.

The final part of the book, 'Policy, organisation and training', reflects Klaus's growing interest in the legislation for special needs and the influence that he has had in its implementation in a positive direction for pupils with SENs and the professionals supporting them. Klaus has played a very influential role in relation to the education legislation in this country, from his work following the 1981 Education Act to the conceptual and analytical work and lobbying on both the 1988 Education Reform Act and the 1993 Education Act and its Code of Practice (DfE & WD, 1994). In Chapter 9, Jennifer Evans draws on the work of the DES-funded evaluation of the 1981

Act of which Klaus was co-director. Brahm Norwich and Ingrid Lunt (Chapter 10) describe some of the developments among schools working together as 'clusters' and ways in which a collaborative mode may prevail in the current educational climate. In Chapter 11, Peter Evans describes some of the work of the OECD with which Klaus has been closely associated as consultant. As a fellow lobbyist, Margaret Peter (Chapter 12) has written about pressure groups, particularly in relation to special educational needs. In the final chapter in this section, Peter Mittler, a colleague of long standing and since undergraduate times, addresses the very important and fundamental area of training and professional development for teachers of children with special needs.

In the Conclusion, Chapter 14, Ingrid Lunt and Brahm Norwich have written an appreciation of Klaus's work and contribution and have attempted to trace some of the conceptual and professional threads and developments of Klaus's career. This chapter has provided an opportunity for a reflection on these developments and on the relationship of psychology with education and how special needs education reflects this.

The chapters in this book develop many of the themes central to the current debate and discussion in this field, and provide a perspective on current and future aspects of these issues. The introduction of the National Curriculum and its assessment arrangements through the 1988 Education Act has altered attitudes to teacher assessment and its practice in schools. This has affected the conceptualisation and practice of special educational professionals, including educational psychologists. Changes in the resourcing of pupils with SENs introduced by this legislation have led to questions concerning the identification of pupils and the appropriate and effective targeting of resources. The considerable expansion of special needs support services following the 1981 Education Act and the concomitant growth in expertise have resulted in developments in teacher training in this area, though it has been argued that these developments do not go far enough. Based on the White Paper *Choice and Diversity* (DfE, 1992), the recent education legislation has raised the potential of conflict for schools between competitive and collaborative tendencies, one aspect of which is developed in Chapter 10 on cluster groups of schools focusing on special educational needs. The Code of Practice (DfE & WD, 1994) of the 1993 Education Act provides a challenge for all professionals in the field and raises fundamental questions in the identification of children with SENs and the ways in which schools, to a large extent through the curriculum, make provision at an early stage in the identification process.

The national changes in the education system in the UK provide challenges and opportunities for progress in the special needs field. Progress since the Warnock Report (DES, 1978) has meant increased entitlement, choice and rights for pupils with SENs and their parents. Funding changes now require greater accountability and may permit more flexibility in the resourcing of special provision. Collaboration between the enormous number of groups with interests in the field – as exemplified during the passage of the legislation – has shown that the special needs lobby has power and influence. Nevertheless, recent changes in the context of national financial constraints in the education budget have also highlighted the vulnerability of pupils with SENs. It is our hope that this book will provide both some ideas and inspiration to support those interested in the field of SENs in their endeavours to ensure the best provision for the more vulnerable members of the school system.

References

Department for Education (DfE) (1992) *Choice and Diversity: A New Framework for Schools*, London: HMSO.

Department for Education & the Welsh Office (DfE & WO) (1994) *Code of Practice on the Identification and Assessment of Special Educational Needs*, London: HMSO.

Department of Education and Science (DES) (1978) *Special Educational Needs: Report of the Committee of Inquiry into the Education of Handicapped Children and Young People* (The Warnock Report), Cmnd 7212, London: HMSO.

Part I

Provision for special needs

2 Early identification of special educational needs

Geoff Lindsay

A constant theme in the education of children with special educational needs (SENs) is that of early identification. The argument is simple, and superficially persuasive. In order to help children with SENs we should identify their difficulties as soon as possible. By so doing, we shall then be in a position to provide intervention which will remedy the problem, or at least provide amelioration, or prevent the development of more serious difficulties.

Klaus Wedell became interested in this area through his work with children with cerebral palsy and as a practitioner educational psychologist. In the former case, the medical services had a history of screening neonates and babies in their early lives in order to identify significant disorders and developmental delays. With respect to the latter – like every other educational psychologist, I imagine – Klaus became aware of children who had difficulties which had not been recognised until a stage several years after early intervention might have been introduced for the child's benefit. For example, in the late 1960s and early 1970s it was quite common for children with significant problems with literacy not to be identified until at least the beginning of the junior phase of education (about 7 to 8 years of age).

Klaus Wedell made important contributions to the early work of educational screening in this country, to facilitate the early identification of educational difficulties. This commenced with his investigations of the perceptuo-motor disabilities of children with cerebral palsy (e.g. Wedell, 1960, 1964 and 1971). For example, in the 1960 paper, Klaus demonstrated that perceptual impairment is not a general concomitant of cerebral palsy but is mainly associated with bi-lateral and left-sided spasticity. As this work progressed, Klaus shifted his focus of interest from those children with clear evidence of brain damage – e.g. cerebral palsy – to the range of children who appeared to have some of the same characteristics, but in a milder form. For example, many children with cerebral palsy have difficulties in organising not only their motor functioning but also their perception. These children have problems in making sense of the information which is either coming into their consciousness from the outside world (e.g. through visual perception) or from their 'inside' world of proprioception.

In his book *Learning and Perceptuo-motor Disabilities in Children* (1973), Klaus Wedell gave an analysis of the components of the perception/decision-making/motor output sequence. In this he presented evidence for two important concerns. First, it is both possible and necessary to discriminate between the component elements of perceptuo-motor processes. Second, he demonstrated the importance of recognising the interaction between these processes. A weakness in one component might have an interactive influence on another element in the process. Also, and perhaps of greater importance, there was evidence for strengths in some areas supporting functioning in weaker aspects. In addition, there appeared to be variation among the children concerned: children with apparently similar problems tend to progress differentially.

In his 1971 paper, Klaus showed that, although many children with visual perceptual problems have difficulty with reading, many others do learn to read satisfactorily. While children scoring highly on 'readiness' tests tend subsequently to make good progress, the prediction for children who do badly is less reliable. These findings led to the proposal of the process which came to be known as 'compensatory interaction' (Wedell & Lindsay, 1980; Lindsay & Wedell, 1982). This issue will be considered in more detail later in this chapter.

Klaus Wedell's interest in the field of early identification was supportive of developments in the UK, including the work of Sheila Wolfendale, then in Croydon, who developed the Croydon Checklist (Wolfendale & Bryans, 1979), Lea Pearson, who co-authored the Bury Infant Check (Pearson & Quinn, 1986), and myself, who developed the Infant Rating Scale (Lindsay, 1981a). In 1975, he convened the influential Priorsfield Symposium in Birmingham, drawing together researchers from Europe, the USA and the UK (Wedell & Raybould, 1976).

But these initiatives were not concerned only with the development of instruments. In earlier research (Lindsay, 1974), I had been concerned to explore the technical qualities of a screening instrument which was being used in one large city. The evaluation revealed that the instrument (Tansley, 1973) had significant technical weaknesses. The sample size of the original development project had been small (93 children in total), inter-rater reliability was poor; there was no evidence for construct validity, and predictive validity was less impressive than either another test (the Bender-Gestalt) or a sample of handwriting.

As a result of this study, I was interested in exploring the model of early identification derived from the concept of compensatory interaction. This required examining more thoroughly the potential for the early identification of learning difficulties, both the use of standardised instruments and other approaches, particularly a system of teacher in-service training, leading to a system of monitoring all children's progress (Lindsay, 1979a). I developed the Infant Rating Scale (Lindsay, 1981a), which was subject to evaluative study (Lindsay, 1979b, 1981b). Subsequently, the model was taken up by the headteacher of a junior school, leading to the Junior Rating Scale (Abraham & Lindsay, 1990).

Approaches to screening

The early identification of developmental delays, disorders or special educational needs is not as simple a process as early workers had hoped. On the contrary, this field is fraught with conceptual and methodological issues which, unfortunately, are not always either recognised or addressed. For example, a number of local education authorities (LEAs) have wished to develop programmes of early identification. In many cases, this has been approached by drawing together expert professionals with the task of devising a suitable method. These professionals might include teachers, advisers (in the days when such educational personnel existed in reasonable numbers) and psychologists. However, the project is often limited to development, with little evaluative research. It is as though the professional views of those concerned should be enough. The resultant procedure may then be 'published' in-house as a technique for the LEA, rather than as a commercially-available method published by a recognised test publisher, open to peer review in the normal scientific manner.

However, as I have argued elsewhere (Lindsay, 1974, 1988), the technical quality of the procedures is important – just as much as if these were indeed tests published by recognised test publishers. Their purpose may be to identify difficulties and to lead to decisions on the future education of the children concerned. These are major decisions, and instruments of less than satisfactory quality can result in significant errors. In my review of instruments available at the time (Lindsay, 1979a), I expressed concern that the technical qualities of many instruments available as published tests left something to be desired. Therefore, the use of those 'home grown' instruments is of even more concern, as they frequently lacked information which allowed a proper evaluation.

Another difficulty that became apparent was the differential predictability of children at the extremes as opposed to the centre of a continuum. In essence, the scores of children performing well or very badly at, say, age 5 years on early identification instruments tend to have high and significant correlations with criterion measures (e.g. reading) at age 7 or 8 years. However, those children scoring in the borderline 'at risk' region tend to show low, non-significant correlations and hence more fluctuating developmental status relative to peers (e.g. Lindsay, 1979a). This finding has been replicated by Hagtvet (1993) in Norway. This poses a technical problem in the development of the instruments, as the use of correlation statistics on the sample as a whole masks this factor, but it also suggests an important aspect of differential predictability which should be addressed in any programme of early identification.

Baseline assessment

Interest in early identification of learning difficulties in the UK has changed over recent years, and in particular as a result of changes in legislation. Two major Acts of parliament have been influential in this respect, the 1988 Education Reform Act, and the 1993 Education Act. Before considering some examples of methods, I shall examine the educational political context.

The 1988 Education Reform Act

The Education Reform Act (ERA) has an impact on baseline assessment in two different ways, leading to interest in 'value added' measures and alternative educational measures to allocate the special needs element in the delegated schools budget formula. These will now be explored in detail.

One of the main intentions of the ERA was to increase schools' accountability. The government's method has been to introduce the publication of information on schools, in particular their assessment results and their rates of non-attendance. Consequently, we have seen the rise (and partial fall) of league tables, ranking schools on such measures. The government's intention was to publish not only GCSE and A-level results, but also the outcomes of National Curriculum assessments at the end of Key Stages.

This proposal caused much dissatisfaction among teachers in inner-city schools and others in circumstances of significant disadvantage. In particular, the teachers were concerned that many children came into school with developmental delay, and the children's progress would not be recognised if measures of attainment only were used. This concern led to interest in the measurement of children's attainments and abilities on entry to school, or *baseline assessment*. Thus, in this case, the aim is not to identify children's difficulties *per se*, in order to help plan for their development, but rather a second purpose is evident: to provide a baseline from which their progress may be measured. Lindsay (1993) has highlighted the need to distinguish level of attainment from rate of progress. This is essentially an educational rather than socio-political initiative and owes an allegiance to the effective schools movement. There has been much research investigating how schools, in particular those at secondary level, differ in the degree to which they 'make a difference' (e.g. Rutter et al., 1979).

A number of LEAs have attempted to introduce such schemes, but often this has been carried out in the same way as the introduction of screening programmes in the 1970s, without systematic evaluation of the instruments' technical qualities and educational usefulness. An example of such an initiative at school entry which has had evaluation built into its development concerns the reworking of the Infant Rating Scale (IRS). In order to bring this up to date, following the introduction of the National Curriculum, a new scale was developed, using the same approach as for the IRS. The expertise of experienced educationists was drawn upon, and an evaluative study was conducted to examine the scale's technical qualities. The original intention was to develop a replacement for the IRS, and therefore that the scale should be used as an instrument by the teacher to assist the children's development by identifying difficulties and needs. However, at the beginning of this development it became clear that there was a need to attempt to add the purpose of setting a baseline of attainment at 5 years against which the infant school might evaluate its influence. This has led to the Infant Index (Desforges & Lindsay, 1995), discussed on pages 13–14.

More recently, a third purpose for baseline assessment has come to the fore. This also derives from the ERA, but a different section. Under the 1988 Act, the majority of finance available to LEAs for the running of schools is delegated to the control of governing bodies. This procedure is termed Local Management of Schools (LMS). Under present regulations, at least 85 per cent of the potential schools budget determined by the LEA must be delegated. Control over some services or tasks must remain with the LEA (e.g. the funding and management of the psychological service). This finance must be delegated by a common formula which is transparent and equitable, within certain parameters.

The main component of this formula is pupil numbers, as the government's intention was to reward financially those schools which attracted extra pupils – the assumption being that these were 'better' schools, or at least the parents would think so. However, the regulations also allowed the LEA to have other budget lines making up the formula, and the majority, if not all, of LEA formulae for delegating finance to schools included a heading of 'SEN', usually determined by the proxy measure, eligibility for free school meals. This is a factor reflecting social disadvantage which research has shown to be highly correlated with SEN in general, especially learning difficulties and emotional and behaviour difficulties (e.g.

Essen & Wedge, 1982).

However, LEAs and schools have become concerned about the use of such proxy measures, and many have sought to change to educational measures to determine the funding for SEN. This is an important issue, not only in terms of the educational rationale but also because the amounts of money involved may be significant to some schools. A number of LEAs have introduced assessments of pupils, for example at Year 3 and Year 7 – at entry to junior and secondary schools (or Key Stages 2 and 3). However, what should be done to determine the formula for Key Stage 1, at infant school entry? Group testing of children, as at the ages of 7 and 11 years, is not acceptable or practical. Why not use the baseline assessment?

Thus we see a third rationale for the use of baseline assessment. What started out as a development of earlier attempts to identify children's difficulties at an early stage has been changed (subverted?) into methods of measuring 'value added' or of allocating finance. Further, such methods may also be used in the future to provide the basis for the allocation of the SEN element of the schools' budgets under the LMS scheme. There are two issues that present themselves. First, is this mixture of purposes helpful, or will there be a tendency to lose sight of the original purpose, namely to identify individual children's patterns of development in order to provide appropriate teaching? Second, do the measures have the technical quality to allow safe judgements to be made? This is an important, though often neglected concern in itself, but perhaps is of even more importance when there are various purposes, each of which may make slightly different demands on the qualities of the instrument.

The 1993 Education Act and Code of Practice

The 1993 Education Act, and in particular the Code of Practice (DfE & WO, 1994) have provided a further impetus both to early identification and the approach and direction it might take. Under the Code, all schools are required to have in place systems for the identification of SEN, together with monitoring and review processes. A five-stage process of identification and assessment is proposed, based upon the belief that about 20 per cent of children nationally will have SEN at some stage of their school careers, with about 2 per cent having long-term and complex needs. This legislation has put a responsibility on schools to ensure that they have appropriate systems in place. In the present context, the important issue is that such processes must commence in some form from school entry.

Thus, although there is no national framework of the kind provided by end-of-Key Stage assessments, the Code does provide an obligation to act, and some guidance in the form of the criteria for SEN and provision. It is for schools to develop their own systems, although LEAs may help to set up common approaches in their areas. Therefore, the Code has provided a new impetus to early identification for the purposes of helping individual children, rather than the other purposes that have arisen out of the 1988 Education Act. Methods of early identification are now becoming of renewed interest to teachers. It will be important, therefore, that the approaches used are sound.

Examples of initiatives in early identification

Wolfendale (1993) and Blatchford and Cline (1992) have provided useful summaries of a number of examples of baseline assessment approaches. For example, Wolfendale describes several methods categorised by approach, namely Teacher Scoring/Rating; Teacher Descriptions; Child Self-assessment; Child Tasks; Parent Descriptions and LEA–National Curriculum Link. In fact, there is some degree of overlap between the categories, but the typology is useful. In this section, I shall give examples of three more recent initiatives which have different aspects of interest.

Infant Index

The Infant Index (Desforges & Lindsay, 1995) was mentioned above in the context of one LEA's response to the demands of the 1988 Education Reform Act. Originally it was designed to help teachers produce a profile of their 5-year-olds, for the purpose of identifying SEN in particular, but also to provide a baseline measure against which the children's progress, and hence the school's effectiveness, might be evaluated.

The first stage in its development was to seek the views of a number of experienced reception class teachers, who were asked: 'What ten things do you expect a child to be able to do at school entry in order to be able to reach National Curriculum Level 2 at the age of 7?' No further guidance was given, and a range of responses was expected. The responses were grouped and matched against National Curriculum attainment targets where appropriate. For example, many items related to language skills; others related to behavioural development. A total of 16 items was drawn up, for each of which three levels were produced. For example, the three levels of writing are:

a   can write own name
b   uses pictures or symbols or isolated words or phrases to communicate meaning
c   produces a short piece of written prose.

The items are arranged into four subscales, for ease of presentation:

- Language and Literacy Skills
- Mathematical Skills
- Social Behaviour
- Independent Learning

A pilot study of 16 schools led to some amendments to the content, including the reduction of items to 15. The revised Infant Index was then trialled on 25 per cent samples of two cohorts of children at school entry, in the September and January intakes respectively. The properties of the scale were examined – in particular the coherence of its structure – through factor analysis. This suggests a two-factor solution, namely Basic Skills (comprising the Language and Literacy Skills and Mathematical Skills subtests) and Behaviour (comprising the Social Behaviour and Independent Learning subscales). These are currently called Composite Scores. Hence the Infant Index can provide Item, Composite and Total Scores. These different types of score allow comparisons of a child's strengths and weaknesses, comparisons between children and comparisons between schools.

A further series of minor amendments have now been executed, and the final standardisation has been carried out on the September 1994 intake. Reliability studies are currently in progress. Predictive validity studies were to have used National Curriculum Key Stage 1 assessments, but have been postponed owing to the teachers' industrial action, refusing to carry out the assessment process, and doubts about the technical qualities of such assessments.

Dyslexia Early Screening Test

The interest in specific learning difficulties continues at the high level it attained ten or twenty years ago. Although the debate is now more measured and without the heat of the past (e.g. Pumfrey & Reason, 1991) there is still much controversy, not about the existence of children with significant difficulties in developing functional literacy but about the degree to which such children form distinct groups, of dyslexics and non-dyslexics (see Stanovich, 1994 for a recent review and presentation of a particular position).

Against this background, Nicolson and Fawcett have developed the Dyslexia Early Screening Test (DEST) (1994a) and the Dyslexia Screening Test (DST) (1994b), informed by the earlier research on the cognitive characteristics of dyslexics. On the basis of a series of interesting experiments where dyslexics and controls were asked to carry out single and joint processing tasks, they found that the dyslexics were particularly impaired on the latter. Nicolson and Fawcett (1990) argued that these experiments provide support for the existence of a disability which is more fundamental than the language-processing problems which are now generally considered to be the essential characteristics of dyslexics. If this is the case, they argued, it might be possible to identify dyslexics before the stage when reading is developing, with the benefits of early intervention being made available.

They have produced a computer version of the DEST (Fawcett et al., 1993) and are now trialling a prototype pencil and paper version. At the present time, they have data on 180 5-to-6-year-old children, as part of a development study (Fawcett, personal communication). The DEST comprises 11 varied tests. Assessment of motor organisation includes reaction time, bead-threading and postural stability. Language tests include rapid naming, nonsense passage reading, phonemic segmentation, and a 'one minute reading test'.

Early results from the research are considered by the authors to be encouraging (Fawcett & Nicolson, 1994), but it is not yet possible to evaluate the effectiveness of the instrument until the current fieldwork is available for analysis. There are two main questions which arise with regard to the DEST. First, does it show appropriate technical qualities of validity and reliability, as a means of identifying those children who would, without special help, show significant literacy difficulties at 7 or 8 years? Second, does the DEST discriminate successfully between those children termed dyslexic and others with difficulties with literacy?

Middle Infant Screening Test (MIST)

The Middle Infant Screening Test (Hannavy, 1993) is a recent example of an approach which focuses on face validity and educational connectedness, rather than technical validity. The test is designed to be administered to children in their fifth term in school (a minimum age of 5 years 8 months is recommended). It is administered to groups of up to 20 children by the teacher and one other adult. The aims of the MIST are:

- to give a profile of class performance
- to screen out children who are in the lowest 20 to 25 per cent of their peer group in reading and writing
- to pinpoint significant difficulties and confusions which are contributing to poor reading and writing
- to yield information on which to base a follow-up programme.

The MIST comprises six subtests which have recognised links with literacy development: Listening Skills, Letter Sounds, Written Vocabulary,

Three-phoneme Words, Sentence Dictation, and a further Listening Skills task. The results of the test are scored against cut-offs for each subtest. A child who scores below the cut-off on three or more tests is regarded as in need of extra help to develop literacy. The author has produced a programme of intervention, 'Forward Together', which accompanies the test.

The MIST has the benefit of a thoughtful application of known elements of literacy development, and the back-up of an associated intervention programme. On the other hand there are no data to support the technical quality of the instrument. For example, there is no evidence that failure on three tests is the correct level to determine implementing the programme. No standardisation has been carried out. It is suggested that, although the test is designed to identify 20 to 25 per cent of children, a school might vary the cut-off on the class data in order to keep to this proportion if their population characteristics produce a different result. Thus, in many respects, the MIST is similar to the many instruments which were being produced in the 1970s, based upon sound educational rationale, designed to identify children 'at risk' but with little or no concern for the need to examine the technical qualities of the assessment technique.

Comment

Blatchford and Cline (1992) suggest four purposes for the assessment of children on school entry at age 5:

- as a basis for measuring future progress
- gaining a picture of the new intake
- gaining a profile of the new entrant
- identifying children who may have difficulties in school.

In their paper, Blatchford and Cline evaluate six sample approaches against the following criteria: theoretical integrity, practical efficacy, equity and accountability. They make the point that, while there is now statutory assessment at the end of Key Stages 1 to 4, there is no such requirement at school entry, but some form of assessment happens anyway. In some cases, this may be the result of an LEA initiative, in others, the school takes the lead, or even an individual teacher. But there is no national framework or guidance.

The six methods evaluated by them vary in the extent to which they meet their criteria, and the same is true of the three techniques described here. It is still the case that instruments are being produced with little or no psychometric support. The instruments reported here are either clear about this (MIST) or are in development, but with the intention of providing appropriate information. However, there is still a potential concern, and the Canadian experience is interesting. Simner (1994) reports that the Canadian Psychological Society became concerned about advertisements for pre-school screening tests, where 75 per cent of the 24 advertisements analysed contained claims that were not supported by the available evidence.

Pearson and Lindsay (1986) suggested a checklist for early identification procedures, to aid practitioners in evaluating the methods available. Blatchford and Cline (1992) have also produced a helpful set of guidelines, linked to their four criteria. (See also the section 'Future developments' later in this chapter.)

Compensatory interaction

The concept of compensatory interaction proposed by Wedell (e.g. Wedell, 1978; Wedell & Lindsay, 1980) stressed that children's SEN should be considered as the result of the interaction between their own abilities and disabilities and the strengths and weaknesses in their environments. The model proposed is presented in Figure 2.1. Here it is presented as two

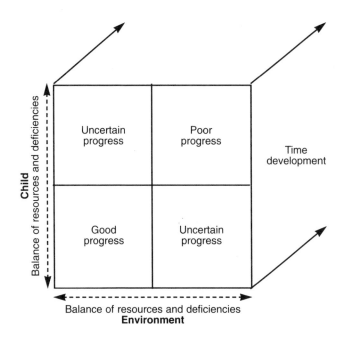

Figure 2.1   A model of compensatory interaction
Source: Wedell and Lindsay (1980)

dichotomous variables, but in fact it was always conceptualised as two continua. Note also the third dimension of time, as it was hypothesised that the nature of the interactive equation of the other two dimensions might well alter over time. This has indeed been shown, for example by the studies of children moving in and out of categories of risk associated with social disadvantage and the degree to which continuities and discontinuities are apparent in children's development (e.g. Rutter, 1989; but see also Luthar, 1993). Research on the development of children with specific and general reading difficulties has also indicated that, while some maintain their relative retardation, others move out of the 'problem' group as they move through primary school (e.g. Share et al., 1987).

This concept of compensatory interaction has also been used and developed further by Adelman in his projections concerning the field of learning disabilities into the next twenty-five years (Adelman, 1992). He points to the difficulties which have bedevilled this field with respect to definitions, notwithstanding Hammill's optimistic perspective (Hammill, 1990). Adelman refers to the trend towards a transactional perspective in understanding behaviour, and proposes a conceptualisation very similar to that of Wedell ten years earlier:

> The value of a broad transactional perspective, then, is that it shifts the focus from 'Is there a neurological deficit causing the learning problem?' to 'Are the causes to be found primarily in:
>
> - the individual (e.g. a neurological dysfunction; cognitive skill and/or strategy deficits; developmental and/or motivational differences);
> - the environment (e.g. the primary environment, such as poor instruction programs, parental neglect; secondary environment, such as racially isolated schools and neighbourhoods; tertiary environment, such as broad social, economic, political, and cultural differences); or
> - the reciprocal interplay of individual and environment?' (Adelman, 1992, p. 18)

Adelman stresses the benefits of differentiating types of learning problems along a causal continuum, as shown in Figure 2.2. Here the continuum ranges from children with Type I problems, where the cause is essentially located in the environment, through to Type III, where the cause is essentially intrinsic to the individual. In the middle, Type II are those problems which are a result of an interaction between environment and the individual.

In his paper, Adelman's interest was focused on problems of definition, whereas Wedell's interest went beyond that to questions of the nature of the

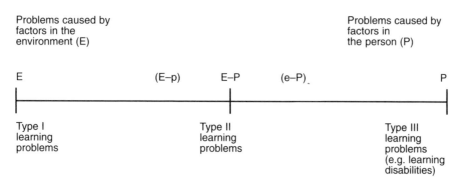

**Figure 2.2   A continuum of learning problems reflecting a trans-
actional view of the locus of primary instigating factors**
Source: Adelman (1992)

compensatory process. That is, rather than using this model to decide which children are really learning-disabled, the issue is one of identifying how any individual makes use of the resources available, and therefore what other resources are necessary in order for that child to progress.

Over the past ten years, the number and severity of such influences has been of interest to a number of researchers. For example, Hallahan (1992) has hypothesised that the increase in the numbers of children identified as learning-disabled in the USA is not an artefact but a true reflection of an increase in their number. To support this contention, Hammill argues for the influence of two factors. First, he suggests that:

> social/cultural changes puts the development of children's central nervous systems (CNSs) at increasing risk of disruption. Second, they have placed an increasing degree of psychosocial stress on children and their families – a stress that has deleterious consequences for children's social support systems. (Hallahan, 1992, p. 524)

Future developments

In this chapter, I have traced the issues concerning early identification since the 1960s. There have been many attempts to develop techniques which will identify children's learning difficulties and SENs at an early stage. Such initiatives are still in vogue, and the Dyslexia Early Screening Test described here is one of the most recent. There also continues to be interest in identifying children's SEN and other disabilities at the pre-school stage. It was apparent ten years ago (e.g. Lindsay, 1984) that some disorders, including phenylketonuria, had both a direct and significant effect on children's development and could be identified with a high degree of accuracy, using cost-effective, easily-administered techniques. However, the success of other screening methods – particularly those which attempted to identify the child before the difficulty arose, the 'at risk' stage – showed much less impressive results (Lindsay & Wedell, 1982; Wedell & Lindsay, 1980; Wedell & Raybould, 1976).

The present position is very similar. It will be interesting to see the results of the DEST evaluation, for example, but will it prove to be any more effective than the batteries developed in the 1960s and 1970s (e.g. DeHirsch et al., 1966)? Within medicine, there are now a large number of disorders which are subject to identification and surveillance, but still there are many where the methods available do not warrant large-scale population screening programmes. Interestingly, identification and surveillance are now being conceptualised by the British Paediatric Association's Working Party on Child Health Surveillance within a 'child health promotion', rather than a 'disability' framework (Hall, in press).

When considering future directions, it is also worth considering the criteria that should be met by a programme of early identification of SENs. If screening tests are to be used, they should be:

- simple, quick and easy to perform and interpret
- accurate – giving a true measure of the aspect of development being investigated
- reliable – including in-rater and test-retest reliability
- sensitive – producing a positive finding when the child has the difficulty
- specific – giving a negative finding when the child does not have the difficulty.

Guidance on early identification programmes (e.g. Hall, in press) also recommends – particularly for health promotion objectives – that, in addition, the programme as a whole should meet other criteria, including:

- the condition or developmental difficulty should be important
- a screening stage should link efficiently with an assessment stage
- the type of difficulty should have an agreed definition (a particular problem with dyslexia, for example)
- intervention at an early stage should have a positive influence on prognosis.

However, research has consistently shown that, for psycho-educational difficulties, such requirements are difficult to meet. The new guidance contained in the Code of Practice actually meets the major requirements of a programme of identification and intervention for children with SEN. It is based upon a model of continuous monitoring of children's progress, using teachers and parents at the early stages, gathering data systematically on the children. These data are considered by the professionals and parents and lead to intervention – which may in turn, for some children, lead to further assessment by specialists (e.g. educational psychologists, speech and language therapists). Screening tests are subordinated within this process, but in most cases the intention is not to categorise (e.g. 'dyslexic' or 'autistic') but rather to build up a functional analysis of the children's difficulties and needs.

Thus, looking to the future, we can see a continuation of two different strands of development in the early identification of SEN *per se*. Some researchers will continue to be interested in trying to identify at an early stage specific groups of children, developing assessment methods for this purpose. This work will be informed by the developments in fundamental psychological research. I venture to predict that the main areas of interest will be dyslexia, autism (e.g. Baron-Cohen et al., 1992) and attention deficit with hyperactivity disorder.

On the other hand, practitioners will primarily be addressing early identification within the framework of the 1988 and 1993 Education Acts, and the other influences of the educational legislation are likely to continue to interact with the primary purpose of any early identification procedure. The reasons for assessing children at school entry, for example, are now several, and it will be important for schools and LEAs not only to develop systems which are technically and ethically sound, robust and defensible but which are linked to clear purposes.

Finally, it is important to return to the major theoretical issue identified here – namely, compensatory interaction. This process is fundamental to the development of children and hence to our understanding of how methods of early identification might operate. In this respect, the Code of Practice may again be seen as a positive move, as it builds in a process of continuous monitoring. Thus we can see the importance of the ideas that Klaus Wedell has been promoting over the past thirty years.

Postscript

Klaus Wedell was my tutor at the University of Birmingham when I trained as an educational psychologist (1973–4). Although turned down at my first attempt, as I was considered 'too young', I was encouraged by Klaus to reapply the following year, when I was successful. The Birmingham team of Klaus, Brian Roberts and Ted Raybould was a formidable group, a very good example of a team of professionals with very different personalities, interests and strengths who knitted together to provide an excellent training experience. Klaus acted as my personal supervisor, and was undoubtedly the major formative influence on my development as an educational psychologist. He acted as the supervisor of my MEd, and then my PhD research project, the latter carried out when I was working in Sheffield as an educational psychologist. Both were concerned with early identification of learning difficulties. This support enabled me to undertake research in an LEA – an activity which is still regrettably rare.

Klaus was also instrumental in my involvement with the British Psychological Society (BPS), persuading me to be nominated for the committee of the Division of Educational and Child Psychology (DECP), of which he was then Chair. We worked together on the DECP survey of psychological services for children, and Klaus encouraged me to develop my work with the BPS further. This has been a major and most enjoyable element in my own professional career, and my regret is that Klaus was unable to continue with his own involvement. However, I was honoured to be the co-proposer, along with Ingrid Lunt, of Klaus for the title Honorary Fellow of the British Psychological Society.

Over recent years, I have been fortunate to work with Klaus on various steering groups and seminars. In addition, we have met to discuss matters concerned with SEN or the profession of educational psychology. As always, Klaus has been both committed and helpful.

I have no doubt that Klaus has been the foremost formative influence on my career, and hence, through me, on the careers of a generation of educational psychologists I trained at Sheffield, and the children, parents, teachers and other colleagues with whom I have worked. This chapter has been a small repayment for the debt I owe to Klaus.

References

Abraham, J. & Lindsay, G. (1990) *The Junior Rating Scale*, Windsor: NFER-Nelson.

Adelman, H.S. (1992) 'LD: The Next 25 years', *Journal of Learning Disabilities*, 25, pp.17–22.

Baron-Cohen, S., Allen, J. & Gillberg, C. (1992) 'Can autism be detected at 18 months? The needle, the haystack, and the CHAT', *British Journal of Psychiatry*, 161, pp.839–43.

Blatchford, P. & Cline, T. (1992) 'Baseline assessment for school entrants', *Research Papers in Education*, 7, pp.247–69.

DeHirsch, K., Jansky, J.J. & Langford, W.S. (1966) *Predicting Reading Failure*, New York: Harper and Row.

Department for Education & Welsh Office (DfE & WO) (1994) *Code of Practice on the*

Identification and Assessment of Pupils with Special Educational Needs, London: HMSO.

Desforges, M. & Lindsay, G. (1995) *The Infant Index*, London: Hodder and Stoughton.

Essen, J. & Wedge, P. (1982) *Continuities in Childhood Disadvantage*. London: Heinemann.

Fawcett, A. & Nicolson, R. (1994) 'Computer-based diagnosis of dyslexia', in C. Singleton (ed.) *Computers and Dyslexia*, Hull: Dyslexia Computer Resource Centre.

Fawcett, A., Pickering, S. & Nicolson, R. (1993) 'Development of the DEST test for the early screening for dyslexia', in S.F. Wright & R. Groner (eds), *Facets of Dyslexia and its Remediation*, Amsterdam: Elsevier Science Publishers.

Hagtvet, B.E. (1993) 'From oral to written language: A developmental and interventional perspective', *European Journal of Psychology of Education*, 8(3), pp.205–20.

Hall, D. (in press) *Health for all children* (3rd edn), Oxford: OUP.

Hallahan, D.P. (1992) 'Some thoughts on why the prevalence of learning disabilities has increased', *Journal of Learning Disabilities*, 25, pp.523–8.

Hammill, D.D. (1990) 'On defining learning disabilities: An emerging consensus', *Journal of Learning Disabilities*, 23(2), pp.78–84.

Hannavy, S. (1993) *Middle Infant Screening Test and Forward Together Guide*, Windsor: NFER-Nelson.

Lindsay, G. (1974) 'The identification of children with learning difficulties', unpublished MEd (Educational Psychology) dissertation, University of Birmingham.

Lindsay, G. (1979a) 'The early identification of learning difficulties and the monitoring of children's progress', unpublished PhD thesis, University of Birmingham.

Lindsay, G. (1979b) 'The Infant Rating Scale: Some evidence for its validity from a selected sample of children', *Occasional Papers of the Division of Educational and Child Psychology*, 3, pp.27–41.

Lindsay, G. (1981a) *The Infant Rating Scale*, Sevenoaks: Hodder & Stoughton.

Lindsay, G. (1981b) 'The Infant Rating Scale', *British Journal of Educational Psychology*, 50, pp.97–104.

Lindsay, G. (ed.) (1984) *Screening for Children with Special Needs*. London: Croom Helm.

Lindsay, G. (1988) 'Early identification of learning difficulties: Screening and beyond', *School Psychology International*, 9, pp.61–8.

Lindsay, G. (1993) 'Baseline assessment and special educational needs', in S. Wolfendale (ed.) *Assessing Special Educational Needs*, London: Cassell.

Lindsay, G. & Wedell, K. (1982) 'The early identification of educationally "at risk" children: Revisited', *Journal of Learning Disabilities*, 15, pp.212–17.

Luthar, S.S. (1993) 'Annotation: Methodological and conceptual issues in research on childhood resilience', *Journal of Child Psychology and Psychiatry*, 34, pp.441–53.

Nicholson, R. & Fawcett, A. (1990) 'Automaticity: A new framework for dyslexia research?' *Cognition*, 30, pp.159–82.

Nicolson, R. & Fawcett, A. (1994a) *The Dyslexia Early Screening Test: V2.0 Pilot*, University of Sheffield, Department of Psychology.

Nicolson, R. & Fawcett, A. (1994b) *The Dyslexia Screening Test: V1.0 Pilot*, University of Sheffield, Department of Psychology.

Pearson, L. & Lindsay, G. (1986) *Special Needs in the Primary School*, Windsor: NFER-Nelson.

Pearson, L. & Quinn, J. (1986) *The Bury Infant Check*, Windsor: NFER-Nelson.

Pumfrey, P. & Reason, R. (1991) *Specific Learning Difficulties/Dyslexia*. Windsor: NFER-Nelson.

Rutter, M. (1989) 'Pathways from childhood to adult life', *Journal of Child Psychology and Psychiatry*, 30, pp.23–52.

Rutter, M., Maughan, B., Mortimore, P. & Ouston, J. (1979) *Fifteen Thousand Hours*, London: Open Books.

Share, D.L., McGee, R., McKenzie, D., Williams, S. & Silva, P. (1987) 'Further evidence relating to the distinction between specific reading retardation and general reading backwardness', *British Journal of Developmental Psychology*, 5, pp.35–44.

Simner, M.L. (1994) 'Canada's reaction to misleading advertisements for pre-school screening tests', *School Psychology International*, 15, pp.277–86.

Stanovich, K. (1994) 'Annotation: Does dyslexia exist?', *Journal of Child Psychology and Psychiatry*, 35, pp.579–95.

Tansley, A. (1973) 'Special education treatment in infant schools: A 6 and a half year screening', *Educational Development Centre Review*, 14, pp.6–11.

Wedell, K. (1960) 'The visual perception of cerebral palsied children', *Journal of Child Psychology and Psychiatry*, 1, pp.217–27.

Wedell, K. (1964) 'Some aspects of perceptual-motor development in young children', in J. Loring (ed.) *Learning Problems of the Cerebral Palsied*. London: Spastics Society.

Wedell, K. (1971) 'Perceptuo-motor factors', in B. Keogh (ed.) 'Early Identification of Children with Potential Learning Problems', *Journal of Special Education*, 4, pp.223–31.

Wedell, K. (1973) *Learning and Perceptuo-motor Disabilities in Children*, London: John Wiley.

Wedell, K. (1978) 'Early identification and compensatory education' paper presented at the NATO International Conference on Learning Disorders, Ottawa.

Wedell, K. & Lindsay, G. (1980) 'Early identification procedures: What have we learned?' *Remedial Education*, 15, pp.130–5.

Wedell, K. & Raybould, E.C. (1976) 'The early identification of educationally "at risk" children', *Educational Review, Occasional Publications No. 6*. University of Birmingham.

Wolfendale, S. (1993) *Baseline Assessment: A Review of Current Practices, Issues and Strategies for Effective Implementation*, London: Trentham Books.

Wolfendale, S. & Bryans, T. (1979) *Identification of Learning Difficulties: A Model for Intervention*, London: National Association for Remedial Education.

3 Children with specific perceptuo-motor difficulties: Where do we stand now?

Sheila Henderson

A teacher affects eternity; he can never tell where his influence stops.
H.B. Adams (1838–1918)

I have listened to many extolling the virtues of linking psychological theory and educational practice, but no one has taught me more about how to achieve it than Klaus Wedell. My first direct experience of his boundless enthusiasm for this task was obtained in a pub in Oxford more than twenty years ago. On this occasion, we discussed the unexpected perceptuo-motor problems that can be found among children who appear physically normal, do not exhibit any classic neurological signs and are verbally gifted; we touched upon the idea that this kind of dissociation might have implications for a strict interpretation of Piaget's theory of cognitive development, but, equally important, we wondered how teachers could be led to an understanding of these difficulties and their implications for a child's progress in the classroom.

Many terms have been used to describe children who lack the motor competence necessary to cope with the demands of the classroom and, indeed, of everyday life. Some, such as 'physical awkwardness' or 'perceptuo-motor dysfunction', seem confined to a largely descriptive level. Others seem to carry us beyond mere description, implying the existence of a distinct clinical entity or cluster of entities, e.g. 'clumsy child syndrome', perhaps even embodying some general assumptions about the underlying nature of the dysfunction, e.g. 'dyspraxia'.

Over the years, a growing number of clinical and educational studies have allowed us to make progress in understanding the natural history and consequences of this 'syndrome' (a word cordially detested by Wedell for its categorical implications). These studies have not only contributed to the view that the postulation of a separable disorder of movement skill acquisition – requiring aetiological, diagnostic and remedial attention in its own right – is a fruitful enterprise but have also led to the formal endorsement of the syndrome in recent editions of the diagnostic manuals published by the World Health Organisation (WHO, 1992) and the American Psychiatric Association (APA, 1994). The entry in the WHO manual is headed 'Specific developmental disorder of motor function' and in the APA manual, 'Developmental Coordination Disorder' (DCD).

While recognition by official bodies such as the WHO helps to raise the profile of a particular developmental problem amongst professionals in both medicine and education, it does not help us to understand the possible causes of the difficulties these children experience. The question of what underlies the problem has been framed in different ways, but from a psychological viewpoint, the information-processing approach has served us well. With the publication of his book entitled *Learning and Perceptuo-motor Difficulties in Children* (1973), Klaus Wedell established himself not only as one of the first to illustrate how this kind of modelling could be put to good use in the investigation of perceptuo-motor difficulties in children but also one of the best illustrators of its practical value.

In this chapter, my attempt to summarise the progress that has been made in understanding and providing for children with (specific) perceptuo-motor difficulties is divided into two sections. In the first section, my focus is on the natural history of this 'syndrome' and its consequences. In the second section, attention turns to a different level of enquiry in which the processing deficits that might underlie inadequacies in the planning and execution of motor acts are of interest.

The natural history of Developmental Coordination Disorder

Until quite recently, the prognosis for children identified in their early years as being deficient in the acquisition of movement skills was assumed by most pediatricians to be benign. From this comfortable stance, it was easy to slide into a relaxed position in which inaction was the considered view. The widely-held belief that the child could be relied upon to 'grow out of' coordination difficulties conjures up the comforting image of a reliably autonomous recovery process, whereby those who have at any particular time fallen behind their peers in motor development are continuously being gathered back into the fold of normality.

From the safe shelter of the retrospective viewpoint, it is all too easy now to enquire how a few poorly-documented case histories in which recovery was reported could ever have sustained the weight of these assumptions, seeming to establish the reality of a process not only effortless and complete but with the inevitability required to justify a serene and universal prescription of non-intervention. However, in order to make progress on these difficult issues, two fundamental requirements had to be satisfied: a longitudinal methodology had to be adopted, in harness with the employment of standardised, norm-referenced tests (see Henderson, 1993 for a complete review of such studies).

In 1983, Knuckey and Gubbay published the first longitudinal study of children selected exclusively on the basis of their motor disability. They described an eight-year study of 24 'clumsy' children and age-matched controls, first seen between the ages of 8 and 12. At follow-up, the 'clumsy' group remained consistently less proficient on all of the motor tasks, but there did seem to be individual differences in the extent to which change had taken place. In order to explore this variation further, Knuckey and Gubbay made an arbitrary decision to divide the 'clumsy' group into three subgroups on the basis of the severity of their impairment at first testing. Perhaps not surprisingly, this analysis revealed that the children who had originally been the most 'clumsy' lagged furthest behind at follow-up, while others appeared to have 'recovered'. On the basis of these results, Knuckey and Gubbay took an optimistic view, suggesting that it is only the most severely 'clumsy' children who fail to catch up. However, this conclusion needs to be viewed with some caution. In addition to the arbitrary nature of the subdivision of the 'clumsy' group, half of Knuckey and Gubbay's sample was lost to follow-up. Moreover, it looked as though some of the test items employed were incapable of revealing differences between the groups because they were too easy.

In 1992, my colleagues and I reported the outcome of a ten-year follow-up of 17 'clumsy' children matched pair-wise to controls between the ages of 5 and 7 (Losse et al., 1992). When these children were teenagers, three different evaluations of their motor performance were obtained. They were tested on a standardised test of motor competence, the TOMI (Stott et al., 1984) and on a well-developed battery of neuro-developmental tests (O'Connor et al., 1986), both administered by assessors blind to the original classification of the children. In addition, the physical education (PE) component of their school records over the ten-year period was consulted by independent teachers, who were also unaware of the original classification. There was good agreement between these three sources of information. Almost all of the children identified as having motor difficulties soon after they began primary school still had similar problems as teenagers. Our objective measures revealed a distinct lack of coordination, as did the many comments from their teachers. Although some 'clumsy' pupils were described as trying hard in PE, none achieved a high achievement rating on the scales used by the schools. In other subjects, problems in art and crafts and difficulty with handling equipment in science were frequently noted, with untidy handwriting and poor presentation of written work being almost universal themes. Outside school, some of the children with difficulties had succeeded in finding sports that they enjoyed, but we had no way of knowing how proficient they were. In summarising the implications of our findings, we drew a less optimistic conclusion than Knuckey and Gubbay (1983), emphasising our failure to find support for the benign view of 'clumsiness'.

Two subsequent investigations have provided further clarification of the prospects for children identified as 'clumsy' in their early years (Geuze & Borger, 1993; Cantell et al., 1994). In the latter, Cantell et al. tracked the progress of the largest group of children with a coordination problem yet to be studied. At the age of 5 years, the entire population of a Finnish town was screened for movement difficulties. Out of a total of 1,138 children, 115 were described as having delayed motor development. Although there was some attrition at successive testings, 81 were retested at age 15 on a very extensive battery of perceptual and motor tests. From this group, 37 turned out to have substantial movement difficulties, and 44 appeared to have improved considerably. However, when the 'improved' group was compared to the stable 'clumsy' group and the controls on the individual items of the test battery, their performance turned out to lie between the two extremes on every item, indicating a slight residual deficit.

In sum, regardless of whether the metric used is a neuro-developmental examination administered by a paediatrician, a standardised motor test administered by a psychologist or a report written by a teacher, these studies consistently show that spontaneous recovery is far from universal. Moreover, although a number of recent studies have shown that intervention can improve performance (e.g. Laszlo et al., 1988; Schoemaker et al., 1994), this remains in dispute, and none has included very long-term tests of retention. Consequently, until we can predict which child will recover spontaneously and which will not, then we must abandon the view that 'we can simply wait and see', and put far more effort into finding effective approaches to intervention.

Associated deficits

Children can be found whose lack of competence in the motor domain contrasts sharply with their academic and social success. Such isolated deficits are undoubtedly thought-provoking, but the salience of such cases often causes their prevalence to be overestimated. Far more common are children whose movement problems are associated with behavioural or educational problems of various types. Among this group are children who find it difficult to concentrate at school and cannot sit still, children who are unhappy in school because they are bullied or socially isolated, and children who cope with their clumsiness by becoming the class clown. Not to be forgotten, also, are those children who withdraw completely from participation, remaining unnoticed for too long.

Fortunately, the conclusion that there is a strong association between poor motor coordination and social-emotional problems in childhood no longer has to rest on anecdotal evidence. The publication of Wall et al.'s (1990) comprehensive review was swiftly followed by several studies which extended our knowledge of the range of difficulties these children encounter. For instance, Schoemaker and Kalverboer (1994) demonstrate that, even as young as 6, children's lack of confidence in their physical competence invades other domains. Not only did the children with movement problems judge themselves to be less competent socially on the Harter Scale, but they also rated themselves as more introverted and anxious than their well-coordinated peers. An interesting feature of this study is that Schoemaker and Kalverboer were among the first to seek converging evidence by soliciting the views of parents and teachers as well as consulting the children themselves. Recently, we have been able to confirm these findings in a rather different context (Jongmans et al., in press). We asked prematurely-born 6-year-olds with isolated movement problems, isolated reading problems and a combination of the two to complete the pictorial version of the Harter Scale. The children's judgements of themselves exactly mirrored their areas of competence as measured on standardised tests. Those who were poorly-coordinated but could read well rated themselves relatively low on the physical and high on the cognitive component; those who were well-coordinated but read poorly produced the opposite pattern, and those with problems in both areas rated themselves as low in both.

At the other end of the age spectrum, evidence of the co-occurrence of social, emotional and coordination problems is also accumulating. Using the adult version of the Harter Scale, two of the longitudinal studies mentioned in the previous section (Losse et al., 1992; Cantell et al., 1994) showed that 'clumsy' teenagers are very aware of their physical difficulties. However, whereas the English teenagers in our study had a very poor perception of themselves socially, those in the Finnish study did not. It is possible that this difference can be accounted for in terms of cultural differences in attitude to disability, but this would have to be investigated further.

Although inevitability is never claimed, many studies have demonstrated that being 'clumsy' in the early years carries with it an increased risk of other learning difficulties later. For instance, in the early 1980s, Drillien and Drummond (1983) observed that motor problems in the pre-school period were predictive of later school problems. Numerous later studies also attest to the co-occurrence of coordination problems with other learning difficulties in the primary school years (e.g. Hadders-Algra et al., 1988). In addition, all four of the longitudinal studies mentioned above showed that these problems do not miraculously disappear in secondary school. Indeed, for some children, the restrictions imposed by their motor difficulties seem to result in school performance that is substantially below that which would have been predicted on the basis of their IQ, and this seems especially true when the movement problems are accompanied by problems of attention (Gillberg et al., 1982; Gillberg et al., 1983; Gillberg & Gillberg, 1989; Gillberg et al., 1989).

The high incidence of problems associated with 'clumsiness' in children raises a number of issues. The co-existence of motor difficulties with impairments of attention, language or reading creates difficulties in the areas of classification, differential diagnosis and aetiology. For example, the overlap has led some to question the very existence of a separable childhood syndrome centred on motor dysfunction, while others are concerned with the procedures and criteria for assigning children to specific groups. Among those who study the aetiology of developmental disorders generally, the question of whether early brain damage can affect later development in a way that leads to highly specific impairments is always an issue (see Caron & Rutter, 1991 for a general discussion of issues concerned with co-morbidity).

On the other hand, these overlapping conditions have to be distinguished from the social-emotional concomitants of 'clumsiness' which are common to many childhood disorders and are often assumed to stem from the fact that normally-developing children are intolerant of those who are 'different'. Consequently, they are treated as secondary symptoms in official classification systems and are not formally recorded. Whether this primary/secondary relationship is actually the case or not has never been properly investigated. Moreover, although these impairments may not be considered as core symptoms of the disorder, they present substantial problems for the practitioner.

As Wedell has elegantly pointed out in many of his papers, understanding children's problems can only be achieved effectively by considering the *whole* child in the social and educational context in which he/she lives. Although the educational system still has some way to go in providing adequately for children with this particular type of difficulty, progress is being made, and awareness of the consequences of failing to offer help in school has certainly increased.

Experimental studies of children with perceptuo-motor difficulties

> The question why? is increasingly being asked in special education. Educators and others concerned are no longer satisfied with finding *that* children are failing in school or in their social and intellectual development. They want to know *why* they are failing. (Wedell, 1973)

In 1973, Wedell opened his discussion of perceptuo-motor disabilities and learning by using four children's attempts to copy a sequence of simple line drawings to achieve two objectives: to illustrate the potential of the information-processing approach as a means of identifying possible sources of difficulty in a child's performance, and to point to the diagnostic/practical value of this approach (see Figure 3.1).

Sequence 1 points to a dissociation between what a child 'knows' and what he/she can do; the child is able to perceive his/her own failure but is unable to act upon the feedback this provides. Sequences 2 and 3 illustrate the need to distinguish between deficits which are either purely sensory or purely motor and those which involve translation between these systems. They also show how well some children are able to compensate for their difficulties in spite of an impairment. Sequence 4 illustrates the fact that there are children who possess the requisite sensory and motor apparatus to perform a task but whose cognitive disabilities are such that they are unable to use this apparatus effectively.

As his essay develops, Wedell proceeds to use a simple information-processing model as a framework for reviewing a substantial body of research on perceptuo-motor deficits and their possible effects on school achievement. Since it is impossible to provide an update on all of the work reviewed in 1973, I have elected to illustrate the way that thinking in this area has progressed by focusing on studies which explore the relationship between vision, kinaesthesis and motor output, leaving aside those concerned with the efficiency of the effector system and the temporal aspects of motor control.

Sensory information and task demands in simple actions

In addition to form-copying, poorly-coordinated children find it hard to perform many other skills which are necessary for successful progress at home and at school. Fastening buttons, tying shoe laces, using a knife and fork, cutting with scissors and writing are a few of the most frequently mentioned examples. What these skills have in common is the requirement to process complex sensory information and form an abstract representation

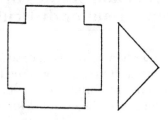

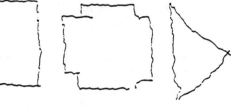

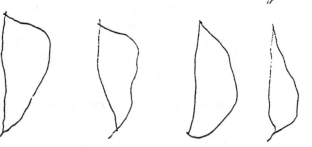

(1)

(2)

(3)

(4)

Figure 3.1   Pattern copies made by children with different types of handicaps

Source: Wedell (1973)

of the task parameters in order to plan the appropriate movement sequences. Perhaps not surprisingly, therefore, the search for deficits at the sensory/perceptual end of the processing chain has motivated much of the experimentation on this topic. Also predictable is the focus on the visual and kinaesthetic modalities, since they are the two senses most involved in movement control (kinaesthetic or proprioceptive information is that derived from sensors in the joints, muscles and tendons).

In 1973, Wedell began his review of the literature on oculo-motor defects and perceptuo-motor performance by noting that existing research had largely focused on the possible consequences for reading. Although we still know rather little about the wider developmental consequences of oculo-motor defects such as squints, nystagmus and lack of stereopsis, a number of studies have recently appeared which address and confirm Wedell's surmise that, as far as the development of adequate motor competence is concerned, children are able to compensate rather well for such deficiencies (e.g. Mon-Williams et al., 1994; Jongmans et al., submitted). However, the approach taken in these studies has been to determine whether any oculo-motor deficit can be detected which reliably distinguishes between 'clumsy' and control groups, and it is tacitly assumed that any inconsistency in the estimation of an individual child's oculo-motor performance consists merely of error variance. However, Wedell was prepared to consider alternative methodologies. Finding himself confronted with the very rare and fascinating case of a child with a predictably varying deficit – a squint which was only present on alternate days – he seized upon nature's generous provision of an experimental manipulation unavailable to us in the laboratory and performed a within-subject analysis of the concomitants of squint. By comparing performance on days when squinting was present or absent, Wedell was able to show that the boy was much slower on visuo-motor tasks, such as inserting pegs in a board and completing form boards, on the squinting days than on days when his oculo-motor control was normal. Interestingly, too, it seemed that the boy's oculo-motor problems generalised to other aspects of his behaviour, in that his mother found him more difficult to deal with on squinting days. This example provides a vivid illustration of the potential power of the case study approach to illuminate childhood problems. It is a great pity that nobody seems to have replicated the findings.

In contrast to the paucity of research on the effect of oculo-motor defects on perceptuo-motor competence, the idea that visual perceptual deficits might be the cause of 'clumsiness' has received a great deal of attention. The fate of one particular line of enquiry might serve to illustrate the problems that have been encountered. Between 1982 and 1988, Hulme and his co-workers published a sequence of studies in which they showed that 'clumsy' children were poor on a variety of perceptual tasks. These tasks included matching the length of lines, discriminating between objects of different shapes and sizes, and making size constancy judgements (e.g. Hulme et al., 1982; Lord & Hulme, 1987a). The investigation began with a demonstration that children described as 'clumsy' were less accurate than normal children at matching the length of two rods, whether they were allowed to look at them or feel along them, but that only performance on the task requiring *visual* matching correlated significantly with the children's composite scores on everyday motor tasks. Having pointed out that correlations are unable to sustain the logical weight of causal conclusions, Hulme et al. nevertheless argued that the results of this study supported the view that the deficit that underlies clumsiness is a visual one.

In another attempt to demonstrate that a deficit in visual perception causes clumsiness, Lord and Hulme (1988) examined visual discrimination and drawing in children with coordination problems. As before, the two groups of subjects differed significantly on both tasks. However, rather than assessing the relationship between the perceptual measures and motor competence for the entire sample, as they had done in 1982, this time Lord and Hulme elected to focus only on the correlations *within* each of the groups. What they found was that only the correlation within the 'clumsy' group reached statistical significance. That for the control group was negligible. To accommodate this finding, they introduced the very interesting possibility that lack of perceptual competence might only affect motor ability at the lower end of the scale. In other words, once perceptual competence reaches a certain threshold level, then motor control systems can function normally. Unfortunately, there were problems with this study too. First, the results just described contradicted the data obtained in 1982, in which the equivalent correlation was actually higher for the control group. Second, the interpretation was patently *post hoc*.

Two recent studies have attempted to replicate Hulme et al.'s findings without success. Although both Powell and Bishop (1992) and Henderson et al. (1994) found that poorly-coordinated children had difficulty on Hulme's visual perceptual task, neither found that the children's perceptual scores correlated with their motor competence scores. On the basis of their findings, both of these groups rejected the notion of a causal link between visual perceptual problems and clumsiness and favoured the idea that these two deficits may simply co-occur in some children. Moreover, as Henderson et al. point out, a true test of the hypothesis that visual perceptual problems cause 'clumsiness' would require that one start with a group of children with visual perceptual problems, rather than with a group defined as 'clumsy'.

Kinaesthetic deficit

The other perceptual explanation of Developmental Coordination Disorder

(DCD) currently in vogue is that proposed by Laszlo, Bairstow and colleagues (e.g. Laszlo et al., 1988), who argue that the critical deficit is to be found in kinaesthesis. As Hulme did for vision, Laszlo and Bairstow began their investigation by examining the relationship between their kinaesthetic test (the KST: Laszlo and Bairstow, 1985) and measures of movement skill. They report, for example, a significant correlation between KST performance and a writing task (Bairstow & Laszlo, 1981). However, Elliott et al. (1988) and Sugden and Wann (1988) present data which is inconsistent with these findings.

In spite of various criticisms of the psychometric properties of their test (e.g. Doyle et al., 1988), Laszlo and Bairstow pursued the hypothesis that clumsiness is caused by a kinaesthetic deficit by undertaking an intervention study. Training studies are uniquely powerful tools for identifying the causes of behavioural abnormalities. If it can be shown that treatment to alleviate a specific deficit has an effect not only on the specific difficulty but also on the more general problem it is believed to cause, then this constitutes good evidence that the specific deficit truly did underlie the general problem. This is precisely what they did.

Children selected by their teachers as 'clumsy' were first confirmed to be so on a variety of standardised motor tasks. The children were then divided into four groups and given different kinds of intervention, including both kinaesthetic training and intervention described as being more traditional. The results showed that those children who were trained on the two components of the KST not only made much more accurate kinaesthetic judgements but also improved dramatically on the TOMI, a standardised test containing a combination of gross and fine motor tasks. Those who received other kinds of intervention did not.

In view of the fact that this type of intervention appeared to offer such a cost-effective solution to the treatment of children with DCD – in total each child receives only three hours of intervention from a professional with no special training – it seemed absolutely essential to replicate it, a task now undertaken by two separate groups, one in Canada (Polatajko et al., 1995) and one in the UK (Sims et al., submitted). The results of these two studies were not identical, but in neither case is there strong support for Laszlo's approach.

Alternative approaches to studying the relationships between perception and action

So far, we have discussed two approaches which place a rather narrow construction on the cause of clumsiness. Both share the view that the boundaries of the difficulty are those of a sensory modality, and that the deficit can be diagnosed by tests of 'visual functioning' or 'kinaesthetic functioning' which can be administered in isolation from the realm in which clumsiness is exhibited. No clear picture emerges from either line of enquiry. Why might this be so?

Throughout his book on perceptuo-motor difficulties in children (Wedell, 1973), Wedell emphasised the fact that, even when children experience the same day-to-day difficulties, the underlying causes may be quite different. Unfortunately, while most researchers in this field concur that it is unlikely that a *single* deficit accounts for these difficulties, to this day, most behave as if they were seeking a unitary cause. Two groups of children, divided on the basis of their everyday life competence in the motor domain, are compared on a task designed to reveal the locus of *the* processing defect. Group differences form the focus of the analysis, and individual differences are rarely considered. Moreover, when differences have been demonstrated, few consider the possibility that the difference is a *consequence* of the primary problem, as opposed to the *cause* of it – another point made by Wedell but so far ignored by his successors.

A number of recent studies have made limited attempts to address these issues, all of which start from the position that children whose everyday life problems may be similar might nevertheless exhibit different patterns of underlying impairment. While some have addressed the problem by reporting data on individual children in their samples (e.g. Rosblad & Hofsten, 1992), others have used clustering techniques to search for subgroups among the spectrum of children with similar functional problems (Hoare, 1994; Miyahara, 1994). For example, using six tests, including the kinaesthetic test devised by Laszlo and Bairstow (1985), the visual perceptual tests used by Hulme and colleagues and four somato-motor tests, Hoare (1994) found that her sample of 80 children with movement difficulties fell into five clusters. Two findings relevant to the present discussion emerged. First, differences between the profiles in relation to the two perceptual tests supported the idea that neither of these deficits is an *essential* component of DCD. In the case of the visual tasks, there were children who scored both above and below 1 standard deviation from the mean. Similarly, for the kinaesthetic tasks, there were differences in profile, with some children performing well on the kinaesthetic tasks and others failing badly. Second, in three clusters, there was a dissociation between visual and kinaesthetic performance, with some children showing good performance on one set of tasks and poor performance on the others, and vice versa.

In our own investigations of prematurely-born children, we have also used cluster analysis as a way of searching for subgroups among children who are 'clumsy', but, for purposes of external validation, have added an experimental analysis of the children's performance on relevant tasks (Jongmans, 1993). There is space to provide just one example.

We began by focusing attention on only one of the six clusters which emerged from our study, a group of children who appeared to have exceptional difficulty with form board tasks. By showing that this particular group differed from the other 'clumsy' children on a series of related 'constructional' tasks which were not included in the cluster analysis, we were able to suggest that the concept of a specific deficit in this area of perceptuo-motor performance might be valid. As a second approach, we then demonstrated that the way these children performed the form board task differed from those without similar movement difficulties – especially in response to changes in the characteristics of the task.

While the use of cluster analysis represents a methodological advance in the study of 'clumsiness' in children generally, it does not in itself take us further forward in understanding the links between the co-occurring deficits in perception and movement, if links there be. Having declared the approaches discussed so far essentially bankrupt, a number of investigators have proposed a quite different approach to the question of how the perceptual system drives action. The position taken is that one can only study the relationships between perception and action when both are functioning together. In their experiments, therefore, it is the strategies adopted by clumsy children and their normal peers in performing simple, relatively natural tasks that become the focus of attention, while at the same time, attempts are made to constrain these strategies by systematically manipulating the sensory information available to guide action.

Using a paradigm first used on normal children, Hofsten and Rosblad (1988), in collaboration with my own group, have investigated how children with poor coordination performed a finger-positioning action, when the availability of vision and kinaesthesis was manipulated. There were three conditions. In a vision-only condition, the target was visible, and the child's task was to reach under a table and place a finger in the same position (the pointing hand was never visible). In a kinaesthesis-only condition, target location was indicated by placing the non-reaching finger on the target. There was also a condition in which both sources of position information were available. There were no time constraints. Taken together, these two studies included 45 children with coordination difficulties, and despite minor procedural differences, the results were strikingly similar. When the target remained visible, the clumsy group performed as accurately as their normal peers. Moreover, addition of kinaesthetic information did not improve the performance of either group. When only kinaesthetic information about target location was available, both groups were less accurate, but the decrease for the clumsy group was much more striking (Rosblad & Hofsten, 1992; Henderson et al., in preparation).

We have also studied a task which is even more familiar to the child. Barnett (1993) compared normal and 'clumsy' children, spanning a broad range of ages, on time taken to complete a buttoning task. The task was performed with and without vision. With this task, we found a difference emerging between the groups even when vision was available, but once again the removal of vision had a greater impact on the 'clumsy' group. Moreover, the younger the subjects, the greater the difference between groups on the time measure. This difference emerged even more strikingly from qualitative ratings of the strategies adopted.

So far then, we have seen that the difference between the performance of 'clumsy' and normal groups is qualified by task demands, age and the sensory information available to guide performance. At present, the precise reason for the sensitivity of 'clumsy' children to the withdrawal of visual information is unclear. One consequence of withdrawing vision is that the task becomes more difficult, which makes it hard to disentangle any peculiarly visual aspects of the manipulation from the more general tendency for impairment to show up more clearly as task difficulty increases. Another somewhat global interpretation asserts that doing things with your eyes shut is a strange and unnatural activity, at which an inflexible processor will encounter exceptional difficulties. Rather more particularly visual is the role of looking in focusing attention (difficulty in maintaining attention to a task is a commonly reported concomitant of clumsiness). Probably the most direct interpretation of the consequence of withdrawing vision, however, is that it deprives the child of a specific source of spatial information that may be used in the planning and execution of movements. Where lack of visual information exacerbates the difficulties of a 'clumsy' group, this might be due to the 'unveiling' of a defect in the sensory systems which are left to carry the burden of movement control (e.g. vestibular or kinaesthetic information). However, an alternative view is that there is a fundamental interdependence of the sensory systems that furnish us with spatial information. Vision might have a special status in calibrating environmental action space.

General conclusion

Although the two sections of this chapter provide quite different perspectives on developmental perceptuo-motor difficulties, they converge on the conclusion that these difficulties frequently obstruct the child's ability to translate intellectual competence into educational attainment, either directly through impairment of classroom skills or by a more general deleterious effect on socialisation and self-esteem. In spite of increased awareness of the disorder, such difficulties often remain a puzzle to many classroom teachers, standing apart from other specific learning difficulties. The onus now is on researchers to provide an account of the problem that affords insights into the nature of a particular child's difficulties and informs classroom practice.

From this necessarily selective review of the literature, two issues stand out as critical. The first concerns the description of children's movement difficulties. In this regard, we need to distinguish the advancement of scientific investigation from the requirements of educational practice. For research purposes, it is essential that the data provided allow an informed comparison of one study with another but also a definition of the precise population of children with difficulties to which a set of findings may be generalised. For practical purposes, it is important to decide what information is most relevant to decisions about the appropriate provision for the child and the useful role of classroom teacher and therapist. Within Wedell's framework for assessing a child's needs, this means that we describe not only the general profile of the child's strengths and weaknesses but also the aspects of the environment that are either facilitatory or inhibitory to any programme of work that might be planned.

The second issue concerns the appropriate unit of analysis for the formulation of theory and remedial strategy – whether the unique individual or 'types', groups and syndromes. Recently, Hofsten (1993) has provided vigorous support for the single-case approach. He starts from the strong assumption that 'every malformation [to the developing nervous system] is more or less unique and so is the subsequent reorganisation of the system'. This leads him to assert that 'it is only through the study of individual pathological systems that we can make progress in understanding these systems and through them the organisation of the motor system in general'. This viewpoint has some force. As noted earlier, some of the conflicting results obtained in the studies reviewed might have been illuminated by presentation of individual subjects' data. The information lost when the individual's data are collapsed into a group mean may be that which is essential to characterise a particular child's difficulties and its practical implications. However, what is required at this early stage of understanding is a plurality of approaches directed towards various levels of generality. In particular, we need to construct bridges that allow the evacuation of the extremes, on one hand, of oversimplified generalisations about the cause of a purportedly unitary disorder, and on the other, a narrow focus on the unique individual that has no regard for the scientific cannons of parsimony or the resources of the educational system. Group studies need to have constant regard for the heterogeneity of the disorder and the possibility of detecting and delineating subtypes, while those prosecuting the single-case approach need to be constantly striving to detect larger patterns and profiles and to formulate generalisations.

Postscript

I have known Klaus Wedell for twenty years, most spent in the same department. We're both about thirty years older now! He hasn't changed much. In his office, the piles of paper have got deeper. (Have my papers got deeper, I wonder?) In a rare summer, the top layer bathes in the Bloomsbury sunshine long enough to turn a sickly yellow before the deciduous memo tree drops its autumnal load atop. Like the artichoke, Klaus's own memo pad violates a principle of physics – the leaves somehow growing in number as they are voraciously plucked. Perhaps his hair is whiter now. (Or have my views become more black and white?) When it comes to important things, Klaus is incapable of changing. Always willing to counsel. To advise. To linger over a problem (thereby missing the next one entirely). Prepared to care. To turn a cool and penetrating gaze upon the special needs of the world, while favouring his interlocutor with a crooked grin.

References

American Psychiatric Association (APA) (1994) *Diagnostic and Statistical Manual of Mental Disorders – Fourth Revision*, Washington, DC: APA.

Bairstow, P.J. & Laszlo, J.I. (1981) 'Kinaesthetic sensitivity to passive movements and its relationship to motor development and motor control', *Developmental Medicine and Child Neurology*, 23, pp.606–16.

Barnett, A.L. (1993) 'A Study of Manual Competence in Clumsy Children', unpublished PhD thesis, London University.

Cantell, M.H., Smyth, M.M. & Ahonen, T.P. (1994) 'Clumsiness in adolescence: Educational, motor, and social outcomes of motor delay detected at five years', in S.E. Henderson (ed.) *Developmental Coordination Disorder, Special Issue of Adapted Physical Activity Quarterly*, 11, pp.115–29.

Caron, C. & Rutter, M. (1991) 'Co-morbidity in child psychopathology: Concepts, issues and research strategies', *Journal of Child Psychology and Psychiatry*, 32, pp.1,063–80.

Doyle, A.J.R., Elliott, J.M. & Connolly, K.J. (1986) 'Measurement of kinaesthetic sensitivity', *Developmental Medicine and Child Neurology*, 28, pp.188–93.

Drillien, C. & Drummond, M. (1983) Developmental screening and the child with special needs: A population study of 5000 children', *Clinics in Developmental Medicine*, 86, London: Heinemann Medical Books.

Elliott, J.M., Connolly, K.J. & Doyle, A.J.R. (1988) 'Development of kinaesthetic sensitivity and motor performance in children', *Developmental Medicine and Child Neurology*, 30, pp.80–92.

Geuze, R. & Borger, H. (1993) 'Children who are clumsy: Five years later', *Adapted Physical Activity Quarterly*, 10, pp.10–21.

Gillberg, C., Rasmussen, P., Carlstrom, G., Svenson, B. & Waldenstrom, E. (1982) 'Perceptual, motor and attentional deficits in six-year-olds: Epidemiological aspects', *Journal of Child Psychology and Psychiatry*, 23, pp.131–44.

Gillberg, I.C. & Gillberg, C. (1989) 'Children with preschool minor neurodevelopmental disorders IV: Behaviour and school achievement at age 13', *Developmental Medicine and Child Neurology*, 31, pp.3–13.

Gillberg, I.C, Gillberg, C. & Groth, J. (1989) 'Children with preschool minor neurodevelopmental disorders V: Neurodevelopmental profiles at age 13', *Developmental Medicine and Child Neurology*, 31, pp.14–24.

Gillberg, I.C., Gillberg, C. & Rasmussen, P. (1983) 'Three year follow-up at age 10 of children with minor neurodevelopmental disorders: School achievement problems', *Developmental Medicine and Child Neurology*, 25, pp.566–73.

Hadders-Algra, M., Huisjes, H.J. & Touwen, B.C.L. (1988) 'Perinatal risk factors and minor neurological dysfunction: Significance for behaviour and school achievement at nine years', *Developmental Medicine and Child Neurology*, 30, pp.482–91.

Henderson, S.E. (1993) 'Motor development and minor handicap', in A. Kalverboer and R. Geuze (eds) *Motor Development in Early and Later Childhood: Longitudinal Approaches*, Cambridge: Cambridge University Press.

Henderson, S.E. & Sugden, D.A.S. (1992) *The Movement Assessment Battery for Children*, London: Psychological Corporation.

Henderson, S.E., Barnett, A. & Henderson, L. (1994) 'Visuospatial difficulties and clumsiness: On the interpretation of conjoined deficits', *Journal of Child Psychology and Psychiatry*, 35, pp.961–9.

Henderson, S.E., Jongmans, M. & Barnett, A.L. (in preparation) 'The effect of removing vision on the accuracy of a simple pointing task – a comparison of clumsy and normal children'.

Hoare, D. (1994) 'Subtypes of developmental coordination disorder', in S.E. Henderson (ed.) *Developmental Coordination Disorder, Special Issue of Adapted Physical Activity Quarterly*, 11, pp.158–69.

Hofsten, C. von (1993) 'Studying the development of goal directed behaviour', in A.F. Kalverboer, B. Hopkins & R. Geuze (eds) *Motor Development in Early 2nd Later Childhood: Longitudinal approaches*, Cambridge: CUP.

Hofsten, C. von & Rosblad, B. (1988) 'The integration of sensory information in the development of precise manual pointing', *Neuropsychologia*, 6, pp.805–21.

Hulme, C., Biggerstaff, A., Moran, G. & McKinley, I. (1982) 'Visual, kinaesthetic and cross-modal judgements of length by normal and clumsy children', *Developmental Medicine and Child Neurology*, 24, pp.461–71.

Jongmans, M.J. (1993) 'Perceptuo-motor competence in prematurely born children at school age: Neurological and psychological aspects', unpublished PhD thesis, University of London.

Jongmans, M., Demetre, J., Dubowitz, L. & Henderson, S.E. (in press) 'How local is the impact of a specific learning difficulty on the premature child's evaluation of his own competence?' *Journal of Child Psychology and Psychiatry*.

Jongmans, M., Mercuri, E., Henderson, S.E., de Vries, L., Sonksen, P. & Dubowitz, L. 'Visual function of prematurely born children with and without perceptual-motor difficulties'. Submitted to *Early Human Development*.

Knuckey, N.W. & Gubbay, S.S. (1983) 'Clumsy children: A prognostic study', *Australian Pediatric Journal*, 19, pp.9–13.

Laszlo, J.I. & Bairstow, P.J. (1985) *Perceptual-motor Behaviour: Developmental Assessment and Therapy*, London: Holt, Rinehart and Winston.

Laszlo, J.I., Bairstow, P.J., Bartrip, J. & Rolfe, V.T. (1988) 'Clumsiness or perceptuo-motor dysfunction?', in A. Colley & J. Beech (eds) *Cognition and Action in Skilled Behaviour*, Amsterdam: North Holland.

Lord, R. & Hulme, C. (1987a) 'Perceptual judgements of normal and clumsy children', *Developmental Medicine and Child Neurology*, 29, pp.250–7.

Lord, R. & Hulme, C. (1987b) 'Kinaesthetic sensitivity of normal and clumsy children', *Developmental Medicine and Child Neurology*, 29, pp.720–5.

Lord, R. & Hulme, R. (1988) 'Visual perception and drawing ability in clumsy and normal children', *British Journal of Developmental Psychology*, 6, pp.1–9.

Losse, A., Henderson, S.E., Elliman, D., Hall, D., Knight, E. & Jongmans, M. (1992) 'Clumsiness in children: Do they grow out of it? A ten year follow up study', *Developmental Medicine and Child Neurology*, 33, pp.55–68.

Miyahara, M. (1994) 'Sub-types of learning disabled students based upon gross motor functions', *Adapted Physical Activity Quarterly*, 11, pp.368–83.

Mon-Williams, M.A., Pascall, E. & Wann, J. (1994) 'Opthalmic factors in developmental coordination disorder', in S.E. Henderson (ed.) *Developmental Coordination Disorder, Special Issue of Adapted Physical Activity Quarterly*, 11, pp.170–9.

O'Connor, P., Shaffer, D., Stokman, C. & Shafer, S.Q. (1986) 'A neuro-psychiatric follow-up of children in the Collaborative Perinatal Project: A longitudinal study of neurological signs in childhood', in S. Mednick & M. Hanway (eds) *Longitudinal Research in the United States*, New York: Praeger Scientific Publications.

Polatajko, H.J., Macnab, J.J., Anstett, B., Malloy-Miller, T., Murphy, K. & Noh, S. (1995) 'A clinical trial of the process-oriented treatment approach for children with developmental coordination disorder', *Developmental Medicine and Child Neurology*, 37, pp.310–19.

Powell, R.P. & Bishop, D. (1992) 'Clumsiness and perceptual problems in children with specific language impairment', *Developmental Medicine and Child Neurology*, 34, pp.755–65.

Rosblad, B. & Hofsten, C. (1992) 'Perceptual control of manual pointing movements in children with motor impairments', *Physiotherapy, Theory and Practice*, 8, pp.223–33.

Schoemaker, M.M. and Kalverboer, A.F. (1994) 'Social and affective problems in children who are clumsy: How early do they begin?' in S.E. Henderson (ed.) *Developmental Coordination Disorder, Special Issue of Adapted Physical Activity Quarterly*, 11, pp.130–41.

Schoemaker, M.M., Hijlkema, M.G.L. & Kalverboer, A.F. (1994) 'Physiotherapy for clumsy children: An evaluation study', *Developmental Medicine and Child Neurology*, 36, pp.143–55.

Sims, K., Henderson, S.E., Hulme, C. & Morton, J. 'Kinaesthetic training for clumsy children: An evaluation', submitted to *Developmental Medicine and Child Neurology*.

Stott, D.H., Moyes, F.A. & Henderson, S.E. (1984) *The Henderson Revision of the Test of Motor Impairment*, San Antonio, Texas: Psychological Corporation/London: Psychological Corporation.*

Sugden, D. & Wann, C. (1988) 'Kinaesthesis and motor impairment in children with moderate learning difficulties', *British Journal of Educational Psychology*, 57, pp.225–36.

Wall, A.E., Reid, G. & Paton, J. (1990) 'The syndrome of physical awkwardness', in G. Reid (ed.) *Problems in Movement Control*, Amsterdam: North-Holland.

*   This text has now been expanded to include intervention guidelines – see Henderson & Sugden, 1992.

Wedell, K. (1973) *Learning and Perceptuo-motor Disabilities in Children*, London: John Wiley.

World Health Organisation (WHO) (1992) *The ICD 10 Classification of Mental and Behavioural Disorders*, Geneva: WHO.

4 The management of specific learning difficulties (dyslexia): Challenges and responses

Peter D. Pumfrey

Summary

How much is literacy worth to you? How much is literacy worth to our children and to society? How much is literacy worth to the individual pupil with specific learning difficulties (dyslexia, hereafter SpLD)?

In our culture, literacy enriches both culturally and economically. Whatever its causes, illiteracy isolates and impoverishes. In principle, there is general agreement that illiteracy, irrespective of its causes, should be minimised. In practice, there are many barriers. In relation to the identification and alleviation of special educational needs (SENs) in general and of SpLD in particular, policies and practices currently being developed in England and Wales represent one constructive but inevitably contentious approach to similar problems experienced in other educational systems. The challenge can be summarised as: resources finite; priorities contentious; knowledge partial; demand infinite.

This chapter is set within the context of continuing changes in administrative and financial policies and practices affecting education in England and Wales. It considers some of the issues involved in the management of SpLD at national, local, school and individual levels.

Legal recognition of specific learning difficulties and dyslexia as disabilities under the provisions of the 1981 Education Act led, during the period 1983 to 1993, to the development of a range of local education authority (LEA) policies and practices addressing this area of SENs. In the period up to about 1988, a significant expansion took place in the resources devoted to the identification of pupils experiencing such difficulties, and the specialist educational support services provided for them. Since then, there is evidence of retrenchment. The establishment of a National Curriculum under the provision of the Education Reform Act took place in 1988. The devolution of decision-making and financial resources from LEAs to schools under the Local Management of Schools (LMS) provisions, coupled with the studies of special education policies and practices published in 1992 by the Audit Commission, highlighted concerns about identification, incidence, statementing practices and provision for pupils with SENs under the theme of 'accountability'. With English as one of the core subjects in what is called 'an entitlement curriculum' aimed at raising educational attainments, the challenges to mainstream schools and their governors presented by pupils having SpLD are inevitably highlighted. There is a growing demand by parents for Statements of Special Needs and the resources linked to these. 'Who pays?' is a key question.

Deriving from earlier Education Acts and based on the 1993 Education Act, a *Code of Practice on the Identification and Assessment of Special Educational Needs* and *The Education (Special Educational Needs) (Information) Regulations 1994* were jointly published by the Department for Education and the Welsh Office (DfE & WO, 1994a, 1994b). Circular 6/94 on *The Organisation of Special Educational Provision* was also published (DfE, 1994a). Extensive consultations on these documents had taken place. Their provisions took effect from 1 September 1994. Their implications for LEAs, schools, governors, teachers, pupils and their parents are considerable. For example, these developments have far-reaching financial consequences for LEAs, schools and their governors. The increased demand by parents for specialist professional services for their children presents an eminently understandable but very considerable and continuing management problem. Dependent on possible changes in its legal responsibilities and on the amounts of money and central services retained by an LEA, policy and provision are likely to continue to differ across the country, as they do already (Bibby, 1995). Despite the legal duties of LEAs, schools, governors and parents concerning the education of pupils with SpLD, and despite the five-stage model of SEN provision advocated by the DfE, the latest government proposals will still leave many issues concerning the identification, incidence and alleviation of SpLD unresolved.

A series of important court decisions concerning the rights and responsibilities of LEAs, schools, governors, parents and children sought to clarify particular legal points concerning pupils with SpLD. Such legal decisions have significantly affected, and will continue to affect, the development of the policies and practices of LEAs in particular. This chapter will consider some of the effects of recent legislation, of LMS and of such parts of the 1993 Education Act, its associated Circulars and Regulations as bear on provision for pupils with Specific Learning Difficulties (Dyslexia), and the effects of related legal decisions. Ways in which management issues have been addressed in particular LEAs, schools and individual cases will be described and discussed.

In this changing scene, one statement can be made with confidence. An increasingly litigious parental lobby has been considerably stimulated. It can be confidently predicted that calls on the services of members of the legal profession specialising in education law will increase dramatically in the immediate future.

Introduction

In *The Times Educational Supplement* (13 November 1992) Her Majesty's Chief Inspector of Schools and Head of Office for Standards in Education (OFSTED), Professor Stuart Sutherland, commented on the management of education. He made the point that, whatever aspect of education you are considering, 'If you can't measure it, you can't manage it.' In my opinion, this point is central to the efficient and socially just identification and alleviation of SpLD, and to any appraisal of the accountability of the system of provision for such pupils. Sadly, the importance of such explicit measurement in decision-making concerning resource allocation in special education is insufficiently appreciated (Elliott, 1990; Sawyer, 1992; Pumfrey, 1994).

The torrent of publications intended to improve the educational system for pupils with SENs continues in full spate. The revised OFSTED *Handbook for the Inspection of Schools*, published in July 1993, includes technical guidance on the evaluation of provision for pupils with SENs in mainstream schools (OFSTED, 1993). Reference to pupils with specific difficulties that affect progress in the acquisition of literacy more than in other areas of the curriculum is made in the 'Technical Papers'. In October 1993, the DfE and the WO published a 122-page consultative document entitled *Draft Code of Practice on the Identification and Assessment of Special Educational Needs and Draft Regulations on Assessments and Statements* (DfE & WO, 1993). In December 1993, the DfE published over 500 further pages of double-spaced typescript comprising eight Draft Circulars and five sets of Draft Regulations on SENs. Among these was the 46-page *Draft Circular on the Organisation of Special Education Provision*. Together with *Draft Regulations on Schools' Policies on Special Educational Needs and Provision by LEAs of Special Educational Needs Support Services*, it was published on 29 December (DfE, 1993). Final versions of these documents appeared in 1994 (DfE & WO, 1994a, 1994b; DfE, 1994a). The changes in policies and practices envisaged are to be 'cost neutral'.

Aims

With reference to pupils with SpLD in mainstream state schools, the aims of this chapter are as follows:

1   to outline and comment on administrative aspects of the management of SpLD within the current legislative procedures in England and Wales
2   to consider some of the implications of these, and the challenges they present at national, local, school and individual levels
3   to point to promising practices at each of these levels.

Contexts

Educational

Sixteen years ago, the *Report of the Committee of Inquiry into the Education of Handicapped Children and Young People*, chaired by Mary Warnock, summarised its thrust in the four points listed in Table 4.1.

Table 4.1   Views of the Warnock Committee

- The aims of education are the same for all children. The means to achieve these might be different for pupils with SENs, as might the extent to which the aims can be reached.
- SENs are not caused solely by deficiencies *within* the child. They result from interaction between the strengths and weaknesses of the child, and the resources and deficiencies of the environment. SENs occur in a continuum of degree of severity, and so it is not meaningful to attempt to draw a hard and fast time between the 'handicapped' and the 'non-handicapped'.
- All schools have a responsibility to identify and meet pupils' SENs and all children and young people with SENs should be educated alongside their peers, as long as their needs can be met and it is practicable to do so.
- Parents, and as far as possible the children and young people with SENs themselves, have the right to share in the decisions about how their needs are met.

(*Source:* DES, 1978)

The Warnock Committee rejected the labelling of 'handicaps' and the categories that had developed over time. The subsequent 1981 Education Act supported this move. The Department of Education and Science discontinued the collection of data on pupils by category of handicap. Categories were 'out'; a continuum of SEN was 'in'. The concept of SENs was developed and related to learning difficulties, as shown in Table 4.2.

The notion that categories had been discarded by this approach was untenable. Two superordinate categories replaced less inclusive ones. Pupils were categorised as either having or not having SENs. It was asserted that approximately 1 in 6 of pupils at any given time, and 1 in 5 at some time during their education, will have SENs. The basis for these figures is highly contentious. It has been argued that the concept of SENs has served its useful awareness-raising function and should now be abandoned and replaced with a more precise formulation and quantification of inter- and intra-individual differences (Pumfrey & Mittler, 1989). There is a central paradox. All children are the same: they are all different. In a very real sense, *every* child is special by virtue of his or her uniqueness. The differential allocation of inevitably limited resources from public funds to any individual or group of pupils deemed to have SENs requires a decision-making system that is open, justifiable, replicable, can be evaluated, is perceived by the general public as equitable, and therefore merits the consequent demands on the public purse.

The Dyslexia Institute, the British Dyslexia Association and other voluntary bodies exist to further the interests of individuals having SpLD (Crisfield & Smythe, 1993). All such groups are in competition with parallel bodies equally concerned with a wide range of other identified categories of disability. All represent entirely legitimate manifestations of concern in the community. All are involved in raising public and professional awareness and in advocating their particular cause.

At present, because the concept of a continuum of SENs confounds qualitative and quantitative aspects of inter- and intra-individual differ-ences, the term means almost whatever a user wishes it to mean. The relative and highly subjective concept of SENs is deeply embedded in current thinking and in the law relating to education. In the absence of an agreed operational definition, the concept's manifold weaknesses ensure that it will continue creating administrative confusions and complex legal battles. As such, the concept makes work for many professionals. Its future would appear assured until more professionals question its validity and utility (Pumfrey & Mittler, 1989).

The 1981 Education Act owed much to ideas within the report of the Committee of Inquiry chaired by Mary Warnock (DES, 1978), the recently-elected President of the British Dyslexia Association (National Organisation for Specific Learning Difficulties). Ten years after the 1981 Education Act, she said in the House of Lords debate held in December 1991:

I put on a white sheet so far as concerns the report which tried to remove the categorisation of children. I think now that that was a rather trendy mistake, because children are necessarily referred to by the category of their disabilities and it is necessary to have some way of referring to those children as a whole and according to their individual needs. There was a terrible time, to the alarm and horror of my children, when the children covered by the 1981 Act were known as 'Warnock children'. (Warnock, 1991)

Table 4.2   Special educational needs, learning difficulty and special educational provision

A child has *special educational needs* if he or she has a learning difficulty which calls for special educational provision to be made for him or her.

A child has a *learning difficulty* if he or she:

a   has a significantly greater difficulty in learning than the majority of children of the same age
b   has a disability which either prevents or hinders the child from making use of educational facilities of a kind provided for children of the same age in schools within the area of the local education authority
c   is under 5 and falls within the definition at (a) or (b) above, or would do so if special educational provision was not made for the child

A child must not be regarded as having a learning difficulty solely because the language or form of language of the home is different from the language in which he or she is or will be taught.

Special education provision means:

a   for a child over 2, educational provision which is additional to, or otherwise different from, the educational provision made generally for children of the child's age in maintained schools, other than special schools, in the area
b   for a child under 2, educational provision of any kind.

(*Source:* 1993 Education Act, Section 156, quoted in DfE & WO, 1993, 1994 para 2.1).

While the idea of one overall continuum of SENs is suspect, in principle, continua and categories of SENs are not necessarily mutually exclusive. If either proves to be of utility in the management of SENs, they are both to be welcomed, provided that they can be theoretically justified, empirically quantified and validated. For example, the wide range of voluntary organisations concerned with particular disabilities appreciate the communicative value of the label that identifies their particular concerns. Even then, within a category, there are degrees of disability. Pupils with SpLD do have distinguishing characteristics. Even so, SpLD is not unitary: it is unquestionably a variable syndrome. Pupils deemed to have SpLD can differ markedly in the degree and nature of their specific difficulties. Their differing patterns of aetiologies, presenting symptoms and responses to interventions emphasise the importance of explicitly assessing the nature and degree of their inter- and intra-individual differences. As operational definitions determine the formal incidence of a condition in a population at a given point in time, measurement is central to effective management.

Legal

For governors, teachers and parents, one of the most helpful books in this area is that by Chasty and Friel (1993).

Court judgments

In 1984, a High Court judgment by Lord Justice Waller in the case of *Regina* v. *Surrey County Council* provided an important protection for LEAs:

> There is no question of Parliament having placed on the local education authority the obligation to provide a child with the best possible education. There is not duty on the authority to provide a Utopian system or to educate him or her to his or her maximum potential. (Pumfrey & Reason, 1991)

As will be seen below, this point has very recently been reaffirmed in the High Court in defence of two LEAs, when the parents of pupils with SpLD challenged the provision the authority had made for their sons' earlier education. Subsequently, in the case of *R* v. *Hampshire County Council ex parte J*, Mr Justice Taylor ruled that 'dyslexia' was clearly a disability, and therefore the 1981 Education Act requirements applied. The pupils had a learning difficulty that required an assessment. Following the LEA's assessment, three questions should be asked:

● Does the child have SENs?

- If so, what provision is required?
- Can this be provided by the LEA within their normal or special resources?

The child's Statement should specify what provision is required. The LEA must provide this and review the child's progress on at least an annual basis.

In January 1993, two cases were brought against Hampshire and Dorset LEAs respectively. Each authority was accused of failing to provide an appropriate education for a student suffering from dyslexia. These were important cases, where parents were seeking substantial compensation. In the High Court, Mr Justice Otton ruled that there was no case to answer. The reason was that authorities had a duty to the public, but not to individuals which would allow them to sue. Both plaintiffs were given leave to take their case before the Court of Appeal.

The Chairman of the Education Law Association, an expert in special needs cases, was subsequently quoted as saying: 'Authorities can more or less do what they like without any risk of penalty.' The Assessment and Statementing Adviser to the British Dyslexia Association, Ann Brerton, said: 'Any authority which is minded to break the law seems free to do so.' Dr Chasty, then a member of staff of the Dyslexia Institute, is reported as saying: 'It [the judgment] will be interpreted by most education authorities as giving them carte blanche to make less good provision than they otherwise would have done.'

Another ongoing case merits mention. A boy, 'S', with SpLD, had been assessed by the staff of the Essex LEA and a Statement of SENs issued. The pupil's subsequent educational progress was considered unsatisfactory by the parents. S was assessed by a psychologist, who recommended that the child receive nine hours' additional help per week. The parents also wanted their son to be educated in a specialist school. The LEA decided that seven hours' additional tuition within the mainstream school would meet the pupil's needs. The case went to a local appeal committee and was referred back to the LEA. The LEA decided not to amend the Statement. The parents then appealed to the Secretary of State, John Patten, as allowed under the 1981 Education Act. In November 1992, Mr Patten decided that the boy should be offered 40 minutes' additional help per day within the mainstream school. The case then went to the High Court on appeal. In the interim, the parents paid for the boy's education in a special school at their own expense. In January 1994, after his review of the case, it was reported that Mr Justice Sedley had quashed the Secretary of State's decision. The Secretary of State for Education must reveal his reasons for deciding that a dyslexic pupil should receive less help than the LEA had been prepared to offer. Non-disclosure of specialist advice given to the Secretary of State was interpreted in this case as unfair to the other parties. Leave to appeal has been granted to the Secretary of State (Gardiner, 1994). The outcome of this case could have important consequences concerning the resources provided for pupils with SpLD in mainstream schools. There is evidence concerning the effectiveness of differing periods of weekly tuition on children's reading attainments.

The ombudsman

The local government ombudsman system was established to investigate individual cases of grievance concerning maladministration where no legal route existed. One of the attractions of this system to plaintiffs is that it can offer financial compensation if a legitimate grievance is established. While local authorities are apparently not absolutely bound to pay, so far they have done so. There has been a massive increase in complaints from the families of children with SENs. Between April 1993 and September 1993 it is reported that there were 21 judgments against LEAs; in the previous eight years there had been a total of only 26. In large measure, such complaints are a result of increased public awareness of parents' and their children's rights, and of the ombudsman's function.

Frederick Laws is one of England's three ombudsmen. He is responsible for the South of England, the South West, the Midlands and East Anglia. Until 1991 he had issued a mere 6 reports of SENs. In the period 1992–3 he issued 15 reports against 11 LEAs. Education-related complaints in his area in 1991–2 totalled 193, with 14 concerned with SENs. By March 1993, the parallel figures were 238 and 42 respectively. The major focus of concern is said to be delays in LEA decision-making, in that many LEAs take far longer than the six months recommended (*Education*, 1992; Pyke, 1993b).

The 1990 Children Act

The availability of legal aid for children in their own right was effected in 1990 in Regulations related to the Children Act. In effect, in certain circumstances, the Regulation allows parents to get help with legal fees for their children's cases, irrespective of the parents' own income. Whereas previously parents were being advised by solicitors that they had rights of appeal under the 1981 Education Act, they were also advised that the financial costs to them could be heavy. The case of Oliver Derrick makes the point. In 1992, at the age of 12, Oliver had a reading age of about 7 years. Psychologists are reported as having recommended his attendance at a private school specialising in dyslexia. The LEA (Wiltshire) refused to accept this recommendation and to pay the costs involved. In the High Court, a judicial review of Wiltshire's actions required the LEA to pay the £3,300 per term fees for Oliver's education. Subsequently, his mother sought reimbursement from the county of £15,000 in fees that the family had already paid (Pyke, 1993a). Understandably, there is an increased willingness of parents to go to court.

Special Educational Needs Tribunals

Regional Special Educational Needs Tribunals have been established under the provisions of the 1993 Education Act. These represent an attempt to meet parental concerns. The tribunal is an independent body established to determine appeals by parents against LEA decisions concerning their children's SENs (DfE, 1994b). The tribunal's decision will be binding on both parties to the appeal. The DfE claims that the number of parents making appeals about Statements will not increase. If this proves to be the case, then the parental awareness-raising, market-creating function of the Parents' Charter, will have failed. After all, a key tenet of a materialist, consumer-oriented society is: 'If there isn't a market, create one.' While the DfE intends that the system will cut down on the use of solicitors and barristers, this seems highly unlikely. Already the Education Law Society and the British Dyslexia Association are running training courses on the new tribunals. The first of the 235 cases registered since September 1994 was heard in January 1995. More than half of the cases so far filed concern pupils with specific learning difficulties (dyslexia). The amount of time taken at this first SEN tribunal hearing augurs ill. The first case took a full day, whereas the SEN tribunal budget allowed only half a day per case (Pyke, 1995).

Challenges

How much is literacy worth to an individual and a nation? What sacrifices would each of us as individuals make for our own children? Would you be willing to sell your home and live in a caravan for six years in order to pay for the special education that the state would not provide? Other parents have made similar sacrifices in what they see as the best interests of their child's education. What contributions are we willing to make to help all pupils with SpLD? The overall investment in education is considerable, running at about 5 per cent of GDP. IN 1991 the amount allocated for SENs was £1,500,000,000. This included provision for approximately 170,000 pupils with Statements. The percentage of Statements issued continues to vary markedly between LEAs (Audit Commission, 1992a, 1992b). Since 1985, there has been a steady increase in the number of pupils with Statements being educated in mainstream schools. The proportion of pupils with Statements in mainstream schools rose from 14 per cent in 1985 to 42 per cent in 1991 (OFSTED, 1993).

The *Code of Practice on the Identification and Assessment of Special Educational Needs* seeks to establish more standard procedures across the country. The fundamental principles underpinning the Code and the practices and procedures essential in pursuing these are set out in Tables 4.3 and 4.4. Central to the effective operation of the Code of Practice is the establishment of a five-stage model of SEN provision, as shown in Table 4.5.

The first three of these stages are designed to meet the needs of pupils for whom a Statement may not be required and for whom provision is to be financed by the school from its own delegated budget. With reference to pupils with SpLD who have Statements, Table 4.6, from a large LEA, underlines the problems of management at the LEA level. Such a continuing rate of growth of Statements for pupils with SpLD charged against centrally-held LEA funds, when these are being reduced by virtue of financial

Table 4.3   Fundamental principles underpinning the Code of Practice

- the needs of all pupils who may have special educational needs either throughout, or at any time during, their school careers must be addressed; the Code recognises that there is a continuum of needs and a continuum of provision which may be made in a wide variety of forms.
- children with special educational needs require special educational provision to ensure the greatest possible degree of access to a broad and balanced education, including the maximum possible access to the National Curriculum.
- the needs of most pupils will be met in the mainstream and without a statutory assessment or statement of special educational needs. Children with special educational needs, including children with statements of special educational needs, should, where appropriate and taking into account the wishes of their parents, be educated alongside their peers in mainstream schools.
- even before he or she reaches compulsory school age a child may have special educational needs requiring the intervention of the LEA as well as the health service.
- the knowledge, views and experience of parents are vital. Effective assessment and provision will be secured where there is the greatest possible degree of partnership between parents and their children and schools, LEAs and other agencies.

(*Source:* DfE & WO, 1994)

Table 4.4   The practices and procedures essential in pursuit of these principles given in the Code of Practice

- All children with special educational needs should be identified and assessed as early as possible and as quickly as is consistent with thoroughness.
- Provision for all children with special educational needs should be made by the most appropriate agency. In most cases it will be the child's mainstream school, working in partnership with the child's parents: no statutory assessment will be necessary.
- Where needed, LEAs must make assessments and Statements in accordance with the prescribed time limits; must write clear and thorough Statements, setting out the child's educational and non-educational needs, the objectives to be secured, the provision to be made and the arrangements for monitoring and review, and ensure the annual review of the special educational provision arranged for the child and the updating and monitoring of educational targets.
- Special educational provision will be most effective when those responsible take into account the ascertainable wishes of the child concerned, considered in the light of his or her age and understanding.
- There must be close cooperation between all the agencies concerned, and a multidisciplinary approach to the resolution of issues.

(*Source:* DfE & WO, 1994)

devolution to schools, is impossible to manage on the resources available. Thus, with devolution of monies to schools comes devolution of responsibilities for the first three of the five stages for SENs identification and assessment set out in the 1994 Code of Practice.

The challenge summarised earlier as 'resources finite; priorities contentious; knowledge partial; demand infinite' has to be faced. There are no easy answers. If you are the parent of a child who has SpLD, you are likely to want action on your child's behalf. A Statement continues to be a guarantee of such additional resources. However, the proposed five-stage model of SENs identification and assessment requires that pupils have gone through the school-based Stages 1 to 3 before consideration is given to making a formal assessment. The Regulations propose that there be a statutory six months from the request for an assessment by a parent – or from that point in time when the LEA initiates the formal assessment

Table 4.5 The proposed five-stage model of SENs given in the Code of Practice

Stage 1 Class or subject teachers identify a child's special educational needs and, consulting the school's SEN coordinator, gather information and take initial action.

Stage 2 The school's SENs coordinator takes lead responsibility for managing the child's special educational provision, working with the child's teachers.

Stage 3 Teachers and the SENs coordinator are supported by specialists from outside the school.

Stage 4 The LEA consider the needs for a statutory assessment, and, if appropriate, make a multidisciplinary assessment.

Stage 5 The LEA consider the need for a Statement of Special Educational Needs and, if appropriate, make a Statement and arrange, monitor and review provision.

(*Source:* DfE & WO, 1994)

Table 4.6 Pupils with SpLD and Statements in an LEA

SW LEA

Population: 550,000
Pupils: 78,000

In 1992 the LEA spent approximately 10 per cent of its budget on pupils with SENs.

Year	All SENs Statements		SpLD Statements	
	(N)	(%)	(N)	(%)
1983	1,326	1.7	0	0
1986	1,560	2.0	17	.02
1991	3,120	4.0	567	.73
1993	3,419	4.4	784	1.01
1994	3,087	3.95	not available	
1995	2,841	3.6	not available	

procedure – to its completion. Permissible exceptions to the time limits are specified in the Code of Practice. If past experience is any guide, this is unlikely to be achieved in the absence of any direct sanctions when delay occurs. The former British Rail and British Airways have an agreed scale of compensation to travellers if untoward delays occur. Could not the same be done in the assessment of pupils with SpLD? After all, such an arrangement would be consumer-led and encourage the service provider to keep to an agreed timetable. There is, of course, a 'downside' to such an approach.

The 1988 Education Reform Act required that LEAs delegate an increasing proportion of their funds to schools. This had meant that LEA centrally-supported services, such as the specialist support services for pupils with SpLD, are under increasing pressure. A survey of support services was carried out by the NUT in 1993. Results from a sample of 40 of the LEAs in England and Wales showed that, in 1991–2, almost 11 per cent had made cuts in SEN support services. This proportion is expected to reach 18 per cent in 1993–4. Before April 1993, LEAs retained centrally an average of 88 per cent of the funding for SEN support services. For 1993–4 this dropped to 67 per cent. Six of the LEAs are also reported as having delegated money for educational psychology services.

Additionally, by 1991, the National Foundation for Educational Research (NFER) found that, in a sample of 81 LEAs, 15 per cent reported that schools had made cuts in learning support departments and special needs coordinator posts (Fletcher-Campbell & Hall, 1993). Such posts are now central to the provisions of the 1993 Education Act and the implementation of the Code of Practice. Since the 1988 Education Reform Act, considerable evidence has accumulated suggesting that there has been a deterioration in the provisions for pupils with SENs (Wedell, 1993). The bill that preceded the 1993 Education Act was commented on by Sir Malcolm Thornton, Chairman of the Select Committee on Education, as follows: 'If we really believe that SENs are to be given a better deal under the new legislation than under the old system, then this is the biggest triumph of hope over experience that I have ever encountered' (*The Times Educational Supplement*, 11 December 1992).

The 1994 2.9 per cent pay award for teachers put the budgets of many LEAs and schools under severe pressures. A survey of 1,584 schools was carried out by the Institute of Manpower Studies for the National Association of Head Teachers. This showed that 18 per cent had overspent their budgets in 1991–2: twice the number that the Audit Commission had previously estimated. The General Secretary of the Secondary Heads Association is reported as anticipating that there will almost certainly be teacher redundancies. The 1995 teachers' pay recommendation of 2.7 per cent exacerbates this situation, especially as the government maintains its unwillingness to fund the award from the centre. Governors in some schools in some LEAs are already considering deficit budgets which are almost inevitably going to lead to the LEA taking over the governors' duties. Currently, such uncertainties do not help the morale of teachers or their effectiveness. If there are to be redundancies, where are these likely to fall? Will pupils with SENs suffer?

Another challenge is the length and obscurity of important parts of the Code of Practice and the associated Circular and Regulations. The understandable conceptual ambiguities and disagreements in specifying how SpLD (or any other disability) can be operationally defined presents very serious management problems for LEAs, schools and their governors, pupils and their parents.

Responses

The management of special education is a political issue. As such, policies and practices must command the support of the general public. The voluntary bodies with particular interests in SpLD represent only a part of the population. Table 4.7 considers national and local policies and procedures concerning the education of pupils with SpLD. It is divided into two related sections. The first concerns the scientific and professional bases of good practice. The second section underlines the political and educational importance of the concept of perceived 'Fairness' in resource allocation in a democracy.

'Children of parents with (metaphorically) the longest arms are not necessarily more deserving than those of parents with shorter ones.' Values concerning the type of society in which we and our children wish to live are central to the establishment of educational policies and priorities.

Whitman's words, 'I swear nothing is good to me that ignores individuals', should encourage a healthy scepticism of elaborate, expensive and ever-expanding bureaucratic systems. This is not to say that such systems are unimportant in SEN policy and service development. However, the ground-alder-like creeping propensities of educational bureaucracies require regular doses of informed criticism.

There now follows a small selection of promising practices concerning the revised SEN administration procedures and pupils with SpLD.

The LEA

With a reducing budget, the LEA continues to 'hold the ring' between competitors for limited SEN resources at Stages 4 and 5. The following actions can help in this challenging responsibility.

Table 4.7   National and local policies and administrative procedures governing the identification and education of pupils with SpLD

These procedures must be based on the assumption that SpLD comprise a variable syndrome and that there are both quantitative and qualitative differences between pupils in their developing patterns of abilities and attainments.

The procedure should:

- be based on current multidisciplinary professional understandings concerning the interactive nature of child development in general and of the semiotic function in particular
- build on existing expertise in educational, psychological, ophthalmological and medical services concerning the aetiologies, presenting symptoms, prognoses and responses to various interventions by pupils deemed to have SpLD
- encourage the development of understandings and skills in observation, assessment and teaching
- encourage cooperation between statutory and voluntary services

- be legally cohesive
- be understood by all citizens
- be agreed with by a majority of citizens
- be endorsed by local politicians
- be perceived by the general public and professionals as rational, equitable and acceptable, despite acknowledged limitations
- be regularly and systematically evaluated
- be costed

In common-sense terms, the policies, procedures, priorities and decision-making in relation to resource allocation must be perceived as 'fair'.

In terms of administrative policy and practice, the 'perfect' system does not exist.

The management of SpLD will advance on the basis of theory-driven research, tested in the crucible of the classroom.

1 Ensure that the LEA's SEN policy documents and procedures are updated in line with legislation and based on 'best practice'.

2 The efficacy of the SEN policies and practices must be regularly and systematically evaluated and revised, if necessary. In this, measurement of pupils' standards and progress is of the essence. So too is the cost-effectiveness of different forms of educational provision.

3 Continuing professional development for staff at all levels is essential. Ensure that the LEA legal advisers run courses on the 1993 Educational Act, and the Code of Practice, with particular reference to the five-stage model of SEN provision, and the rights and responsibilities of those involved as both providers and consumers of services.

4 Provide related courses for local councillors (particularly members of the Education Committee), staff of LEA psychological and support services, mainstream and special school staff, school governors, parents and representatives of voluntary and professional organisations concerned with SEN procedures and provision in general and with the identification and alleviation of SpLD in particular.

5 Ensure that the Education Psychological Service, the Education Support Service, the LEA Statementing Officer and the local inspectorate are fully conversant with the LEA's responsibilities, have run courses for the groups listed in item 3 above, and have undertaken training before they are required to attend the regional SEN Tribunals to justify an LEA's decisions.

6 Capitalise on existing strengths. Identify and disseminate examples of good SEN management practice within the LEA and establish links with the voluntary bodies concerned with SpLD.

7 Send staff to (or organise) regional and national conferences on SEN provision under the 1993 Education Act.

8 The Code of Practice contains the concept of what can 'reasonably be provided within the resources normally available to mainstream schools in the area'. This is an issue that, to advantage, could be clarified.

9 Cost everything, including the time of costing everything.

The school

The teaching profession has, collectively, sufficient understanding of the development of children's abilities and motivations to ensure that the vast majority of pupils become literate (Pumfrey, 1991; Owen & Pumfrey, 1995a, 1995b). Although their task is considerably more difficult, children with SpLD are no exception (Pumfrey & Reason, 1991; Reid & Diniz, 1993). The aspiration of the '99 by 99' campaign to ensure 99 per cent literacy by 1999 is entirely achievable. However, unless the general public, and the politicians who represent us, make this aspiration a top priority and provide additional resources, including in-service training (INSET) to keep teachers abreast of current developments, it will not be attained.

1   Ensure that the 'whole-school' SEN policy takes into account the 1993 Education Act, the OFSTED inspection requirements, the final version of the Code of Practice and Circular 6/94 2nd associated Regulations.
2   The SEN coordinator will need a strong administrative and record-keeping support system to enable the school to manage the first three stages of school-based SEN provision efficiently.
3   Help staff develop expertise in the assessment and alleviation of SpLD through award-bearing INSET.
4   Capitalise on the great promise of information technology in teaching and testing pupils with SpLD (Day, 1994).
5   Estimate the costs to the school of the management of services for pupils with SEN in general and SpLD in particular. Table 4.8 indicates how this can be started.

An analysis of the current financing by LEAs of special needs provision for non-Statemented pupils at Stages 1 to 3 of the Code of Practice demonstrates great variability in policies, priorities and practices. Special needs payments *direct* to schools by LEAs are typically based on one or more of: an audit of special needs; socio-economic factors such as the proportions of pupils eligible for free school meals; or assessments of performances. The sums *directly* allocated to schools by different LEAs to address the learning difficulties of children *without statements* range, in England, from zero to £30,627 per 100 pupils. Within LEAs the amounts delegated vary between schools, dependent on the incidence of special needs. 'These dramatic differences must have a profound effect on schools' ability to implement the *Code of Practice on the Identification and Assessment of Special Educational Needs'* (Bibby, 1994). Some LEAs delegate to schools the entire budget for children with special needs who do not have Statements. Other LEAs delegate a proportion to schools and retain the rest for centrally provided services.

> Control of local authority expenditure is, in large measure, determined by central Government. The latter provides about fifty percent of the money used by local authorities through the revenue support grant . . . Sixteen percent of that grant is allocated on the basis of different levels of additional educational needs based on a national index of socio-economic deprivation. . . . The Government estimate that, in order to provide the same standard of education nationally, the additional educational needs expenditure for primary children would range from £18,200 per 100 children in the least deprived authorities to £82,200 per 100 children in the poorest areas (Bibby, 1995).

Table 4.8   Estimated costs in a mainstream school of special needs provision at Stages 1, 2 and 3

Stage 1   Half an hour per week for each child (£23 per hour for 39 weeks)[1]

Annual costs = £448.50 per child

Stage 2   One and a half hours per week for each child at £23 per hour, plus materials for educational programmes (£200) and classroom assistant two hours per week at £5 per hour (£390)

Annual costs = £1,935.50 per child

Stage 3   Two hours per week for each child at £23 per hour. The educational psychologist for two hours per term at £45 per hour would add £270 if this had to come from the school budget. Materials would add £200, classroom assistance £2,340 (five hours per week at £5 per hour) plus a specialist teacher £3,340 (two hours a week at £30 per hour).

Annual costs = £5,579 per child

Assume a sample of 100 pupils.
Assume that about 1 in 5 (20%) have SENs at some time.
Assume that about 1 in 6 (17%) of pupils have SENs at any given time.
Assume that 2 in 100 (2%) have Statements and are funded by the LEA.
Assume that there are 15 pupils with SENs but without Statements.

Assume: 8 at Stage 1 (8 x £44.50)   = £3,588
           4 at Stage 2 (4 x £1,935.50)   = £7,742
           3 at Stage 3 (3 x £5,729)   = £17,187
           2 Statemented by LEA   = NIL (to school: LEA pays).

TOTAL COST PER ANNUM FOR 15 PUPILS = £28,517 (no Statements).

MEAN COST PER NON-STATEMENTED PUPIL PER ANNUM = £1,901

Assume that 4 in 100 have SpLD: COST = £7,605 (no Statement)
Assume that 10 in 100 have SpLD: COST = £19,010 (no Statement)

Note: 1   Highly likely to be inadequate

(*Source:* adapted from Bibby, 1994)

The funds directly delegated to schools for non-Statemented pupils with SEN at Stages 1 to 3 of the Code of Practice affect the threshold at which the LEA is required to make a Statement. The Code of Practice states: 'The main grounds on which the LEA may decide that it must make a statement is when the LEA concludes that all the special provision necessary to meet the child's needs cannot reasonably be provided within the resources normally available to mainstream schools in the area' (DfE & WO, 1994a).

In addition to her longstanding and influential work on SENs, Baroness Warnock is the President of the British Dyslexia Association (National Organisation for SpLD). Addressing the Oldham National Special Educational Needs Conference in May 1995, she is reported as criticising what she saw as the undermining of the Code of Practice by the government's other educational policies (Pyke, 1995b). 'The code essentially depends on having a higher, not a lower, number of teachers proportional to the children, a smaller, not a higher number of children in the class' (Quoted in Pyke, 1995b).

The largest groups of both non-Statemented and Statemented pupils with SENs are those with SpLD. The implications of the funding mechanisms described in Bibby's article are that overall SEN resources are being restricted. Whilst fully accepting that the public purse is not bottomless, in a society in which equality of educational opportunity is purported to be a plank of policy, the issue of resource priorities becomes central, as Baroness Warnock's comments make clear. The DfE is virtually alone in considering that the Code of Practice will be 'cost neutral'.

Governors

Governors have important collective responsibilities for the SENs programme in their school.

1   Governors must be able to explain to parents the policies and practices comprising the school's SENs programme, including the identification and alleviation of SpLD.
2   By virtue of their management responsibilities, governors require training in the legal and financial implications of the SEN provisions in the 1993 Education Act. As SpLD may be one of the most frequently-occurring special educational needs, the governors need to be fully aware of the financial implications for the school budget.

Parents of pupils who may have SpLD

1   If parents think that their child may have SpLD, they should always contact the school in the first instance.

2   Obtain and study the school's SEN policy, and check whether provision is made for pupils with SpLD within the three stages for which the school is responsible.
3   Collaborate with your child's school and staff.
4   Meet both the class teacher and the special needs coordinator.
5   Remember that the staff of the Education Psychological Service and the Education Support Service can provide expert advice on SpLD.
6   Learn about your rights and responsibilities under the 1993 Education Act.
7   Contact local voluntary associations concerned with SpLD.
8   Read about the SEN Tribunals (DfE, 1994b; Pyke, 1995).

Conclusion

The 1993 Education Act takes the market economy concept of education even further. The Code of Practice and Regulations on Assessment and Statements (DfE & WO, 1994) plus Circular 6/94 (DfE, 1994a) are key documents for those concerned with the identification and alleviation of SpLD. Important as they are, neither the Code nor the Circular have the power of law. Despite this, they will have a powerful influence on SEN policies and provision.

Great expectations of what will be done to help pupils with SpLD have been raised. Great responsibilities have been created for schools and their governors. Within a 'whole-school' SEN policy, the school's special needs coordinator is going to be extremely busy in ensuring that the three non-Statemented school-based stages of the identification and assessment process function successfully. The additional ongoing involvements with Statemented pupils, and with those for whom Statements are being prepared, underline the demands of the work.

Support services and LEA psychological services will also be under considerable pressure. Already, one LEA is currently being legally challenged for letting teachers carry out aspects of individual assessment that are the province of qualified psychologists. The timetable set for decision-making in relation to Statements is challenging but possible, given adequate staffing of the psychological services, and provided that the earlier 'within-school' stages are properly completed before statutory assessments are started. These are important caveats. The regional SEN Tribunals are waiting. So are concerned parents and their supporters (Pyke, 1995).

The Code of Practice and Circular 6/94 contain many constructive suggestions for improving the management of SpLD. The development of a common administrative procedure across the country has considerable merit. In view of their implementation being 'cost-neutral', the complexities of the five-stage model suggest that the proposals could have been intended to function as a blocking mechanism to a virtually unstoppable and quite obviously rapidly-growing tide of requests for Statements and the resources attached to these. Parents' expectations concerning the identification and alleviation of their children's SpLD have been raised. Can these expectations be met by the management system proposed by the DfE? It not – as is highly likely – then consumer protection will become a much larger and even more expensive growth sector.

Postscript

Chapter 14, by Ingrid Lunt and Brahm Norwich, provides the essential informed appreciation of Klaus Wedell's work that justifies this Festschrift. Asked to provide some personal comments concerning my contacts with Klaus, I decided that 'free association' was the most appropriate retrieval technique, confident that readers will fully appreciate the attendant dangers, of 'false memory syndrome'. Any tendency to beatification that may be revealed here is, I hope, offset by my awareness that the difference between a halo and a noose is about six inches.

The associations that emerged comprised a very lengthy list of individuals, institutions and idiosyncratic items. On reflection, a subjectively clear grouping could be discerned. One cluster comprised the names of past and current members of the educational and psychological professions, their teaching, research and the institutions with which they were associated. To give the flavour: Mia Kelmer Pringle; Selly Wick House; Albemarle Street . . . The second cluster was a series of extremely idiosyncratic items. From the latter I will select only one (later).

The University of Birmingham Institute, Department, Faculty and School of Education, respectively, have played major roles in the professional development of myself and myriad other colleagues. The linkages between Manchester University's Centre for Educational Guidance and Special Needs and Klaus at Birmingham's Centre for Child Study and, subsequently, the University of London Institute of Education, Department of Educational Psychology and Special Educational Needs were initially institutional and professional ones. These were based on shared values, mutual interests and ongoing involvements in training teachers and psychologists, research, local and national educational policy development, publications, and through professional bodies of which we were both members. Meeting and working with Klaus widened my professional perceptions significantly.

My membership of the Division of Educational and Child Psychology (DECP) Committee coincided with Klaus's involvement as member and officer. It was in this forum, in particular, that I witnessed the courtesy, tact, thoughtfulness and industry that, for me, have characterised my involvements with Klaus. This is not to suggest that he lacks either professional passion, drive or steel! Above the attributes listed towers his vision concerning the nature of a society in which equality of opportunity was, and continues to be, a central challenge. Underpinning that vision is a set of values concerning the worth of the individual. Linked to that is his appreciation of the importance of using the structures and institutions of our community to move towards a more just society. In this latter respect, few psychologists have been as assiduous and as influential as he. Equally, no one is more aware that much still requires to be achieved.

While at Birmingham, his orchestration of a DECP Enquiry into Psychological Services for Children in England and Wales brought together educational and clinical psychologists in regional groups. This 1979 initiative provided opportunities for the constructive and focused cross-divisional discussion that is easily espoused but difficult to achieve in a somewhat fragmented profession. I mention it as one who was involved and who benefited from the *process* as well as from the report by Wedell and Lambourne (1979). The tensions between generic and specialist training in professional psychology came to the fore in relation to the ongoing moves towards harmonisation of professional qualifications across the European Community.

Turning to the idiosyncratic associations, I select only one: newel post. Klaus's eloquent description of the satisfactions that he derived from turning a newel post for a house that he was refurbishing underlined his appreciation of the practical and aesthetic challenges and rewards of craftsmanship. Utility and beauty combined: the spirit of William Morris lives on! I trust that the family home in Longtown and his *pied-à-terre* in London will provide ample scope for continuing his artisan and academic activities.

Over time, there have been significant improvements in concep-tualisations, policies and practices concerning the nature of disabilities. These have culminated in the 1994 Code of Practice and its related Circulars and Regulations. Despite its controversial nature, the concept of special educational needs has helped to this end. Klaus's current involvement with the National Council for Educational Technology on a project to support the work of special needs coordinators in mainstream schools is typically forward-looking.

As a far-sighted, persuasive and informed colleague, Klaus Wedell's contribution to the development of services for pupils with SEN, and thus to *all* pupils, is one of which not only fellow professionals can be justly proud. The newel post and its connotations help make this paragon human.

References

Audit Commission (1992a) *Getting in on the Act: Provision for Pupils with Special Educational Needs,* London: HMSO.

Audit Commission (1992b) *Getting the Act Together: Provision for Pupils with Special Needs,* London: HMSO.

Bibby, P. (1994) 'Dreamland of special needs draft', *The Times Educational Supplement,* 18 February, p.8.

Bibby, P. (1995) 'Nasty bumps on the statements thresholds', *The Times Educational Supplement* (School Management Update), 12 May, pp.8–9.

Chasty, H. & Friel, J. (1993) *Children with Special Needs: Assessment, Law and Practice – Caught in the Act,* London: Jessica Kingsley (2nd edn).

Crisfield, J. & Smythe, I. (eds) (1993) *The Dyslexia Handbook 1993/4,* Reading: British Dyslexia Association.

Day, J. (1994) *A Software Guide for Specific Learning Difficulties,* Coventry: National Council for Educational Technology.

Department for Education (DfE) (1993) *Education Act 1993: Draft Circular on the Organisation of Special Educational Provision, Draft Regulations on Schools' Policies on Special Educational Needs and Provision by LEAs of Special Educational Needs Support Services,* London: DfE, December.

Department for Education (DfE) (1994a) *The Organisation of Special Educational Provision,* Circular 6/94, London: DfE.

Department for Education (DfE) (1994b) *Special Educational Needs Tribunal: How to Appeal,* London: DfE.

Department for Education & Welsh Office (DfE & WO) (1993) *Education Act 1993: Draft Code of Practice on the Identification and Assessment of Special Educational Needs and Draft Regulations on Assessment and Statements,* London: DfE & WO, October.

Department for Education & Welsh Office (DfE & WO) (1994a) *Code of Practice on the Identification and Assessment of Special Educational Needs,* London: Central Office of Information.

Department for Education & Welsh Office (DfE & WO) (1994b) *The Education (Special Educational Needs) (Information) Regulations 1994,* London: Central Office of Information.

Department of Education and Science (DES) (1978) *Special Educational Needs: Report of the Committee of Inquiry into the Education of Handicapped Children and Young People* (The Warnock Report, Cmnd 7212), London: HMSO.

Education (1992) 'Ombudsman: Staffing difficulties no excuse for delaying assessment of special needs', *Education,* 6 March, p.198.

Elliott, C.D (1990) 'The definition and identification of specific learning difficulties', in P.D Pumfrey & C.D. Elliott (eds) *Children's Difficulties in Reading, Spelling and Writing,* London: Falmer Press.

Fletcher-Campbell, F. & Hall, C. (1993) *LEA Support for Special Needs,* Windsor: NFER-Nelson.

Gardiner, J. (1994) 'Judge overrules Patten', *The Times Educational Supplement,* 14 January, p.7.

Office for Standards in Education (OFSTED) (1993) Part 5, Technical Papers: 'Paper 8: Special Educational Needs in Mainstream Schools', in *Handbook for the Inspection of Schools,* London: HMSO.

Owen, P. & Pumfrey, P.D. (eds) (1995a) *Children Learning to Read: International Concerns, Vol. 1, Emergent and Developing Reading,* London: Falmer Press.

Owen, P. & Pumfrey, P.D. (eds) (1995b) *Children Learning to Read: International*

Concerns, Vol. 2, Curriculum and Assessment Issues, London: Falmer Press.

Pumfrey, P.D. (1991) *Improving Children's Reading in the Junior School*, Special Needs in Ordinary Schools Series, London: Cassell.

Pumfrey, P.D. (1993a) 'Specific learning difficulties', in *Working Together at all Ages and Stages*, Rotherham: Rotherham LEA.

Pumfrey, P.D. (1993b) 'Looking at dyslexia through rose-coloured glasses', *Special!*, June.

Pumfrey, P.D. (1994) 'Specific learning difficulties: Research findings and their implications for the initial and in-service education of teachers in the UK', in P. Mittler (ed.) *Proceedings of the European Association for Special Education Conference on Teacher Training*, University of Manchester School of Education.

Pumfrey, P.D. & Elliott, C.D. (eds) (1990) *Children's Difficulties in Reading, Spelling and Writing*, London: Falmer Press (3rd edn, 1993).

Pumfrey, P.D. & Mittler, P. (1989) 'Peeling off the label', *The Times Educational Supplement*, 13 October, pp.29–30.

Pumfrey, P.D. & Reason, R. (1991) *Specific Learning Difficulties (Dyslexia): Challenges and Responses*, London: Routledge (5th edn, 1994).

Pyke, N. (1993a) 'Parents take to the high court', *The Times Educational Supplement*, 15 January, p.6.

Pyke, N. (1993b) 'Complaints flood in', *The Times Educational Supplement*, 17 September, p.4.

Pyke, N. (1995a) 'Special needs tribunals confirm critics' fears', *The Times Educational Supplement*, 27 January.

Pyke, N. (1995b) 'Warnock fears for special needs code', *The Times Educational Supplement*, 12 May, p.7.

Reid, G. & Diniz, F.A. (eds) (1993) *Course Reader: Perspective on Practice*. Edinburgh: Moray House Publications.

Rogers, R. (1993) *A Guide to the Education Act 1993*. London: Advisory Centre for Education.

Sawyer, D.J. (1992) 'Language abilities, reading acquisition and developmental dyslexia: A discussion of hypothetical and observed relationships', *Journal of Learning Disabilities*, 25, pp.82–95.

Warnock, M. (1991) 'Motion – Children with Special Educational Needs', *House of Lords Official Report: Parliamentary Debates, Hansard*, 532 (12), p.973.

Wedell, K. (1993) 'Special Needs Education: The next 25 Years', *National Commission on Education Briefing*, 14, London: NCE.

Wedell, K. & Lambourne, R. (1979) *An Enquiry into Psychological Services for Children in England and Wales*, Birmingham: University of Birmingham, Department of Educational Psychology.

5 Provision for children with communication difficulties

Jannet A. Wright

Introduction

This chapter will begin with a description of communication difficulties, both receptive and expressive, and implications of these for a child's educational progress. This will be followed by a brief historical review of educational provision for these children. It will then focus on the current range of provision for children with communication problems as well as the opportunities and challenges being offered to multidisciplinary teams working with these children and their parents. The chapter will conclude with a consideration of the future concerns for both therapists and teachers in this area of work.

Communication problems or difficulties

Children with communication problems are a heterogeneous group (Byers Brown & Edwards, 1989). It can be helpful to conceptualise such problems on a continuum. A communication difficulty can range from a mild disturbance in the sound system, such as substituting 'w' for 'r' as in 'wabbit', to a severe language disorder when children are unable to understand spoken language and/or express themselves adequately. In the latter case, they may require specialised therapeutic and educational provision throughout their school life.

Communication problems include difficulties with verbal and nonverbal communication. These may co-exist with sensory, cognitive and physical difficulties, or the communication problem can appear to be a specific difficulty. When professionals work with children who have severe cognitive and/or physical problems, their focus is on the communicative function of children's utterances, rather than the structure of their speech and language skills. In the latter case, the child's communication will be investigated at the phonological, semantic, syntactic or pragmatic level as well as at the interactions between these levels. It is important to remember that children with communication problems may have difficulty in understanding spoken language as well as expressing themselves. Comprehension problems can be overlooked, due to the prominent nature of expressive language difficulties.

There are some children who have severe speech and language problems which have been identified by excluding all other causative/contributive factors. These children have been described as having a 'specific' speech and language problem. In the past, they have been described as 'developmentally dysphasic', 'language-impaired' or 'language-disordered'. Children with such a severe and specific communication problem may have been identified before school entry as children with delayed language development.

Many children will have their communication difficulty identified before school entry:

> Although most speech and language difficulties will have been identified before a child reaches school, some children will still have significant speech and language difficulties which impair their ability to participate in the classroom by the time they go to school. (DfE & WO, 1994, para. 3.85)

There are two points raised in this paragraph from the Code of Practice which need further consideration. The first one is the implication that the *majority* of children who have speech and language problems will have been recognised prior to school entry. Although many children are identified via referrals from parents, GPs, health visitors and clinical medical officers, there are, unfortunately, children who will not have their communication difficulty recognised until they start school.

It would seem reasonable to assume that, if a child has a structural abnormality or neurological condition such as a cleft palate or cerebral palsy, where a communication problem is likely to co-exist, these children will be identified in the pre-school years. Early identification of children with delayed language development can happen when parents, relatives and health visitors become concerned. Developmental checks in the pre-school years also provide an opportunity to identify children with speech and language problems. But there will still be many children, despite the reassuring statement from the Code of Practice (DfE & WO, 1994), whose communication problems will not be identified until after they start school. Secondly, the paragraph from the Code of Practice quoted above gives the impression that only a *small* number of children will have communication difficulties 'which impair their ability to participate in the classroom'. In fact, in any classroom there will be children who have considerable difficulty with gaining access to the curriculum or coping with the content of the curriculum. The educational implications of a communication problem are described below.

Educational implications of communication problems

This section will review studies which have tried to relate language impairment to later educational achievement. The majority of the studies, both in the USA and in the UK have ben retrospective.

Children with both 'speech defects' and language difficulties were included in a study by Hall and Tomblin (1978), in Iowa, USA. The authors contacted 36 language- and articulation-impaired clients, thirteen to twenty years after their initial contact with a speech and hearing clinic. By this time, the clients were in their early twenties. The results of their research indicate that the subjects who had language problems also had academic problems. An association between articulation problems and poor school achievement was identified by Drillien and Drummond (1983). They were carrying out a longitudinal study in Dundee, Scotland, and aimed to ascertain the frequency of neurodevelopmental disabilities in a population of 5,334 pre-school children. The authors found an incidence of speech disorders of 5.6 per cent in the pre-school population. This figure rises to 7.5 per cent if those children are included for whom speech difficulties are a secondary problem. The teachers of these children received a questionnaire when the children had been in school for eighteen months to two years. They were asked about the children's academic achievement, and reported poor school achievement in those children who had articulation problems.

Another longitudinal study carried out by a multidisciplinary team in Dunedin, New Zealand (Silva et al., 1983), looked at 857 children. In this study, early identification of a language delay was also linked with some cognitive difficulties. The children had their language skills assessed at 3, 5 and 7 years. The authors made a distinction between children with:

- language delay at only one age – 'transitory language delay'
- language delay at two ages – 'moderately stable delay'
- language delay at all three ages – 'stable language delay'.

They found that 168 children out of 857 had a language delay at one or more of the assessments. When the authors looked at the numbers of children who had low IQ or reading difficulties at 7 years old, between 45.8 per cent and 68.2 per cent of these had had a language delay at 3 years old. The more stable the language delay, the greater the prevalence of later low IQ and reading difficulties. If one bears in mind the quote given earlier from the Code of Practice, it is interesting to note in this study that some children who were not delayed at 3 years were identified as language-delayed at a later stage, after school entry.

If a child has a very specific communication problem, such as 'developmental verbal dyspraxia', there is evidence of difficulty with particular learning strategies; for example, Snowling and Stackhouse (1983) demonstrated that such children have difficulty using a phonetic spelling strategy. In 1992, Stackhouse and Snowling followed up two children they had seen four years before. This time the children were aged 14.6 years and 15.8 years, and they still had marked speech problems. They also had continued difficulties in reading and spelling, supporting a link between spoken-language problems and literacy.

Aram et al. (1984) followed up 20 children of a similar age to those looked at by Stackhouse and Snowling. These children had been studied ten years earlier, when they were all diagnosed as 'language-disordered'. The authors studied the children's academic performance, their speech and language and social adjustment. This group of 20 teenagers had 60 per cent of their Verbal IQs, 80 per cent of their Performance IQs and 70 per cent of their Full Scale IQs within or above the low average range, yet they continued to have language difficulties and had required more special educational attention than their peer group. When Howlin and Rutter (1987) re-analysed the data from 11 children, who had an initial IQ of at least 90, they confirmed that there was an increased rate of educational difficulties.

In a study of 156 children with speech and language problems, who entered Dawn House School in Nottinghamshire between 1974 and 1987, Haynes (1992) reports that almost all had persisting language problems which affected their educational achievement, work prospects and social life. These children had such severe speech and language problems that they had been placed at this special boarding/day language school. Their nonverbal skills were average or above, and they did not have additional significant problems. Yet their difficulties were so severe and pervasive that many aspects of their lives were affected. A prospective study was carried out in the UK by Bishop and Edmundson (1987). They tried to predict which children with language delay in the pre-school years would continue to have language difficulties on school entry. They saw 87 language-disordered children from the North of England. The children were seen at 4 years of age and again at 4.6 and 5.6 years. Bishop and Edmundson (1987) found that the more pervasive a communication problem is, the more problems a child is likely to have. They also found that children with language problems at 5.6 years had difficulty with reading comprehension, spoken-language skills and some nonverbal tasks. These results indicate the way in which a persistent language delay can influence academic achievement.

All of the reported studies provide support for the fact that children who have communication difficulties are at risk of academic failure. Although the labels used to describe these children over the years have often changed, they all had a recognisable language difficulty. The school curriculum is delivered using spoken and written language. All subjects have a linguistic component, and children who have difficulties in this area can be disadvantaged when they enter the school system.

Historical review of provision

The first reference in educational legislation to provision for children with communication difficulties was in the 1945 Handicapped Pupils and School Health Service Regulations, which followed the 1944 Education Act. In fact, 'speech defects' was one of the new categories to be introduced. It was recommended that these children should attend speech clinics where therapists employed by the local education authority (LEA) would see them. However, for children with severe speech and language problems, the late 1940s saw the opening of the first residential school, Moor House School in Oxted, Surrey. It is still open today as a non-maintained special school catering for 80 children aged between 7 and 16 years. Other language schools, which were initially residential, were opened by the charity Invalid Children's Aid Nationwide (ICAN). These were the John Horniman School in Sussex, Dawn House School in Nottinghamshire and Meath School in Surrey. Today, all the schools take a proportion of day pupils. Manchester Education Authority was the first to open a school for children with communication problems, the Ewing School.

By the 1970s, the pressure from both parents and professionals was growing for children with severe speech and language problems to receive both educational and therapeutic support nearer to home. This led to the establishment of language units, whose growth reached a peak in the 1980s.

By the end of the 1980s, there was a considerable number of children with speech and language difficulties in mainstream schools who had Statements of special educational need (SEN). Some of these children had speech and language therapy as an educational provision, but for many it was seen as non-educational provision. If speech and language therapy is included in a child's Statement as part of their SENs provision, then the LEA has a statutory duty to arrange such provision. This was the ruling following the *R* v. *Lancashire County Council ex parte CM* (1989) case, where the judges saw the work of speech and language therapists as educational. However, the debate continues about whether speech and language therapy support for children is seen as 'educational provision', and thus included in Part 3 of the Statement, or included in Part 6 as 'non-educational provision'. In paragraph 4 (34) of the Code of Practice, 'speech and language therapy may be regarded as either educational or non-educational provision, depending on the health or developmental history of each child'.

If a child attending school requires speech and language therapy, the LEA and school are dependent for the provision or organisation of the local speech and language therapy services. The LEA may have to negotiate with more than one health authority to arrange appropriate levels of provision, because the health and education authority boundaries are rarely coterminous. If such negotiations are successful, then a speech and language therapist will be assigned to a specific child or school. In situations where a therapist is working with a child in a school, the LEA and the headteacher have to acknowledge that the therapist remains responsible and accountable to a manager outside the school. If a speech and language therapist is employed by the LEA to work either in a special or a mainstream school, then the therapist will be responsible to either the headteacher or a nominated LEA manager. There are administrative and financial disadvantages for the LEA if the provision of speech and language therapy is seen as 'educational'. The LEA has a legal responsibility to provide therapy and will therefore initially approach the nearest health authority to provide the required support, but if the health authority is unable to meet this request, then the LEA will need to approach other health authorities or employ a speech and language therapist themselves; this can be a time-consuming and costly exercise.

Current situation

The provision for children with speech and language problems is provided by both the education and the health service. The children are seen by both teachers and speech and language therapists. In the best situations, the two professionals work together along with the child's parents to provide a coordinated plan of intervention. Unfortunately, this does not always happen. In this section, the provision by the two services will be described under two separate headings, although the reader will become increasingly aware of how, on occasions, these services come together.

Speech and language therapy provision

The range of services for children provided by speech and language therapy includes assessment, information for the parents, management and therapeutic intervention. The therapist will usually work with other professionals. The therapist may be a member of a loosely-knit team which comes together as and when the needs of an individual child necessitate it. On the other hand, the team may be a well-structured one, such as a hospital-based team dealing with children born with a cleft palate or a community-based team supporting children with severe learning difficulties.

The local arrangements for speech and language therapy service provision are the responsibility of the manager of the speech therapy services but will be influenced by the purchasers within the National Health Service and from LEAs and schools using Local Management of Schools. The details of the arrangements vary from one geographical area to another. Thus a child with a communication problem in Sunderland will come into contact with a service organised in a very different way compared to a child with the same problem in Manchester.

The intensity of therapy which the child is offered will vary between daily, weekly or monthly intervention. Appointments within a health centre, hospital or the child's home can vary from 30 minutes to $1^1/_2$ hours. Usually, at least one parent accompanies the child and joins in the therapy, so that the work the speech and language therapist does with the child can be integrated into the rest of the child's life. Some older children will be offered intensive courses during the school holidays. This has been particularly popular with children who are dysfluent or stammer. For some teenagers, attendance at such a course on a daily basis has been a more acceptable form of therapy, especially if parental attendance is also required.

Historically, it was more common to find a speech and language therapist based at a special school or working there on a part-time basis than in mainstream schools. Children attending mainstream schools usually went to a local health centre for speech therapy. This pattern of intervention is still seen by many NHS managers as cost-effective. A therapist spending a whole morning in a clinic can see three or four children on an individual basis for 45–60 minutes each, rather than spending a whole morning visiting a school to see one child and one teacher. On the other hand, this means that a child coming for the therapy appointments may have to miss up to half a day of school.

The 1981 Education Act resulted in the creation of more posts for speech and language therapists to work in mainstream schools or support children who had Statements in the mainstream. At the same time, there was a move within the profession to work more closely with teachers and children in schools. When speech and language therapy is offered within a school setting, the profession faces the same issues which arise for other support services. These include decisions about whether to see the child in the classroom or to withdraw them for therapy, and establishing how the therapist may have time to talk to the teacher. The way in which the therapist decides to work with the child is an area which can lead to conflict between the professionals involved if not addressed during an initial contact. It may be decided by the school's policy, or by the teacher or the child's own choice, or the goals for that particular school term or year. If the intervention mirrors the provision offered in clinic, it can be difficult to justify school-based therapy. Such intervention needs to involve the teacher and therapist in discussion and joint planning. It is important to note that certain areas of speech and language work need to be done on a one-to-one basis, rather than in a group or within the classroom. These areas need to be identified and decisions taken as to which professional will work on a specified area with a child.

If a school-age child is being seen by a speech and language therapist, it is crucial that the therapist work with the parents and teachers. Without such a partnership, a child is unlikely to make significant progress. A speech and language therapy session either once a week or every day in term time will only be successful if the therapy is integrated into a child's lifestyle. Thus parents need to be involved as much as possible from the point of referral to speech and language therapy.

However, when professionals work with other professional groups, problems may arise from their limited knowledge about each other's specific skills, knowledge and intervention strategies (Norwich, 1990). Teachers and therapists have different contracts, employers, holidays and school duties. All of these can influence a professional partnership. Although there is increased evidence of professional collaboration in certain settings, this is still limited to certain activities.

A survey of 443 speech and language therapists working in England and Wales with children up to the age of 11 years revealed that most collaboration occurred during the intervention stages of therapy (Wright, 1994). All the speech and language therapists in this study believed that collaboration between teachers and therapists was important when working with children who had communication problems. The therapists who took part in the survey were based in either schools or health centres. Their responses to a postal questionnaire indicated that the incidence of collaboration increased after the children had been assessed and the therapy planned. The therapists who were clinic-based rarely carried out any joint assessments with the teacher, although there was evidence of some joint planning once the assessment results were known. It is unfortunate that so few therapists carried out joint assessments with teachers, as this would seem to be an ideal opportunity to increase understanding of each others' skills and knowledge. The therapists who were based in the same school as the teacher were more likely to assess and plan the therapy with a teacher than their clinic-based colleagues. However, over 50 per cent of the school-based therapists still assessed and planned their therapy in isolation. The speech and language therapists who saw children in schools but who were based in health centres saw collaboration with the class teacher as an opportunity to provide continuity of intervention. Therapists expected the teacher to carry on with the therapy programme when they were not in school. Indeed, this expectation of continuity was referred to by the clinic-based therapists as one of the main benefits or advantages of collaborating with teachers.

The introduction of the 1988 Education Act appeared to offer many opportunities for therapists and teachers to work together. 'Speaking' and 'listening' were specifically set as attainment targets in the English curriculum. This was viewed by therapists in a very positive light. Therapists had access to specific details about the curriculum, and many were involved with a whole-school approach to planning and teaching this aspect of the curriculum. This focus on speaking and listening meant that teaching colleagues were alerted to pupils with communication difficulties. When speaking and listening were not included in the standard assessment tasks, there was concern that this area would become marginalised and receive less attention from educationalists and therapists. However, changes to English within the National Curriculum (SCAA, 1994) have again raised hopes among therapists that future planning for children with communication problems will be able to use the aims arising from the move toward Standard English. This will be discussed further below.

Educational provision

Children with speech and language difficulties need the support and skills of their teachers in order to gain access to the curriculum. Unfortunately, this presents problems when very few teachers have had any specific information and experience of children with speech and language problems. There are very few award-bearing courses for teachers working with these children. There are courses at Newcastle University, Sheffield University and one run jointly by Whitefields School in Walthamstow and Kingston University. It is increasingly difficult for teaching staff to be released to obtain a qualification if the course runs during the day. This has led to an increase in the numbers of people attending courses after school or studying in their own time. The commitment to these children is demonstrated by the fact that currently there are around a hundred teachers following the Distance Education Course: Speech and Language Difficulties, run by the Faculty of Education and Continuing Studies at the University of Birmingham. This course has attracted teachers from England, Scotland, Wales and Northern Ireland. Increasingly, there are therapists working in education who want to increase their knowledge in this area.

The teachers taking these courses work in a variety of settings. They may be in mainstream schools, language units, special schools specifically for children with speech and language problems. The children in these different educational settings need a joint assessment that will enable the teacher and therapist to prioritise the child's needs. In some schools, this may form the child's Individual Education Plan.

As stated earlier, it is hoped that the new speaking and listening targets (SCAA, 1994) will help teachers when they are planning the work for these children. The focus on Standard English means that reference is made to key skills such as 'choosing words with precision, learning to ask questions, the correct and consistent use of verb tenses'. This means that the intervention offered by both teachers and therapists can focus on such specific areas as and when appropriate.

Children with communication problems require modifications which may take the form of altering the language used to instruct children in the classroom, or the teacher may need to provide additional methods when spoken language is being used as the means of instruction within the classroom. This could mean the use of signing, additional gestures or visual clues. It may mean that the staff working with these children have to think about their own use of language and what they can do within the classroom to enable children to follow instructions and descriptions of activities. When working on specific projects, the children may need pre- and post-lesson support to understand the vocabulary being used. Children who have word-finding problems will need additional time and opportunities to find ways of remembering and recalling the target vocabulary. If children do not understand the vocabulary being used, they will be at a disadvantage in the classroom. Children with speech and language problems require additional opportunities to acquire any vocabulary and will not learn it incidentally. This can cause confusion for teachers inexperienced in working with children who have communication problems, as they may be used to more incidental learning in a group of children.

The class teacher working in a language unit or supporting a child in mainstream schools will also have to think about the motor-organisational and coordination problems which these children can have. This needs to be kept in mind when a child is working in the classroom on tasks such as writing. The other area which often needs careful consideration regarding provision within the classroom is social skills. Children with communication difficulties need additional help to function within a group and to identify and utilise nonverbal social cues. Specific teaching in this area is often required, and packs such as the *Social Use of Language Programme* (Rinaldi, 1992) have been developed by practitioners to try to help both teachers and therapists include this in the curriculum. In secondary schools, it has been possible to include this area of work within English and Personal and Social Education.

Future concerns

When looking at future provision for children with communication problems, a crystal ball is needed. This is partly due to the fact that professionals from both health and education work with these children, and partly due to the complex, sometimes hidden nature of communication problems. Any future changes in either the health service or the education service will have an impact on service delivery. It is probably safe to say that a continuum of provision will continue to exist for children with speech and language difficulties. In fact, there may be a slight increase in the use of boarding provision by LEAs who cannot provide for children with severe communication problems.

The provision will continue to vary from one geographical area to another. This is due to historical factors and the varying ways in which schools and local authorities respond to the needs of children with communication problems.

In spite of the number of education authorities who have funded speech and language therapy posts, it does not seem likely that the education service across the country will have the money to employ all the speech therapists required to support school-age children with communication problems. Thus professionals managed by two different services will, in most areas, continue to work with these children.

The therapists who are already employed by education services will notice an increased similarity in the outlook of the managers in the health and education services. There is a stronger emphasis on the economic aspects of client intervention. Professionals are pre-contracted for a certain number of sessions for each child referred to them. In some cases, this involves recording the number of minutes that a child needs for each therapy session. This approach to record-keeping is based on face-to-face contacts, while discussion with parents and other professionals is not recorded. The implication of this approach is that these statistics are not valuable, and therefore activities which cannot be recorded within pre-determined codes are not worth doing. This makes collaborative working practices between therapists and teachers difficult to maintain, particularly if they require planning sessions. It also removes the individuality of the child as the central concern, and assumes each phonological or syntactic problem will require the same amount of speech and language therapy or teacher intervention time.

To ensure that the children in their school receive adequate speech and language therapy, some headteachers and governors are choosing to 'buy' speech and language therapy time. However, discussion with headteachers reveals that many see this approach as a way of ensuring that the headteacher has control over the therapist's time. In this arrangement, the therapist is in school seeing children, rather than outside school seeing other children or attending meetings. For the profession of speech and language therapy, this raises concerns over the narrow interpretation that managers in education appear to have applied to the job of the speech and language therapist.

The funding arrangements within the health service have made it necessary for speech and language therapy service managers to be explicit about what they can offer for children with communication problems. The fundholders will make decisions, based on this information, about what will and will not receive funding and how much speech and language therapy time will be bought for children both before and after school entry. In some areas, therapists 'overperformed' in 1994 – in other words, they saw more children than they had predicted. This meant that fundholders faced higher bills than they anticipated. As a result of this, some services were told to see fewer children in the next financial year. This will mean that waiting lists will grow, and children will not receive therapy as early as they should.

As people continue to try to predict the amount of therapy a child needs, there will be a positive response to research which looks closely at what constitutes effective intervention and the most successful way in which it can be offered.

The future for teachers working with children who have communication problems looks equally uncertain. They are not sure whether their jobs will continue to be funded. In a school where a language unit caters for a class of eight or ten children, school governors are likely to wonder whether that teacher could not be redeployed to reduce the size of classes across the school. Teachers working in the language support services have seen their colleagues working in other areas of special needs made redundant, and wonder how long their jobs are secure.

Even if funding continues, it is unlikely that there will be any more money available for training. This is more serious than it looks initially, because research into speech and language development and breakdown continues to advance – in the USA, in the UK, and in other parts of Europe. Teachers working with children who have failed to develop their communication, or with children whose speech and language is developing slowly and in an unusual way, need access to current research. They need to be able to acquire this new knowledge, interpret its relevance to the children they see, and apply it to the classroom situation. If financial support to attend short courses/conferences is not provided, then teaching practices with these children may ossify, and opportunities to apply research to practice will be missed.

The issue of in-class support or withdrawal was discussed earlier in this chapter; however, a new concern has recently been raised by the OFSTED (Office for Standards in Education) inspectors. Taking a child out of the classroom for therapy may mean loss of time spent on areas of the National Curriculum. Therefore, schools are being asked to make explicit their arrangements for ensuring that children are not disadvantaged in curriculum areas if they leave the classroom for therapy.

The final area of concern is always present whatever else is happening in the education and health services: this is the issue of identification of children with communication problems. Some children are identified too late for adequate help to be given, and come to see themselves as failures. Others are 'labelled' in a way that fails to acknowledge their communication problems. This means that information constantly needs to be passed to all the professionals working with pre-school and school-age children, as well as parents, about the characteristics of children with speech and language problems. Information also needs to be available about the services available for these children in the health and education services.

Conclusion

This chapter has described some of the features of communication problems. The evidence from research which demonstrates the academic problems which can arise as a result of speech and language difficulties has been reviewed. The provision for these children, both past and present, has been discussed. The chapter ends with a consideration of some of the future issues facing the professionals working with these children, and ultimately, the children themselves. The main advantage for these children is that speech and language development is a significant milestone for parents. A child who fails to develop in this area is a cause for concern, and many parents seek help when this happens. If parents can be provided with information about the availability of the resources to help their children, they will continue to be the professionals' allies in maintaining and developing services for children with communication problems.

Postscript

I have known Klaus Wedell since 1983, when I began the part-time MA in Psychology and Education for Children with Special Needs at the University of London Institute of Education. Between 1987 and 1993, I was seconded to the Department of Educational Psychology and Special Educational Needs to lecture on language and communication difficulties to students on Diploma and MSc/MA courses in special education. I was also fortunate to have Klaus Wedell as supervisor for my PhD research into collaboration between teachers and speech and language therapists who were working with children with communication problems.

Klaus Wedell was also involved in helping me to design an option on special education which was taught to undergraduates in the BSc (Hons) Speech Sciences course at University College London.

References

Aram, D.M., Ekelman, B.L. & Nation, J.E. (1984) 'Pre-schoolers with language disorders: 10 years later', *Journal of Speech and Hearing Research*, 27, pp.232–44.
Bishop, D.V.M. & Edmundson, A. (1987) 'Specific language impairment as a maturational lag: Evidence from longitudinal data on language and motor development', *Developmental Medicine and Child Neurology*, 29, pp.442–59.
Byers Brown, B. & Edwards, M. (1989) *Developmental Disorders of Language*, London: Whurr Publishers.
Department for Education & Welsh Office (DfE & WO) (1994) *Code of Practice on the Identification and Assessment of Special Educational Needs*, London: HMSO.
Department of Education and Science (DES) (1945) *The Handicapped Pupils and School Health Service Regulations*, London: HMSO.
Drillien, C. & Drummond, M. (1983) *Development Screening and the Child with Special Needs*, London: Spastics International Medical Publications/Heinemann.
Hall, P.K. & Tomblin, J.B. (1978) 'A follow-up study of children with articulation and language disorders', *Journal of Speech and Hearing Disorders*, 43, pp.227–41.
Haynes, C.P.A. (1992) 'A longitudinal study of language impaired children from a residential school', in Fletcher, P. & Hall, D. (eds) *Specific Speech and Language Disorders in Children*, London: Whurr Publishers.
Howlin, P. & Rutter, M. (1987) 'The consequences of language delay on other aspects of development', in Yule, W. & Rutter, M. (eds) *Language Development and Disorder*, Oxford: MacKeith Press.
Norwich, B. (1990) *Reappraising Special Needs Education*, London: Cassell Education.
Rinaldi, W. (1992) *Social Use of Language Programme*, Windsor: NFER-Nelson School Curriculum and Assessment Authority (SCAA) (1994) *The National Curriculum Orders*, London: HMSO.
Silva, P.A., McGee, R. & Williams, S.M. (1983) 'Developmental language delay from three to seven years and its significance for low intelligence and reading difficulties at age seven', *Developmental Medicine and Child Neurology*, 25, pp.783–93.
Snowling, M. & Stackhouse, J. (1983) 'Spelling performance of children with developmental verbal dyspraxia', *Developmental Medicine and Child Neurology*, 25, pp.430–7.
Stackhouse, J. & Snowling, M. (1992) 'Developmental verbal dyspraxia II: A developmental perspective on two case studies', *European Journal of Disorders of Communication*, 27, pp.35–54.
Wright, J.A (1994) 'Collaboration Between Speech and Language Therapists and Teachers', unpublished PhD thesis, University of London.

Part II

Teaching, assessment and
support approaches

6 No easy task: Structuring the curriculum for children experiencing difficulties in school

Judith Ireson and Peter Evans

Introduction

In this chapter, we present some of the findings of the 'Curriculum Research for Pupils with Moderate Learning Difficulties Project'. The project was one of several initiated by the then Department of Education and Science in response to government concern about the low levels of attainment of 'the bottom 40 per cent' of the ability range. The brief of the 'Curriculum Research Project' was to focus on pupils who were experiencing mild learning difficulties in both ordinary and special schools.

The aim of the project was to investigate the processes involved in developing effective teaching through structuring the curriculum for pupils experiencing difficulties in learning. This was to be achieved through the development of procedures which would enable teachers to observe and monitor the progress of their pupils and to make use of the information obtained in this way to evaluate their teaching, the progress of their pupils, and the curriculum. The research was concerned with the ways in which such innovations could be implemented in school and, within the limitations of the duration and scale of the work, with an evaluation of the outcome for pupils and schools.

The project was divided conceptually into three phases. The first phase was a study of primary, secondary and special schools that had been recommended for the way they were developing curricula for children experiencing difficulties in learning. The second phase was a two-year period of action research, during which the information obtained from the first phase was used in an attempt to develop curriculum structuring in a small number of schools. The research focus during this phase was on the ways in which teachers, pupils and the schools as a whole responded to the attempts to introduce change. The final phase of the project, which emerged from the first two phases, was concerned with the preparation of dissemination materials in the form of an in-service training pack designed for use in primary schools (Evans et al., 1990).

An important aspect of the research was the development of qualitative methodology. In particular, techniques were developed which enabled systematic comparisons to be made between schools, both on the basis of interviews, observations and documentation collected during short visits to schools and also from multiple sources of data collected during close involvement with schools during the two-year period of action research. During the first phase of the research, an analytic framework, grounded in the views of the participants, was used to make systematic comparisons of the process of curriculum development in the schools. This framework was taken forward and used alongside the identification of themes emerging in each of the schools during the second phase.

This chapter will focus on some of the main themes to emerge from the second, action research, phase in three primary and two special schools. This research strongly influenced the design and content of the in-service training pack produced in the final phase of the project. The rationale underlying the production of the pack, together with a brief description, will then be provided. Before summarising the relevant outcomes of the action research, however, we give a brief account of key concepts that formed the foundations of the research, and an outline of the comparative analysis of the process of curriculum development in schools.

School contexts, curriculum and learning difficulties

The orientation of the research was underpinned by the researchers' views of schools as contexts for learning, the nature of the curriculum and the process of structuring. Our view of schools as contexts was influenced by Bronfenbrenner's ecological model. He conceived of an ecological environment as 'a set of nested structures, each inside the next' (Bronfenbrenner, 1979, p.3). At the innermost level is the immediate setting containing the developing person. Each person participates in several settings, and the relations between these settings form the next level of analysis. A person's development is also influenced by settings in which he or she is not a participant. Classrooms are settings in school, but they function within the setting of the school, and teaching and learning are influenced by teachers' participation in the school setting. Likewise, the school operates in the wider context of the local social and political milieu and government policies. In so far as curriculum development is concerned, schools provide a setting in which teachers may develop their thinking both about the formulation and development of the curriculum and about children's learning.

The traditional meaning of the term 'curriculum' is a course of study, a description of the knowledge, skills and understanding to be taught, and much curriculum theory has been concerned with the form and content of the school curriculum. Stenhouse (1975), however, draws a distinction between curriculum study and curriculum development, with the latter being concerned with the improvement of teaching and learning. Skilbeck (1984) offers a model of school-based curriculum development, which he conceives as a process of collaborative, structured decision-making.

Interactions between the teacher and learner lie at the centre of the process of teaching and learning (Barnes, 1975; Pring, 1976). Although children are active agents in their learning, teachers must structure the curriculum in ways that help children to learn. Children who experience difficulty in learning in school tend to be less active and independent in their learning and appear to have difficulty in organising learning material spontaneously (Evans, 1988). Therefore, teachers must engage in a process of structuring and adjusting content if they are to engage children in their 'zone of proximal development' (Vygotsky, 1978; Evans, 1993).

A comparative analysis of school-based curriculum development

Although this chapter is concerned mainly with the second phase of the project, a brief account will be given of the model of the curriculum development process proposed in the first phase. This phase was a study of a purposive sample of 30 schools (10 primary, 10 secondary and 10 special schools for children with moderate learning difficulty). Headteachers and teachers with responsibility for special needs were interviewed during one-day visits to these schools, and curriculum documentation was collected. The interviews focused on the way in which the curriculum was developed to meet the needs of children with learning difficulties, and a full account can be found in Evans et al. (1987). Drawing on the work of Miles and Huberman (1984), a set of categories, grounded in the participants' views, was drawn up and used to code the information from the interviews and documentation. A model of the curriculum process was proposed which viewed the process as a dynamic system in which information from the formative assessment of pupils is taken up and used in the evaluation and re-formulation of the school curriculum (Evans et al., 1987; Ireson et al., 1989, 1992; Redmond et al., 1988). Schools differed in the extent to which they had engaged in this process, some having involved the whole staff in formulation, implementation and evaluation over a period of several years. In these schools, curriculum resources had been developed and made available for use by all the staff. Curriculum-based assessment procedures were used to monitor pupil progress, and information from these assessments was used both in deciding on the next steps in teaching and also in the evaluation of the curriculum. As systems, these schools were dynamic and encouraged the flow of information between the staff, so that new ideas and developments were shared and promoted. In other schools the process was less well-developed, curriculum intentions were formulated broadly, curriculum-based assessment was not used systematically to inform curriculum evaluation, and as systems, the schools were less well organised to promote the sharing and use of information.

The differences between the schools, although of interest in their own right, raise further questions about the processes taking place in the schools which give rise to such differences. Although some accounts of developments in individual schools are available, very little research has analysed the process of change in different schools, particularly in this country. Change in organisations generally takes place over a long time-scale and therefore calls for longitudinal research over several years. The second phase of the project was designed to allow for the analysis of the process of change through a two-year period of action research in seven schools. The analytic categories developed during the first phase of the research were carried forward into the analysis of the data collected during the action research. Although primary, secondary and special schools were included in the second phase, this chapter will focus on the developments in the three primary and two special schools. A fuller account of developments in the primary schools will be available (Ireson & Evans, in preparation).

Action research in the schools

Design of the research

As this phase of the research was designed to investigate the processes involved in developing the curriculum in schools over a two-year period, a small sample was selected, comprising 3 primary, 2 secondary and 2 special schools for pupils with moderate learning difficulty. In each school, a teacher was seconded to the project for one-and-a-half days each week, to act as a change agent and curriculum developer in the school, and also as a researcher, responsible for some of the data collection. The project researchers maintained close contact with the schools both through the project teacher and through frequent visits (weekly in the initial stages). A wide range of qualitative data was collected from each school, including teachers' diaries, researchers' field notes, minutes of meetings, examples of pupils' work, vignettes and curriculum documentation. Methods were developed for the systematic analysis of these data (see Evans et al., 1988 for a full account). A limited amount of psychometric data was collected, mainly for the purpose of describing the sample of children included as experiencing difficulty in learning. Single-case (N=1) data were also collected.

The selection of schools

A purposive sample of schools was selected from different local education authorities in the London region. The two special schools were all-age schools catering for children with moderate learning difficulties. One was located in an inner-city area and the other in an outer London borough, each with a roll of 80–90 children. The three primary schools selected were an infant school, a junior school and a primary school situated in mixed housing areas, occupied by families of average-to-low income. A major factor in the choice of schools was that they should be willing to become involved in structured approaches to the development of the curriculum and to their teaching of children experiencing difficulties in learning.

Criteria for the selection of children

The following operational criteria were established for the selection of the sample of children to be included in the study:

1 children who were the subject of a Statement of Special Educational Need.
2 children who were not Statemented but who were recognised by their teachers as having significant difficulties in learning, indicated by low attainment levels and slow progress, which were not directly attributable to behavioural difficulties or sensory-motor impairment.

No specification was made about the exact numbers of children who were to become involved in each school. Rather than determine a fixed number of children, it was planned that each teacher would start by working with one child or a small group of children in their own class and would gradually increase the numbers by working with other teachers. The decisions about these developments were made by the schools in consultation with the researchers.

The selection and induction of the project teachers

In all the schools, it was envisaged that a senior member of staff, who had received some training in special needs teaching, would fill the role of project teacher. As it turned out, two of the three primary teachers who had been identified to take on this role were promoted to positions in other schools even before the project got under way. Although the schools succeeded in finding replacements, these teachers were less senior members of staff and had not been trained in special needs teaching. This had an effect on the pace of developments in the schools and was to be only the first of many staffing changes to occur in the schools over the two-year duration of the project.

A series of meetings of teachers and researchers was held to discuss the teachers' dual role as curriculum developers and as researchers. It was a requirement of the project that the teachers would monitor the progress of a few children in each school and that this should be achieved through the development of curriculum-based assessment. It was expected that this close monitoring would provide teachers with additional evidence of their pupils' learning, which would in turn inform their decisions about the sequencing of the curriculum. Curriculum-based assessment involves an understanding of task analysis, goal-setting and criteria for assessment, all of which were discussed during these meetings and in subsequent meetings with individual teachers.

The role of the researchers

The researchers introduced teachers to a strategy for individualising work for individual children. They encouraged and supported the project teachers as they went through the processes of curriculum-based assessment, developing and implementing individualised programmes, and monitoring progress. They also offered support as the teachers became involved in collaborating with their colleagues and attempting to introduce changes in the school as a whole. When asked for help, the researchers attempted to provide it, but the final decisions were always the responsibility of the school staff.

Developments and issues arising in the schools

Individualising work for children

Establishing starting points for teaching   In each of the schools, the strategy was for the teachers to start by working with individual children who were readily accessible to them and who were thought likely to respond to individualised teaching. Time was organised to allow the teachers to work with the children, to observe their performance on tasks and to begin to find ways of describing strengths and weaknesses, setting targets and monitoring progress. The aim of the observation was to establish what the child knew and could do unaided, so that teaching could start from this point. Two examples, from one of the special schools, illustrate how a simple assessment can provide useful information. The teachers were concerned about the slow progress in reading of two boys, both of whom were working on the Ginn 360 reading scheme. An assessment revealed that both boys could read out of context only a small proportion of the reading scheme vocabulary. This was, in its degree of precision, new information for the teachers, and provided a starting point for further work.

The need to observe raised questions in some cases about *what* to observe. For example, in the infant school, a teacher commented on the difficulty of deciding what to note about a child's reading when there was so much that might be significant. In this instance, the observation was not informed by a clearly-formulated view of progression in reading. This realisation subsequently led to a series of staff meetings to formulate goals and objectives in reading for children in each class. Even with the National Curriculum Attainment Targets in place, similar difficulties may arise.

Setting targets   Having identified a starting point in terms of what a child could already do, the question was what to do next. In some cases, this decision was problematic, and further discussion was required. Three main issues were raised at this point: the focusing of teaching on a small segment of the curriculum; what counted as progression in the curriculum, and the distinction between targets and methods. In focusing on one aspect of the curriculum, teachers allocated teaching and learning time to this activity, rather than to others, and naturally wanted to feel that the time would not be wasted. This is a problem in all teaching, but is more acute when teaching children who are making slow progress. The general strategy adopted was to allocate a small amount of additional teaching time to one aspect of learning. During the remainder of the day, the child participated in normal classroom activities. It was anticipated that the child and the teacher would benefit from experiencing success, and that this would motivate further learning. It was also seen as important to ensure that programmes of work were reviewed at frequent intervals, and adjusted if progress was not being made.

On some occasions, difficulties arose because of uncertainties about the importance of a particular aspect of learning in relation to progression in a subject area. This tended to happen less often in relation to mathematics, which was seen as being more structured, than in relation to reading or more creative activities such as creative writing, which were seen to be more complex. Part of the difficulty also stemmed from the teachers' awareness that learners may take different routes to reach an endpoint in learning. This, combined with lack of clarity about the structure of the subject matter, made for difficulties in setting targets.

The third issue was the relationship between a target and teaching methods designed to help the learner make progress towards that target. There was a sense in which it was felt that if, for example, a target of 100 sight words was set, this implied a particular method of teaching. In practice, the creativity of the teachers was brought into play in designing activities that would help children achieve targets. In the infant school, for example, a teacher who was concerned to develop a reception child's language set a target of recognising 20 words. The class was working on a topic on animals, so the teacher took the child to the local pet shop and developed work around the animals they had seen there, such as cutting out animal pictures and sticking them into a book, painting, playing animal 'Who?' games, and so forth. Gradually, the child was introduced to 'Breakthrough to Literacy', and in the course of time she was able to recognise the written names of the animals and to make up her own sentences. Much more was learned than just the reading of the words. Although this might be seen as an example of good remedial practice, it was found to be necessary to emphasise the use of such methods to class teachers.

Recording progress   The issue of recording pupil progress was taken up at all the schools, although in one of the special schools, developments focused on reformulation of the maths curriculum, and recording was a later development. In two of the schools, record-keeping was discussed at staff meetings. Interestingly, while in both schools the staff first discussed what a record is intended to convey and to whom, the outcomes were quite different in the two schools. Pupil reading profiles were drawn up in one school, whereas in the other school, two types of record were developed: a more detailed version for staff and a briefer version for reporting to parents, inspectors and others. In the junior school, a comprehensive recording system was developed by the project teacher to monitor progress through the reading programme, comprising checklists for use during teaching sessions and summary sheets displaying a child's progress in several aspects of reading over a longer period of time. Although initially there was some feeling that record-keeping was time-consuming and not particularly helpful, there were several comments about the usefulness of records as the project progressed.

It was generally agreed that, to be useful in teaching, records had to be straightforward and quick to complete. However, checklists were perceived to provide superficial information and to imply that learning was linear. An acceptable solution was a four-column grid in which the teacher entered a description of the desired learning, the date(s) when the work had been covered and when the pupil had learned it, a subsequent check that the learning was retained, and a space for comments. There was much discussion about what the criteria would be for learning, and in some cases, teachers' intuitive judgements were developed into criteria for mastery.

The requirement to monitor children's progress provided additional information for teachers, which could be used to modify teaching programmes and establish patterns in children's learning. The junior school project teacher noticed, for example, that when children had acquired a sight vocabulary of 30–40 words, several of them seemed to 'plateau' and stop making progress for a while. This appeared to be a temporary phase which was followed by a steady increase to 100 words, after which the recording was discontinued.

A concern expressed by some teachers was that, in choosing to develop programmes in certain curriculum areas, they were influenced by the requirement to record progress. It was tempting to choose a skill which was easier to record, rather than some other aspect of work, such as creativity, which is difficult to record. This perhaps reflects a more developed understanding of progression in some areas of the curriculum than in others. Where schools had developed agreed frameworks for progression, it was much easier to agree on ways of recording progress. In some schools, the realisation that the curriculum policy was inadequate led those schools to undertake the re-formulation of the curriculum before attempting to develop individualised teaching. One of the special schools rewrote its maths curriculum, while the infant school staff decided to rewrite its language policy.

Changes in classroom practice   Attempts to work with children on an individual basis for teaching or for monitoring progress called for changes in classroom practice. Ancillary help was available in the special schools, and teachers reported changing or extending their use of this help. For example, one teacher arranged that, when ancillary help was provided, children worked in small groups of like ability, while another teacher grouped children in pairs according to their level of attainment in the reading curriculum. In the primary schools, no ancillary help was available, and teachers developed other ways of coping, such as organising the children into mixed-ability groups, rather than into groups of similar ability, and planning to spend short periods of time with individuals. Some teachers were successful in managing to spend several short sessions each week working with individual children, without additional support. Those who achieved this reported that they placed great emphasis on classroom organisation at the beginning of the school year, developing routines so that the children were able to work independently. Those who found it most difficult to work with individual children were those whose normal practice was to teach to the whole class. The project teachers also provided some support, either by taking the whole class while the class teacher worked with a subgroup, or supporting an individual while the class teacher took the lesson.

Organisational themes

Focused discussions

In several schools, teachers and headteachers commented on the discussion generated by the project. The headteacher and the English as a second language teacher in the infant school both participated in discussions with the project teacher and class teacher. The discussions focused on working out strategies for children, not only those included in the project, and provide an example of the way in which the approach generalised within the school. Discussions were seen as valuable in generating more positive approaches towards children's difficulties, with teachers coming to realise that they themselves had the expertise to help overcome the difficulties. In the primary school, there was more discussion, not only between the project teacher and individual class teachers, but with other staff, pooling resources and ideas. Much of this took place during breaks, at lunchtime or after school. One of the special school headteachers joined in the regular discussions between the project teacher and class teachers. It was recognised that the focus of these discussions – on children's learning in relation to the curriculum – enabled the time to be used effectively. The need to find time to work on an individual basis with a child, to plan teaching, to monitor progress and to discuss with colleagues was of paramount importance. The need for time was a recurring issue which will be raised again on pages 98–99, in relation to the re-formulation of the curriculum.

Roles of the head and project teacher

It is clearly impossible for an individual teacher to meet the learning needs of all children. In each of the schools, therefore, ways were sought of collaborating with all the staff to enhance the provision made across the whole curriculum. The context afforded by each school influenced the way in which this collaborative activity developed, and it was possible to identify a number of features of this context as significant: the stance of the headteacher towards developments in the schools, the seniority and expertise of the project teacher, and the level of formulation of the school curriculum. The differences between the two special schools illustrate particularly clearly the way these features influenced developments. In one of these schools, the headteacher gave strong backing to the project. She helped by safeguarding time both for the project teacher and class teachers to meet on a regular basis to discuss their work and also for the class teachers to work with individual children. In the other school, the headteacher delegated responsibility to the project teacher, who was a senior member of staff. This teacher experienced some resistance to change, and encountered additional difficulties because the school curriculum was in the early stages of formulation. Developments in the first of these schools proceeded more smoothly and were more far-reaching than those in the second.

In the junior school, the new headteacher initiated a review of several major areas of the curriculum, introduced an integrated-day organisation and discouraged the use of reading schemes, preferring the 'real books' approach. The project teacher, a senior member of staff trained in special needs teaching, while receiving the headteacher's support for the project in principle, found it necessary to adjust the pace of development to take account of the other demands placed on the class teachers. Although she succeeded in putting in place a reading programme which could be used by class teachers, she felt that much more could have been achieved in other curriculum areas had it not been for all the other changes taking place in the school.

Modification and adaptation of the curriculum

Reading schemes were in use in all the schools at the start of the project, although, as reported above, the junior school headteacher had decided to replace the scheme with a 'real books' approach. A similar move took place in the infant school a year later. Several children who were not making good progress in reading were found to be attempting reading scheme books that were too difficult for them, and two examples were given above (see page 93). Little mention has been made so far of the mathematics schemes that were in use in the primary and junior schools, but similar examples of incorrect placement on the schemes were also evident in mathematics. Rather than replace the schemes, in the majority of schools it was decided to modify and adapt them.

In the junior school, the project teacher modified and extended a reading scheme for use with children making slow progress. These children had been exposed to a 'real books' approach and had developed an enjoyment of reading, but were not making progress towards independent reading, and specifically had not recognised the correspondence between the written and the spoken word. After establishing which of the reading scheme words each child could read out of context, the project teacher developed a set of activities and a resource pack for the class teachers to use. She demonstrated how they might conduct short teaching sessions followed by quick assessments and recording within the context of normal classroom organisation. Her expectation was that, once class teachers started to work with children in this way, they would develop further resources for themselves, but this expectation was not fulfilled. Subsequently, she developed recording sheets and resources, including computer activities, to support the Oxford Reading Tree scheme, which was adopted later by the school. The primary school project teacher also developed resources to support the use of the school reading scheme.

Discussions between the primary class teachers in the special school led to two fundamental modifications to the reading curriculum. The first was the extension of the sight vocabulary, and the second was the creation of additional materials to support and extend the scheme. The proposal to extend the sight vocabulary arose from the teachers' concern to take the scope of the children's reading beyond the structured limits of the reading scheme and to include social and instructional vocabulary. The school was fortunate in receiving support from a media resources officer who created additional materials to support and extend the scheme.

In general, then, teachers were able to make use of reading and mathematics schemes, but only with the creation of additional resources and the inclusion of activities which provided additional practice and helped sustain and motivate children's learning. The recognition of this need for additional activities was associated with a view that establishing a sight vocabulary was a necessary step in learning to read. The realisation that additional resources were needed is consistent with the views expressed by staff in the schools in the first phase of the project, some of whom had invested a great deal of time and effort in producing resources.

Re-formulation of the school curriculum

One of the special schools concentrated its efforts on reformulating the school mathematics curriculum. A start had been made prior to the school's involvement in the research project, and a preliminary document had been drawn up. Staff expressed dissatisfaction with the existing records in maths, which were an adaptation of a published scheme of the checklist type. During the period of involvement with the project, a series of workshops was held. The teachers engaged in a process of re-formulation of the mathematics curriculum at a level of detail which provided them with a framework for the individualisation of the curriculum. Considerable time was devoted to this task, organised in the form of regular teacher workshops and discussions involving all staff. The particular approach adopted was to select, combine and adapt existing commercial schemes to suit their own requirements.

A lengthy process of discussion about the school reading curriculum was set in train in the infant school following the move to a more emergent approach to the teaching of reading. A series of staff meetings was held at which various aspects of reading were discussed. Staff expressed dissatisfaction with the recording of progress in reading, which it was felt should be more individualised and less scheme-based. Each class teacher was asked to think about reading in their own classroom and to make a list of reading objectives. These were assembled into a set of guidelines for the preparation of reading profiles, which were in use as the research came to an end.

Summary of points to emerge from the research

The opportunity to develop individualised teaching raised a number of issues. The requirement to establish a starting point for teaching, in terms of what a child could already do unaided, revealed new information that teachers found useful. It also demonstrated that deciding on a starting point in the absence of a clear view of progression may be problematic. Setting targets for learning raised questions about priorities in teaching and learning at a particular point in time, and about the issue of the separation of teaching methods and targets. Monitoring and recording of pupil progress led to discussions about the purposes of records, what to record and how often, and to developments in all the schools' record-keeping systems. In several schools, these discussions led to a re-formulation of a part of the school curriculum, with records linked to the new framework.

Attempts to individualise teaching called for changes in classroom practice for most teachers. Some found time to work with individuals by teaching pupils to work independently, but classroom support was found to be essential for sustained and regular work with individual children. Project teachers used some of their time providing this support. Time was also needed to modify and extend curriculum resources such as reading and mathematics schemes.

An outcome in all the schools was an increase in the amount of discussion between teachers about children's learning, which was seen to promote more positive approaches to children's difficulties. These discussions were sometimes organised in school time, but more often took place when the opportunity arose, in breaks and lunchtime or after school. Time was a major issue in all the schools, and it was generally agreed that only very limited progress could be made without the allocation of time, both to release teachers to work with individual children and to allow for whole-school discussions. The support and involvement of the headteacher was crucial, both in terms of safeguarding time and maintaining the priority of the work.

Development of *Pathways to Progress*

The outcomes of the research seemed to have pinpointed some issues that were common across a range of teaching situations and to have suggested some useful ways for schools to approach these issues. Towards the end of the second phase of the research, careful consideration was given as to how the findings might be most usefully disseminated to schools. It was decided to produce an in-service training package, based on the research, for use in primary schools. *Pathways to Progress* (Evans et al., 1990) was produced, informed both by the theoretical orientation of the research and by the practical experience in the schools during the action research. The project primary schools were centrally involved in producing materials and in commenting on the development of the pack. The aim of the materials was to emulate the process of curriculum development as articulated during the research. This was achieved by incorporating two major components that were found to be essential in all the schools: a strategy for individualising work for children, and strategies for collaborative problem-solving between the class teachers, special needs coordinator and headteacher. The stated aims of the pack were to:

- bring teachers together in small groups to develop a problem-solving approach to the development of the curriculum for pupils who are experiencing difficulties in learning
- develop the school and classroom organisation so as to provide the necessary learning environment for pupils who are experiencing difficulties in learning
- extend teachers' skills in individual programme-planning and in their assessments of pupils.

These aims were realised through designing a pack with seven free-standing units: an introductory unit setting out the legislative background and theoretical orientation; individual units for the headteacher, special needs coordinator and class teacher; two units on planning individualised programmes, linked to videotaped material illustrating the steps in programme planning; one unit on classroom organisation, and task sheets to accompany activities included in the units. In addition, the pack included information for parents, school governors, school inspectors and advisors, and educational psychologists.

The pack contained several activities to maintain collaboration and discussion between the headteacher, class teachers and coordinator, and to encourage a problem-solving approach. The individualised programme-planning units incorporated a general strategy, with examples drawn from the research project. The strategy consisted of five questions, aimed at:

- identifying a goal to which the pupil should work
- identifying the skills, knowledge and understanding of the pupil, which form the starting point for help
- deciding on a first step and identifying an initial target
- selecting teaching methods most suited to help the pupil make progress
- monitoring the pupil's progress and deciding on action to take in the light of this information.

Issues raised in the research were dealt with in the various units. These included the role of the headteacher, the negotiation and safeguarding of time, the purposes and uses of recording, the adaptation and extension of resources, and whole-school curriculum development. Although the core strategy was a method for designing individualised programmes, this represented a starting point for the teachers and the school, with the overall intention being the development of whole-school approaches.

Discussion

It has long been recognised that, to teach successfully, the teacher must know both the subject matter and the child, and Evans (1985) makes this point in relation to children with special educational needs. Teachers' knowledge of subject matter has been the source of much recent concern in relation to primary school teaching (Alexander et al., 1992), in particular the teaching of National Curriculum maths and science (Bennett & Carre, 1993). Clearly, subject matter knowledge is important, but knowledge of the process by which the curriculum is transacted is also necessary. This process is complex and involves what we refer to as 'structuring', to imply continual adjustment and adaptation as learning proceeds. The research presented here suggests both a strategy which can be used by teachers to engage in structuring the curriculum and also a means of studying the process of structuring. Knowledge of curriculum structuring is particularly important in teaching children who experience difficulty in learning. Much of this knowledge develops through experience and forms an implicit basis for on-line teaching decisions. In the normal course of teaching, there is no particular encouragement to make such knowledge explicit. By adopting the strategy advocated in our research, teachers in the project schools were encouraged to engage in discussions, and gradually started to make explicit and share their knowledge about structuring and adjusting their teaching to enhance pupil learning.

The model developed in this research portrays the process of curriculum development, in the sense of improving teaching and learning, as taking place within the dynamic system of a school. In this process, information from curriculum-based assessment and curriculum evaluation can be used to inform the formulation and implementation of the curriculum in the school as a whole. This is in contrast to a view of curriculum development as a periodic review and rewriting of the school policy documents by the headteacher or curriculum post-holder. The maintenance of a high level of involvement of all members of staff requires management and – particularly in the initial stages – investment of time. Although we have limited comparative pupil outcome data, our research suggests that there may be considerable benefits to both staff and pupils in making a commitment of time to involve all staff. Through creating an environment in which teachers' knowledge is shared and extended, schools can ensure that information available to them is used to enhance the effectiveness of teaching for all children, not only those who are identified as having learning difficulties. As far as actual pupil learning outcomes are concerned, the use of psychometric tests is problematic because of the lack of sensitivity to change at the lower end of the range.

The detailed information obtained in the research regarding teachers' attempts to individualise the curriculum has highlighted the difficulties they encountered. Their initial training does not equip them with the skills to undertake task analyses, establish baselines or set learning targets. In attempting these tasks, they faced many problems and dilemmas. Questions that have been mentioned here include: which of many possible aspects of a child's learning to observe and assess; what the goals and targets of teaching should be; how to sequence learning activities effectively; how to organise the classroom to allow for individual teaching, and how to develop appropriate resources and recording techniques. As they attempted to address these questions, teachers came to realise the need for re-formulation of the school curriculum.

An important aspect of the approach adopted in this research was that the information gained from designing individual programmes and monitoring pupil progress was used in the process of formulating teaching goals and targets. The process of formulation of objectives in our approach was fundamentally different from that of programmes such as Direct Instruction (Engelmann & Carnine, 1982) or SNAP (Ainscow & Tweddle, 1979). These programmes offer the teacher a set of objectives derived by others through a logical analysis of the curriculum. In our approach, the teachers' own formulation of targets and goals played a central role. This not only gave the teachers control over their teaching but also provided them with a tool for developing a better understanding of pupil learning. Their targets and goals were derived from their knowledge, both of the curriculum and of the learning process, and allowed for flexibility and adaptation to individual learning needs and interests.

These findings are particularly relevant at this time, as the Code of Practice (DfE & WO, 1994) is implemented. The Code sets out a five-stage model of response to special educational needs. Stages 1 and 2, which require assessment and response first by the class teacher and then the special needs coordinator, call for teachers to confront many of the questions posed above. As the research has shown, these questions are often problematic, and teachers will need time and support as they attempt to address them. Because the Code is framed in administrative terms, there is a danger that the focus will be on establishing procedures, rather than on enhancing teachers' understanding of curriculum structuring. In the current context, time is at a premium, and teachers are being pressed to implement a wide range of reforms. It is important that time for discussion, informed by evidence of the influence of their teaching on pupil learning, is not seen as a luxury but rather as an essential aspect of developing professionalism.

In conclusion, curriculum structuring can be thought of as taking place at two interconnected levels. In teaching–learning interactions, teachers structure and adjust learning activities responsively to learners' developing knowledge, skill, understanding and emotional response. Similarly, schools as systems may be organised in such a way as to engage in structuring the curriculum, using information from curriculum-based assessment to inform their formulation and implementation. The more effectively schools are organised as systems, the more likely they are to support and enhance the individual teacher's response. Organisational effectiveness is not in itself sufficient, however, and must be accompanied by systematic strategies, such as the one adopted in this research, for moving towards a better understanding of teaching and learning.

Acknowledgements

The project was set up under the direction of Professor Klaus Wedell and Professor Malcolm Skilbeck, with funding from the then Department of Education and Science (now the DfE). Peter Evans was the senior research officer and became project co-director when Professor Skilbeck left for Australia. The authors gratefully acknowledge the contribution of Patrick Redmond and would like to thank the participating schools and pupils for their valuable collaboration in the research. The opinions expressed in this chapter are those of the authors, not necessarily those of the DES.

Postscript

I came to know Klaus when I was a researcher on the 'Curriculum Research for Pupils with Moderate Learning Difficulties Project', based at the University of London Institute of Education from 1984 to 1988. This was one of several large, funded projects under Klaus's direction at that time. We obtained further funding to 1989 to allow for the preparation and production of the *Pathways to Progress* in-service training pack, which was published by the Institute of Education. When the project came to an end, I obtained a lectureship and later a senior lectureship in Psychology of Education in the Department of Educational Psychology and Special Educational Needs.

References

Ainscow, M. & Tweddle, D. (1979) *Preventing Classroom Failure: An Objectives Approach*, Chichester: John Wiley.

Alexander, R., Rose, J. & Woodhead, C. (1992) *Curriculum Organisation and Classroom Practice in Primary Schools: A discussion paper*, London: DES.

Barnes, D. (1975) *From Communication to Curriculum*, Harmondsworth: Penguin Books.

Bennett, S.N. & Carre, C. (1993) *Learning to Teach*, London: Routledge.

Bronfenbrenner, U. (1979) *The Ecology of Human Development*, London: Harvard University Press.

Department for Education & Welsh Office (DfE & WO) (1994) *Code of Practice on the Identification and Assessment of Special Educational Needs*, London: HMSO.

Engelmann, S. & Carnine, D.W. (1982) *Theory of Instruction: Principles and Practice*, New York: Irvington.

Evans, P. (1985) 'Psychology and special educational needs in initial teacher training: Pygmalion revisited', in H. Francis (ed.) *Learning to Teach: Psychology in Teacher Training*, London: Falmer Press.

Evans, P. (1988) 'Towards a social psychology of special education', *Educational and Child Psychology*, 5, pp.78–90.

Evans, P. (1993) 'Some implications of Vygotsky's work for special education', in H. Daniels (ed.) *Charting the Agenda: Educational Activity After Vygotsky*, London: Routledge.

Evans, P., Ireson, J. & Redmond, P. (1987) 'Curriculum research for pupils with moderate learning difficulties', *Interim Report MLD (87) 2*, London: DES.

Evans, P., Ireson, J., Redmond, P. & Wedell, K. (1988) 'Curriculum research for pupils with moderate learning difficulties', *Final Report*, London: DES.

Evans, P., Ireson, J., Redmond, P. & Wedell, K. (1990) *Pathways to Progress: Developing an approach to teaching the National Curriculum to children experiencing difficulties in learning in the primary school*, London: Institute of Education.

Ireson, J. & Evans, P. (in preparation) *Providing Effective Support for Children with Learning Difficulties in the Primary School: What's Involved?*, in P. Evans (ed.) *Our Children at Risk, Part 2*, Paris: OECD.

Ireson, J., Evans, P., Redmond, P. & Wedell, K. (1989) 'Developing the curriculum for children with learning difficulties: Towards a grounded model', *British Educational*

Research Journal, 15(2), pp.141–54.

Ireson, J., Evans, P., Redmond, P. & Wedell, K. (1992) 'Developing the curriculum for pupils experiencing difficulties in learning in the ordinary school: A systematic comparative analysis', *British Educational Research Journal*, 18(2), pp.155–73.

Miles, M.B. & Huberman, A.M. (1984) *Qualitative Data Analysis: A Sourcebook of New Methods*, London: Sage.

Pring, R. (1976) *Knowledge and Schooling*, London: Open Books.

Redmond, P., Evans, P., Ireson, J., & Wedell, K. (1988) 'Comparing the curriculum development process in special (MLD) schools: A systematic, qualitative approach', *European Journal of Special Needs Education*, 3(3), pp.147–60.

Skilbeck, M. (1984) *School-based Curriculum Development*, London: Harper and Row.

Stenhouse, L. (1975) *An Introduction to Curriculum Research and Development*, London: Heinemann Educational.

Vygotsky, L. (1978) *Mind in Society*, London: Harvard University Press.

7 Individual strategies for investigation and intervention

Harry Daniels

Introduction

The last ten to fifteen years have witnessed an increasing concern for the development of individual strategies for investigation and intervention in special education. Klaus Wedell has drawn on the repertoire of behavioural and cognitive approaches to construct a pedagogic strategy which has proved to be a much-valued contribution to the professional practice of the large number of teachers and psychologists he has influenced through his writing and teaching. This chapter will discuss issues that have arisen in the development of contemporary practices. It will also attempt to provide an outline of some possibilities for future development. In doing so, it will attempt to draw on the behavioural, cognitive-behavioural and neo-Vygotskian traditions in instructional practice.

The understanding that the causes of special educational needs (SENs) are to be found in the interactions between the nature of the child and the nature of his or her environment underpins much of the current thinking in the field. Writing in the latter part of the twentieth century, it is, perhaps, too easy to forget the impact that the shift away from within-person descriptions of handicap has made on both legislation and practice in schools. Deficit models were embodied in the framework of the legislation of the middle part of the century. Categories of deficiency of mind and body were used to organise the practices of assessment and intervention in special education. The training of psychological abilities found favour in the developments of the 1960s and 1970s. While these espoused a more elaborate model of ability than was previously the case, they remained firmly rooted in a within-person conception of causation. The emphasis on the testing and training of perceptual motor skills and psycho-linguistic abilities has been the subject of much criticism and has lost much of its influence in practice (Reid & Hresko, 1981; Salvia & Ysseldyke, 1985).

The individual constructivism that Piaget's work introduced to the educational world provided elegant descriptions of developmental stages but was almost silent on pedagogic matters. In its search for instructional strategies, special education turned to the behaviourism of Skinner. It was in the application and adaptation of behavioural theory that significant advances were made in the development of pedagogic initiatives in special education.

A psychological model of compensatory interaction (Wedell, 1980) between child and environment factors became embedded in the final report of the Warnock Committee (DES, 1978), was evidenced in the 1981 Education Act and continues to affect the current legislation. The notion of compensatory interaction cleared the ground for policy initiatives in which good teaching was envisaged as the positive effect which could compensate for the child's balance of deficiencies. This work retained a clear linkage with the earlier US behavioural tradition, although differences were to be found in the extent to which individual processes of thinking and learning were accounted for.

A variety of behavioural approaches have been adopted and adapted to meet the demands of a system which, in large part, rejected the psycho-medical or psycho-educational process models with their within-child assumptions of the causation of learning difficulty. Useful summaries of behavioural approaches to teaching children with learning difficulties are provided in Solity (1991), Lister and Cameron (1986), Cameron et al. (1986) and Faupel (1986). Task Analysis (Howell et al., 1979), Direct Instruction (Carnine & Silbert, 1979), Precision Teaching (Raybould & Solity, 1988) and Assessment Through Teaching (Solity, 1991) have been developed and applied by teachers and psychologists as they strive to develop the 'good teaching' which is desirable but so often absent from the experience of many children with learning difficulties in school (Bennett et al., 1984). The elements of the behavioural teaching model have been presented at different levels of complexity (see Figure 7.1 from Solity & Raybould, 1988, p.75 and Figure 7.2 from Cameron et al., 1986, p.7).

These approaches have attracted criticism for the way in which they conceptualise the learning process. In practice, they have been seen to introduce an amount of inflexibility into instructional practices. They carry with them the dangers of over-reliance on rigid prescriptions for instruction that does not allow for differences between individual learners in their prior knowledge base and acquired strategies.

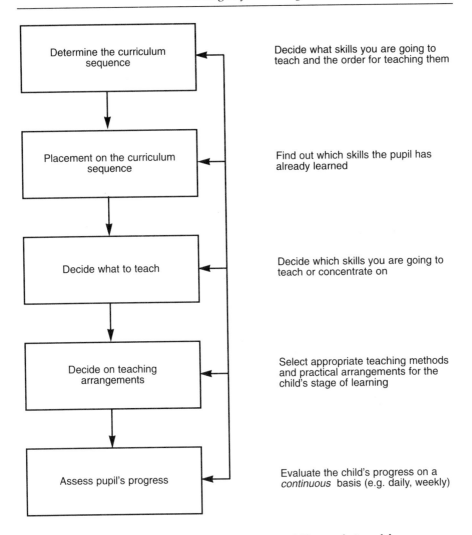

Figure 7.1   The basic model of assessment through teaching
Source: Solity and Raybould (1988, p.75)

Compensatory interaction and intervention

Klaus Wedell brings a consideration of within-child factors to the traditional behavioural approach:

> the teacher also needs to consider 'within child' factors, in order to choose a teaching method which will enable the child to learn effectively . . . The

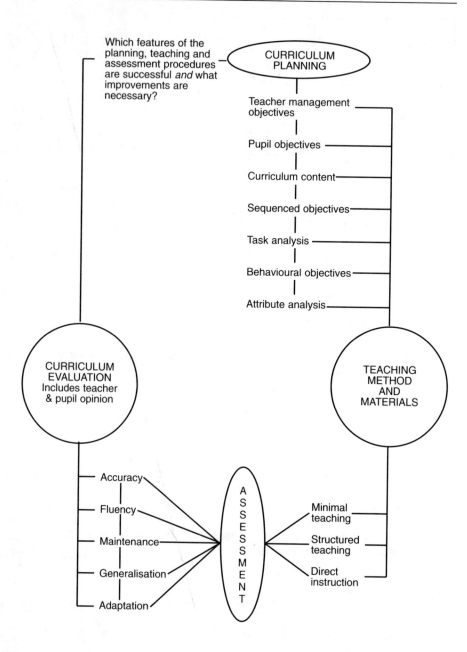

Figure 7.2   The curriculum management feedback loop, showing possible choice points

Source: Cameron et al. (1986, p.7)

teacher will be aware of some relevant aspects of the child from prior observation, but more particularly, she will use her evaluation of the child's response to her teaching as a means of assessing the child. (Wedell, 1989, p.10)

Following the model of compensatory interaction, within-child factors and environmental factors are brought into the analysis of intervention. Importantly, his approach is one in which teachers are encouraged to consider a learner's strengths as well as needs. In so doing, a pupil's own learning strengths may be used as a resource, rather than ignored as has so often been the case in the past. The all too familiar practice of describing learner characteristics in negative terms is avoided. Far too much time has been spent confirming what children *cannot* do, rather than finding out what they *can* do and how it can be used as the basis for new learning.

Dockrell and McShane (1993) provide an outline model of the possible foci for intervention which embodies a cognitive analysis of learner characteristics:

> In addition to the cognitive processes that are central to a task, there is a variety of other mental processes that affect a child's performance. These include executive and motivational processes, which can be regarded as control mechanisms that play a central role in the regulation of the cognitive system . . . These factors . . . constitute additional child variables that must be take into account in the analysis of learning difficulties. (Dockrell & McShane, 1993, p.15)

In Figure 7.3 (from Dockrell & McShane, 1993) the elements of the compensatory interaction model of causation are embodied in the 'Task/Child/Environment' schema and distinguished from the points of intervention in the 'Child Variables/Task Variables/Environment Variables' schema. In this way, they emphasise the need to distinguish the analysis of *needs* for instruction from the analysis of *means* of instruction. Their approach may be located within the rather broad category of intervention strategies described as cognitive-behavioural. The emphasis on cognitive and meta-cognitive factors is also evidenced in a similarly broad emergent category of neo-Vygotskian approaches. Gallimore and Tharp (1990) propose a four-stage model of progression based on a derivation of the well-known Vygotskian concept of the zone of proximal development (ZPD):

> The distance between the actual developmental level as determined by independent problem solving and the level of potential development as determined through problem solving under adult guidance or in collaboration with more capable peers. (Vygotsky, 1978, p.86)

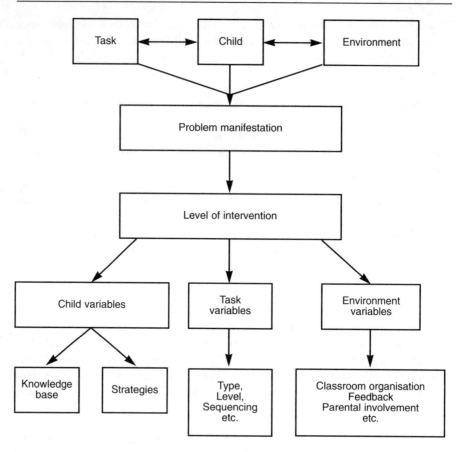

Figure 7.3   Possible foci for intervention
Source: Dockrell and McShane (1993)

In the model shown in Figure 7.4 (from Gallimore & Tharp, 1990), progress is articulated in terms of the relationship between self-control and social control. Many of the models of intervention which espouse a Vygotskian root either explicitly or implicitly draw on Luria's (1979) concepts of verbal regulation and internalisation. They all posit a transfer of control from the social 'other' to the self. The transfer from verbal regulation and assistance by others to self-regulation lies at the heart of many of these models. These same ideas are also employed by those who would describe their work as cognitive-behavioural (e.g. Manning, 1991). One of the important distinctions that may be made between these various models is with respect to the degree of control over the general process of task analysis. In some of the cognitive-behavioural intervention strategies, cognitive and

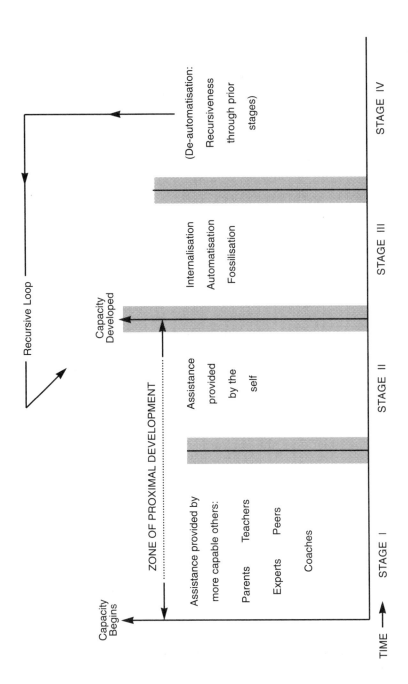

Figure 7.4 The genesis of a performance capacity: Progression through the zone of proximal development and beyond

Source: Gallimore and Tharp (1990)

meta-cognitive task analyses may be performed on the basis of an expert view of the demands of the task and the characteristics of the learner. This task sequence is then employed in instruction. Newman et al. (1989) consider that neo-Vygotskian conceptions of intervention are concerned with learning a task where the breakdown into components is achieved in the social interaction, rather than through a temporal sequence:

> In the traditional approach there is a tendency to break the work down into pieces that can be learned without reference to the forward direction of the sequence. There is no need or opportunity to understand the goal of the sequence while learning the components. Thus, there is a tendency to emphasize rote learning of lower level components. The ZPD approach has an opposite emphasis since the task that is the goal of the sequence is being accomplished interactively from the beginning. The teacher appropriates the child's contributions into her own understanding of the task. There is always an opportunity, therefore, for the child's actions to be made meaningful for the child in terms of the goal of the sequence. (Newman et al., 1989, p.153)

The model places teacher and student in an expert–novice apprentice relationship and emphasises active intellectual interaction within social contexts. The processes involved in social interaction are eventually taken over and internalised by the student to form individual cognitive processes.

Just as the cognitive-behavioural approach may be seen to encompass a continuum of approaches, so the neo-Vygotskian school may be seen to embrace a wide range of intervention strategies. The work of Gallimore and Tharp (1990) may be seen to have more in common with the cognitive-behavioural school than does the approach developed by Newman et al. (1989).

Whereas the cruder forms of behavioural model assume that analysis of the task alone is sufficient, the cognitive-behavioural models additionally consider the demands of the task in terms of the cognitive processes of the learner. The neo-Vygotskian approaches tend to handle such analyses interactively as control over learning and responsibility for it is transferred from tutor to pupil.

The discussion that follows will consider some of the issues that have arisen in the implementation of such models and their underlying assumptions.

Learning hierarchies and task analysis

The process of task analysis has been central in the development of individual programmes for children with SENs. Tasks are broken down into components which may be presented in sequence to develop understanding in progressive stages. In doing this, instruction is developed on the basis of a notion of transfer in which relatively simple learning forms the basis for more complex learning and assists it. Irrespective of the complexity of the task, it is often argued that mastery may be achieved by providing the learner with a hierarchy of subtasks developed through a task analysis undertaken by the teacher or course designer. Learning hierarchies carry with them strong implications for teaching and assessment. Curriculum-based assessment referenced to learning hierarchies can provide information for the skilled teacher about the way in which individual learners skip elements and take alternative routes. Hierarchies can be used as the basis for decision-making concerning individual needs for instruction. Tasks may be submitted to behavioural, cognitive or meta-cognitive analysis, each of which yield their own implications for instruction. The form of analysis depends on the nature of the task.

Gagné (1985) makes an important contribution with his discussion of the types of outcome that learning may have (see Table 7.1).

Gagné argues that different types of learning task demand different conditions for learning:

> Not only do these differ in the performances they make possible; they also differ in the conditions most favourable for their learning. These learning conditions are partly *internal*, arising from the memory of the learner as a consequence of previous learning. In addition, some learning conditions are *external* to the learner and may be deliberately arranged as aspects of *instruction*. (Gagné 1985, p.67)

The clear implication of Gagné's work is that different forms and levels of task analysis are required for different types of task. It is by no means certain that this is taken into account in the design of instructional systems. One of the dangers of some applications of behavioural approaches to instructional planning is that the assumption is made that all learning tasks are essentially of the same type. Newman et al. (1989) present a strident warning of some of these dangers:

> An example of what we are calling the traditional view can be found in Gagné's notion of a learning hierarchy . . . This conception has little to say about teacher–child interaction since its premise is that tasks can be sufficiently broken down into component parts that any single step in the sequence can be achieved with a minimum of instruction. Teacherless computerized classrooms running 'skill and drill' programs are coherent with this conception of change. (Newman et al., 1989, p.153)

Table 7.1   Five major categories of learned capabilities, including subordinate types, and examples of each

Capability (Learning Outcome)	Examples of Performance Made Possible
Intellectual Skill	Demonstrating symbol use, as in the following:
Discrimination	Distinguishing printed *m* and *n*
Concrete Concept	Identifying the spatial relation 'underneath', identifying a 'side' of an object
Defined Concept	Classifying a 'family', using a definition
Rule	Demonstrating the agreement in number of subject and verb in sentences
Higher-order Rule	Generating a rule for predicting the size of an image, given the distance of a light source and the curvature of a lens.
Cognitive Strategy	Using an efficient method for recalling names
Verbal Information	Restating elements of the *Highway Code*
Motor Skill	Printing the letter *R*; skating a figure 8
Attitude	Choosing to listen to classical music

(*Source:* adapted from Gagné, 1985, p.67)

The validity of task analyses

Dockrell and McShane insist that the first stage in identifying what needs must be addressed by intervention is the development of an understanding of the nature of the task:

> Unless a comprehensive and valid description of the task exists, a 'test teach test' strategy will not be possible. An appropriate task analysis of the particular skill or aspect of the curriculum must be developed to provide the basis for assessment. An adequate description of the task allows for an informed assessment of the child's progress and continual adjustment of instructional objectives, materials and strategies. (Dockrell & McShane, 1993, pp.181–2)

However, when discussing the case of mathematics as a subject for instruction, Wood (1988) questions whether enough is known about all the tasks presented to pupils in schools:

> Developing an effective theory of 'where the learner is at' and constructing a workable 'psychology of the subject' present formidable challenges in mathematics . . . we do not possess this level of knowledge in relation to the vast majority of concepts taught in the classroom . . . such knowledge would not provide a map of the learner's terrain though it would improve our sense of direction. (Wood, 1988, p.209)

Resnick and Ford (1981) discuss rational task analyses based on what psychology suggests happens in mathematical learning. They contrast this with empirical task analysis, which is based on observations of what children actually do, or appear to do. When researching the understanding of number concepts in low-attaining 7–9 year-olds, Denvir and Brown (1987) attempted to identify a framework which describes pupils' order of acquisition of number concepts and to devise teaching and activities which would extend the pupil's understanding of number. Using a categorisation of word problems, a hierarchical framework of inter-related skills was constructed and diagnostic tests used to establish what understanding of number individual pupils already possessed.

A teaching programme was implemented to 'teach' skills which were considered to be 'next skills' in the hierarchy or further on in the hierarchy, and the pupils' acquisition of skills was later tested. The results showed that such an approach was useful for describing each pupil's knowledge of number and in establishing which cognitive skills were most likely to be learned. However, it was 'less useful as a predictor of precisely which, or how many, skills a pupil actually learned' (Denvir & Brown, 1987, p.97). Some of the individuals involved did not acquire the skills being taught but made progress in different parts of the hierarchical framework.

If task analysis is used in the classroom as a process for clarifying and understanding the pupil's learning, then it can become an invaluable support for a reflective teacher. The process involves making teaching intuitions explicit, in the form of proposed learning sequences. These proposed instructional sequences then form the basis of teaching/learning experiments in which pupil responses are used as data which is fed back into the instructional design phase. Teaching becomes problem-solving. Teaching sequences are regarded as the object of teacher/researcher activity.

Instructional transmission and learner response

Sadly, there have been too many instances of examples of teaching objectives (e.g. those offered in Ainscow and Tweddle, 1979) being literally photocopied and used inflexibly as definitive instructional pathways. All the power of the approach as a heuristic device is lost. The strengths of the task analysis approach are to be found in a classroom situation in which the teacher is looking for tools with which to understand the learning process, rather than programmes to follow. Recent reports of surveys of classroom practice suggest that the 'culture' of many classrooms does not involve careful scrutiny of pupil responses to instruction as part of the preparation for instructional planning:

> About a tenth of the schools made good use of their records to plan work for classes and individuals. However, in most of the schools there was some inflexible planning in that the work already planned would be done whatever the assessment evidence. (HMI, 1993, p.26)

If it is the case that a large proportion of the teaching in mainstream classrooms is *not* informed by the responses that learners make to instruction, then, perhaps, one useful way of conceptualising special needs support would be in terms of the amount of attention that is paid to a learner's responses to instruction. The extent to which a learner needs support could be thought of in terms of the level of detailed response to learning characteristics that is required in planning. Given that the economics of schooling determine a certain degree of uniformity in instruction, then the degree of diversity in presumed learner behaviour will always, to some extent, be bounded. Special need may be thought of in terms of the degree to which more sensitive and detailed account needs to be taken of the way in which an individual thinks and learns. Following the neo-Vygotskian imperative advanced by Newman et al., this account would be taken in the pedagogic interaction between teacher and learner, rather than by the teacher working as an analyst alone. In terms derived from the jargon of computing, the distinction is between 'on-line' and 'remote' analysis.

The dominant Piagetian emphasis in, particularly, primary schooling in the UK has been on the arrangement of contexts (classrooms, seating arrangements, resources, materials, etc.) in which development can take place and understanding acquired. In contrast, the behavioural approach to special needs work has, in practice, often been associated with transmission-based pedagogies in which pathways for learning are predetermined. Cobb et al. (1992) present an approach that avoids the traps of both consensual *laissez-faire* and over-determined instructional procedures. In the 'on-line' model of teaching, teachers as well as students modify their interpretations in the light of their developing understandings of each others' learning activity. The teacher can then use the pupil's understanding as the point of contact with the direction which they wish to pursue in instruction. In this way, a teacher can help a pupil to make sense of a task in terms of his or her own learning history and understanding. In itself, the assumption that a learner assembles individual task components into a complete package presents some potential difficulties. These are made manifest if and when a particular learner gets 'stuck' at a particular stage in a learning hierarchy. In some cases, it may not be at all clear to a learner why they are attempting to solve a particular stage in an analysis whose ultimate purpose is obscure. Put simply, a child may not know *why* on earth it is being required to perform a particular task:

> However, the time spent on number in some of the schools was excessive and ineffective; insufficient attention was given to sorting out whether errors were careless or represented misconceptions that needed particular attention. Excessive practice frequently led to boredom and inaccuracies. (HMI, 1993, p.3)

There is considerable evidence that many pupils find themselves in situations where they do not understand what they are supposed to be learning and why, nor do they benefit from teaching which treats the errors they make as vital 'windows' on the learning process. It is precisely this kind of what Campione (1989) calls 'on-line diagnosis' that vanishes in a pedagogic context which is dominated by a curriculum script (Putnam, 1987). A 'curriculum script' may be expressed in the form of a syllabus, a set text or a series of objectives in a learning hierarchy. Arguably, the higher the level of specification of the script, the greater the need for 'on-line diagnosis'. In practice, this is not always the case.

One factor that is often forgotten in the discussion of the reasons why rigidity masks the desired responsiveness of the 'teach-test-teach' strategy is that of teacher confidence. Many teachers find themselves required to support learners in curriculum areas with which they themselves are unfamiliar.

> In almost all the schools, however, some teaching of mathematics was carried out by teachers with no initial qualifications or relevant experience or recent in-service training (INSET) in mathematics. (HMI, 1993, p.4)

Gallimore and Tharp (1990) argue that involvement in their own 'assisted performance' instructional programme has beneficial effects for teachers as well as pupils. They argue that school reform is highly dependent on the extent to which teachers have both the confidence to change and competence to develop new curriculum initiatives. The emphasis on teacher as learner within their approach carries with it the need for systems that support teacher and learning as well as pupil progress.

Individual intervention or curriculum and systems development?

Ainscow and Tweddle (1979) provide an example of the application of an individual intervention strategy to special needs education. There have been many critiques of this approach, not least by Ainscow and Tweddle (1988) and Ainscow (1991), which focus on the potential for excessive attention to the individual at the expense of a wider systems/whole-school view. This echoes the earlier sociological critique of the process of individualisation in special education made by Shapiro (1984), amongst others.

There would seem to be two elements to this concern. The first is a psycho-pedagogical concern. Does the 'individual gaze' of much special needs intervention have effects on the individual's learning possibilities? This will be discussed in the next section. The second is a curriculum management and development concern. Within this there are again two elements:

- Do schools make curriculum plans for meeting a diversity of learning needs?
- Is this planning process informed by the ways in which individual learners respond to the curriculum?

There have been a number of attempts to make behavioural individual intervention strategies more ecologically sensitive. Glynn (1983, 1985) has discussed the analysis of the settings or contexts in which individual programmes are implemented, particularly with respect to the prospects for the development of independent learning as against learning which is highly situated as a direct consequence of a limited application of behavioural technology. Certainly, generalisation of learning is regarded as a critical issue in the design of individual intervention programmes. Brown and Campione (1986), Stokes and Baer (1977) and Baumgart et al. (1982) have proposed procedures to alleviate some of the concerns for transfer of training that arise within the more constrained behavioural approaches. However helpful these suggestions are, they fail to connect individual intervention strategies with the more general curriculum processes.

Bennett et al. (1984) discuss the notion of 'curriculum mismatch' in their work on the quality and level of task set in classrooms, and emphasise that 'there is little to be gained from high pupil involvement on tasks that are either not comprehensible or worthwhile'. Baroody and Hume (1991) pursue a similar line of analysis, and argue that most children who experience difficulty in learning mathematics are victims of instruction that is not suited to how children think and learn. They invoke the notion of children becoming 'curriculum-disabled'. The interactional or transactional model of SEN argues for an understanding of the causes of learning difficulty which takes account of within-child *and* environmental factors in a dynamic system of interchanges. The notion of curriculum disability may be taken to be a simple environmental account. This is, perhaps, not a helpful reading of the concept. It would perhaps be better to consider the work of Baroody and Hume as one which establishes *the case for* an interactive model, given that so many of the practices in education have either explicitly or implicitly announced a conventional within-person deficit model of causation.

In the language of the Code of Practice (DfE & WO, 1994) this issue becomes a concern as to whether there is a reciprocal relationship between curriculum practice and the various stages of individual education planning. The connection between the curriculum planning process and strategies for assessing and meeting individual needs must be kept alive if the Code of Practice is to function as a general support for difficulty in learning, rather than as a mechanism for managing limited resources.

The data that is generated from teaching individual pupils is both expensive to glean and vital for the general planning process. As has been noted above, one of the tragedies of the current situation is the limited extent to which the detailed understanding of pupils which is gathered from individual teaching, as and when it occurs, is rarely fed back into the whole-group development cycle. This wastage cannot be afforded in a system in which the possibility of detailed individual attention is severely constrained. The impact of the individual 'gaze' of many special needs systems may be bi-directional: it may cause learning difficulty to be considered in isolation from the general curriculum process, and it may isolate the curriculum from feedback from individual teaching strategies.

Theoretical developments

As has been argued above, the test-teach-test strategy of individualised intervention will usually only function satisfactorily if it involves the re-formulation of teaching plans in the light of the pupils' learning experiences. It has also been suggested that many applications of objectives-based individual programmes have evidenced a rigid adoption of procedures, rather than their adaptation to meet the needs of particular circumstances and learners. Thus there have been problems with the embedding of the behavioural approach in the practices of teaching in schools. However, there is also the need to consider the developments in psychological theory which themselves may come to exert more influence in future. The application of socially-situated theories of learning may come to enjoy more influence in classrooms. Wood engages with this issue in the learning and teaching of mathematics:

> the notion of individualised instruction needs careful thought . . . it destroys any learner if they are left alone in trying to solve problems that make no sense to them . . . if the meaning of mathematical concepts are not rooted or renegotiated in shared practical activities, it seems unlikely that children will learn much more. (Wood, 1988, p.208)

Underlying this statement is a concern for the nature of the psychological model which informs individual intervention strategies. Wood's emphasis is derived from an interpretation of social constructivism:

> This . . . precludes an approach to teaching that is based on universal and invariant 'steps' or 'stages' . . . rather it invites interaction, negotiation and the shared construction of experiences. (Wood, 1988, p.210)

The theoretical antecedents of much practice in special needs education may still be traced to an individualist perspective. If, following Vygotsky (1987), individual learning is to be construed as the internalised results of social activity mediated through sign systems such as speech, then appropriate instructional methods need to be developed. Arguably, the twentieth century has witnessed the theoretical enhancement of the child as an active learner as part of a culturally-situated community, rather than an isolated individual; as a constructor of knowledge, rather than a receiver. The teacher's role within this theoretical shift has been transformed from the transmitter of pre-given understanding to the mediator between informal meanings and those which are taken to be socially valued at a particular time. The concept of the Zone of Proximal Development stresses the need for educational settings which involve cooperation *and* guidance.

Vygotsky also distinguished between scientific concepts – as provided by instruction – and everyday concepts, and argued that a mature concept is achieved when the scientific and everyday versions have merged. Unlike everyday concepts, scientific concepts are schooled and systematic. The emphasis on the interdependence between the development of scientific and everyday concepts is not always appreciated. Vygotsky argued that the systematic, organised and hierarchical thinking associated with scientific concepts becomes gradually embedded in everyday referents, and thus achieves a general sense in the contextual richness of everyday thought. Similarly, he argued that everyday thought is given structure and order in the context of systematic scientific thought. Vygotsky argued that it is in communication that social understanding is made available for individual understanding. Within schooling, word meanings themselves form the object of study. As Minick (1987) has argued, the differences between communication *with* words and communication *about* words marks the significant difference between communication in everyday life and communication within schooling. Communication about words within schooling leads to the development of scientific concepts within the individual. In this way, communication mediates between the society of schooling and the individual. What follows from this definition is the notion of guided interaction which is responsive to individual learning needs and is based on dialogue.

Bruner (1986) used the term 'scaffolding' to describe how the more experienced tutor structures learning tasks to promote higher mental processes. This 'scaffolding' interpretation has inspired teaching approaches that explicitly provide support for the initial performance of tasks to be later performed without assistance. Some of the theoretical work which has been developed in the wake of Vygotsky lays considerable emphasis on the teaching and learning process and the interaction of teacher and taught (see Reid & Addison Stone, 1991 and Palincsar et al., 1991 for reviews). 'Reciprocal teaching' is a term used by Palincsar and Brown (1988) to refer to an individual tutoring strategy whereby both teachers and students assume the role of 'the teacher'. The adult or student 'teacher model' aids learners in the internalisation of similar comprehension strategies. The teacher or more capable peer structures the students' learning through four strategies (Palincsar, 1986, p.119):

1   *Summarising* – identifying and paraphrasing the main idea in the text
2   *Question-generating* – self-questioning about the type of information that is generally tapped on tests of comprehension and recall
3   *Clarifying* – discerning when there has been a breakdown in comprehension and taking the necessary action to restore meaning (e.g. reading ahead, re-reading, asking for assistance)
4   *Predicting* – hypothesising what the structure and content of the text suggest will be presented next.

The post-Vygotskian approach also theorises an important role for the content of instruction. If it is to be effective in the formation of scientific concepts, instruction must, according to Davydov (1988), be designed to foster conscious awareness of conceptual form and structure and thereby allow for individual access and control over acquired scientific concepts. It must also foster the interaction and development of everyday concepts with scientific concepts. Davydov provides an elaborate epistemological and conceptual framework with which to approach questions of instruction and learning. The details of this approach are beyond the scope of this chapter. However, it is important to note that he advocates a form of task analysis which reverses the flow of the conventional Western approach. He advocates the direct teaching of the conceptual 'kernel' in instruction. His emphasis is the teaching of the general case, and then moving to its application:

> Learning activity, which ushers children into the sphere of theoretical knowledge and ensures the development in them of the bases of theoretical consciousness and thought, is the leading reproductive activity that is inherent in the younger school-age period. The structure of this activity includes such components as educational and cognitive needs and motives, the academic task, and the appropriate actions and operations. The specific nature of the learning task consists in the fact that through resolving it the children master a general mode for the resolution of all the particular tasks of a given type. (Davydov, 1988, p.30)

Thus his approach requires a psychology of subjects for instruction. Such an analysis may form part of the 'guidance' within a responsive pedagogy. Hedegaard (1990) provides a clear example of an instructional approach which has developed from this theoretical tradition.

Conclusion

In order to build on the advances that have been made in the teaching of children who experience difficulty in learning, it would seem that there are three points of departure:

1   A more responsive pedagogy needs to be introduced into general curriculum and individual intervention strategies. General curriculum development cycles and the individual intervention strategies must be interconnected and inform each other.
2   An attempt should be made to develop more sophisticated psycho-pedagogical analysis of the types of learning embedded in curriculum content.
3   In order to try to avoid some of the rigidity that creeps in to the application of so many individual intervention strategies, teachers need appropriate forms of training which will leave them with the blend of confidence and competence required to respond to learners. Intervention may then operate as experimental teaching, rather than the mechanical imposition of inert, pre-ordained formulae.

Postscript

I first met Klaus Wedell when I became a student in the then-named Department of Child Development and Educational Psychology at the Institute of Education. At the time, I was working in a special school. His influence enabled me to find my own position on many of the school practices which I had previously considered to be common sense. Several years later, I joined the renamed Department of Educational Psychology and Special Educational Needs as a member of staff. Throughout my association with Klaus as a colleague, I have always been impressed by his self-effacing and yet principled stand on academic and professional matters. His approach to individual strategies for investigation and intervention embodies the careful interrogation of relevant aspects of problems, together with tentative suggestions for making progress. The major impact he made on my thinking was through the insistence that working with individual children must always be undertaken using a strategy for problem-solving rather than applying ready-made 'solutions'. He has always maintained the need for a clear sense of direction, but understood that there are many different pathways by which progress may be achieved.

References

Ainscow, M. (1991) 'Towards effective schools for all', in G. Upton (ed.) *Staff Training and Special Educational Needs: Innovatory Strategies and Models of Delivery*, London: David Fulton.

Ainscow, M. & Tweddle, D. (1979) *Preventing Classroom Failure*, London: Methuen.

Ainscow, M. & Tweddle, D. (1988) *Encouraging Classroom Success*, London: David Fulton.

Baroody, A.J. & Hulme, J. (1991) 'Meaningful mathematics instruction: The case of fractions', *Remedial and Special Education*, 12(3), pp.54–68.

Baumgart D., Brown L., Pumpian I., Nisbet J., Ford A., Sweet M., Messing R. & Schroeder, T.M. (1982) 'Principle of partial participation and individualised adaptations in educational programs for severely handicapped students', *Journal of the Association for the Severely Handicapped*, 7(2), pp.17–27.

Bennett, N., Desforges, C., Cockburn, A. & Wilkinson, B. (1984) *The Quality of Pupil Learning Experiences*, London: Lawrence Erlbaum.

Brown, A.L. & Campione, J.C. (1986) 'Training for transfer: Guidelines for promoting flexible use of trained skills', in M.G. Wade (ed.) *Motor Skill Acquisition of the Mentally Handicapped: Issues in Research and Training*, North-Holland: Elsevier Science Publishers.

Bruner, J. (1986) *Actual Minds, Possible Worlds*, Cambridge, Mass.: Harvard University Press.

Cameron, R.J., Owen, A.J. & Tee, G. (1986) 'Curriculum Management (Part 3): Assessment and Evaluation', *Educational Psychology in Practice*, October 1986, pp.3–9.

Campione, J.C. (1989) 'Assisted assessments: A taxonomy of approaches and an outline of strengths and weaknesses', *Journal of Learning Disabilities*, 22(3), pp.151–65.

Carnine, D.W. & Silbert, J. (1979) *Direct Instruction Reading*, Ohio: Charles E. Merrill.

Cobb, P., Yackel, E. & Wood, T. (1992) 'A constructivist alternative to the representational view of mind in mathematics education', *Journal for Research in Mathematics Education*, 23(1), pp.2–33.

Davydov, V.V. (1988) 'Problems of developmental teaching: The experience of theoretical and experimental psychological research', *Soviet Education*, 30(8), pp.1–97.

Denvir, B. & Brown, M. (1987) 'The feasibility of class administered diagnostic assessment in primary mathematics', *Educational Research*, 29(2), pp.95–107.

Department for Education & Welsh Office (DfE & WO) (1994) *Code of Practice on the Identification and Assessment of Pupils with Special Educational Needs*, London: HMSO.

Department of Education & Science (DES) (1978) *Report of the Committee of Inquiry into the Education of Handicapped Children and Young People* (The Warnock Report, Cmnd 7212, London: HMSO.

Dockrell, J. & McShane, J. (1993) *Children's Learning Difficulties: A Cognitive Approach*, London: Blackwell.

Faupel, A. (1986) 'Curriculum Management (Part 2): Teaching Curriculum Objectives', *Educational Psychology in Practice*, July 1986, pp.4–15.

Gagné, R.M. (1985) *The Conditions of Learning and Theory of Instruction* (4th edn), New York: Holt, Rinehart and Winston.

Gallimore, R. & Tharp, R. (1990) 'Teaching mind in society', in L.C. Moll (ed.) *Vygotsky and Education: Instructional Implications and Applications of Sociohistorical Psychology*, Cambridge: Cambridge University Press.

Glynn, T. (1983) 'Building an effective teaching environment', in K. Wheldall and R. Riding (eds) *Psychological Aspects of Teaching and Learning*, London: Croom Helm.

Glynn, T. (1985) 'Contexts for independent learning', *Educational Psychology*, 5(1), pp.5–15.

Hart, B. & Risley, T.R. (1980) 'In vivo language intervention: Unanticipated general effects', *Journal of Applied Behavioural Analysis*, 13, pp.407–32.

Hedegaard, M. (1990) 'The ZPD as basis for instruction', in L.C. Moll (ed.) *Vygotsky and Education: Instructional Implications and Applications of Sociohistorical Psychology*. Cambridge: Cambridge University Press.

Her Majesty's Inspectorate (HMI) (1993) *Mathematics Key Stages 1, 2, 3 and 4 Fourth Year, 1992–93: The implementation of the curricular requirements of the Education Reform Act*, London: HMSO.

Howell, K.W., Kaplan, J.S. & O'Connell, C.Y. (1979) *Evaluating Exceptional Children: A Task Analysis Approach*, Ohio: Charles E. Merrill.

Lister, T.A.J. & Cameron, R.J. (1986) 'Curriculum Management (Part 1): Planning Curriculum Objectives', *Educational Psychology in Practice*, April 1986, pp.6–14.

Luria, A.R. (1979) *The Making of Mind*, Cambridge: Cambridge University Press.

Manning, B.H. (1991) *Cognitive Self-instruction for Classroom Processes*, Albany, NY: State University of New York.

Minick, N. (1987) 'The Development of Vygotsky's thought: An introduction', in R.W. Rieber and A.S. Carton (eds) *The Collected Works of L.S. Vygotsky: Volume 1*, New York: Plenum Press.

Newman, D., Griffin, P. & Cole, M. (1989) *The Construction Zone: Working for Cognitive Change in Schools*, Cambridge: Cambridge University Press.

Palincsar, A.S. (1986) 'Metacognitive strategy instruction', *Exceptional Children*, 53(2), pp.118–24.

Palincsar, A.S. & Brown, A.L. (1988) 'Teaching and practising thinking skills to promote comprehension in the context of group problem solving', *Remedial and Special Education*, 9(1) pp.53–9.

Palincsar, A.S., David, Y.M., Winn, J.A. & Stevens, D.D. (1991) 'Examining the context of strategy instruction', *Remedial and Special Education*, 12(3), pp.43–53.

Putnam, R.T. (1987) 'Structuring and adjusting content for students', *American Educational Research Journal*, 24, pp.13–48.

Raybould, E.C. & Solity, J.E. (1988) 'Precision teaching and all that', *British Journal of Special Education*, 1(1), pp.32–3.

Reid, D.K. & Addison Stone, C. (1991) 'Why is cognitive instruction effective? Underlying learning mechanisms', *Remedial and Special Education*, 12(3), pp.8–19.

Reid, D.K. & Hresko, W.P. (1981) *A Cognitive Approach to Learning Disabilities*, New York: McGraw Hill.

Resnick, L.B. & Ford, W.W. (1981) *The Psychology of Mathematics for Instruction*, New Jersey: Lawrence Erlbaum.

Salvia, J. & Ysseldyke, J. (1985) *Assessment in Special and Remedial Education*, Boston: Houghton Mifflin.

Shapiro, H.S. (1984) 'Ideology, hegemony and the individualizing of instruction: The incorporation of progressive education', *Journal of Curriculum Studies*, 16(4), pp.367–78.

Solity, J. (1991) 'An overview of behavioural approaches to teaching children with learning difficulties and the National Curriculum', *Educational Psychology*, 11(2), pp.151–67.

Solity, J. & Raybould, E. (1988) *A Teacher's Guide to Special Needs: A Positive Response to the 1981 Act*, Milton Keynes: Open University Press.

Stokes, T.F. & Baer, D.M. (1977) 'An implicit technology of generalization', *Journal of Applied Behaviour Analysis*, 10, pp.349–67.

Vygotsky, L.S. (1978) *Mind in Society: The Development of Higher Psychological Processes*, Cambridge, Mass.: Harvard University Press.

Vygotsky, L.S. (1987) 'Thinking and Speech', in R.W. Reiber and A.S. Carton (eds) *The Collected Works of L.S. Vygotsky: Volume 1 – Problems of General Psychology*, London: Plenum Press.

Wedell, K. (1989) 'Some developments in the concepts and practice of special education' (unpublished manuscript).

Wedell, K. (1980) 'Early identification and compensatory interaction', in R.M. Knights and D.J. Bakker (eds) *Treatment of Hyperactive and Learning Disordered Children: Current Research*, Baltimore University Park Press.

Wood, D. (1988) *How Children Think and Learn*, Oxford: Blackwell.

8 Some reflections on the role of educational psychologists

Peter Farrell

Introduction

There are a great many areas which could be covered in a chapter on the role of educational psychologists. I have chosen to focus on the impact of legislation and government circulars, as this seems to be the issue with which educational psychologists (EPs) are continually preoccupied and which has direct impact, not only on the development of the role, but also on the employment prospects for new entrants into the profession. The chapter is therefore divided into five sections. The first traces the growth and expansion of educational psychology services since the early 1970s. The second discusses some of the studies which have evaluated their effectiveness. The third explores the impact of statutory work on the role. The fourth considers the effects of the 1993 Education Act and the Code of Practice (DfE & WO, 1994), and the fifth raises the issue of whether EPs should continue to be employed by local education authorities (LEAs).

The growth and expansion of educational psychology services

If judgements about the value and effectiveness of a profession were based solely on the growth in the numbers of people who chose to join it, then the profession of educational psychology would be a success by anybody's standards. According to the Summerfield Report (DES, 1968), in 1966 there were only 354 EPs in England and Wales, and some LEAs did not employ any. By January 1994, government figures, reported in the January 1995 edition of *Education*, stated that there was a total of 1,514.2 full-time equivalent (FTE)

EPs in posts in England and Wales. This represents a $4^1/_2$-fold increase over a 26-year period – an impressive rise which is not matched by increases in other services, for example education welfare, learning and behavioural support services. Indeed, the continued existence of LEA-funded support services remains in jeopardy, whereas educational psychology services are, for the present, firmly rooted within LEAs and financed by them.

The rise in the number of EPs is closely associated with new legislation and associated Circulars and with the publication of reports commissioned by the government. One of the most influential of these was the Summerfield Report, the only government-initiated report which is exclusively devoted to the role of EPs. Two of its important recommendations were firstly, that every LEA should employ EPs, and secondly, that the ratio of psychologists to school children should be 1 to 10,000. As a result, LEAs began to expand their services, a move which was accelerated, in 1970, by the transfer to LEAs of the responsibility to educate children with severe learning difficulties and by the rise in pre-school provision. Indeed, a survey into the role of EPs carried out by the Division of Educational and Child Psychology (DECP) of the British Psychological Society (Wedell & Lambourne, 1980) reported that EPs considered the demands on their work had increased considerably as a result of these two developments. Further growth in educational psychology services occurred following local government reorganisation in 1974, when several new LEAs were formed, many headed by recently-qualified EPs with little or no experience of leading a team. This was followed, in 1975, by Circular 2/75 introducing the new special education (SE) procedures which again, according to the DECP report (Wedell & Lambourne, 1980) increased the workload of EPs, since, for the first time, the government indicated that all pupils requiring special educational provision should be assessed by an educational psychologist. Developments during the 1970s resulted in the number of EPs employed in England and Wales approaching 1,100 by the end of the decade.

Perhaps the most significant government-led initiative came with the publication of the Warnock Report (DES, 1978) and the subsequent passing of the 1981 Education Act. The report's recommendation that each LEA should appoint 1 EP to every 5,000 children aged 0–19 and the 1981 Act itself led to a further increase in the number of EPs. Government figures, referred to above, stated that by January 1985 there were 1,173.4 (FTE) EPs working in England and Wales; this figure had increased to 1,496.6 by January 1992. Although the number of EPs has grown steadily since the 1981 Act became law, the HMI report on educational psychology services (DES, 1990) stated that no LEA in their sample had reached the Warnock recommended ratio of 1 EP to 5,000 children.

The 1993 Education Act and the subsequent Code of Practice on the identification and assessment of children with special needs (DfE & WO, 1994) is another example of a government-led initiative which seems to have resulted in a further growth in the number of EPs. Indeed, at the time of writing (December 1994), many LEAs appear to be expanding their services and are having difficulties in filling their posts. The potential impact of the 1993 Act and the Code of Practice on the role of EPs is referred to again later in this chapter.

The evaluation of educational psychology services

There is prima facie evidence that educational psychology services are effective. The fact that the number of EPs has grown so substantially over the past twenty-five years is a powerful indication that their services are valued. Successive governments have presumably been impressed by the valuable contribution that they make, as one of the main effects of legislation has been to lead to a growth in the size of the profession. Similarly, there is no sign that referrals to EPs are dropping, and services consistently report that they are under pressure to keep up with existing demands.

However, to say that educational psychology services are effective just because they have expanded is too simplistic. Services wishing to plan improvements to the quality of their work require more detailed evaluative data. Such services are likely to refer to the results of several small-scale evaluations of different LEAs which have been conducted over the past fifteen years (e.g. Wright & Payne, 1979; Evans & Wright, 1987; Lindsay, 1991; Dowling & Leibowitz, 1994; Morgan, 1994). They may also draw on the findings of the HMI report (HMI, 1990), which is the only recent survey which has evaluated the work of EP services across the country.

There is insufficient space in this chapter to report on the detailed findings of these and other studies. However, there are some key themes emerging from most of them which are worth noting. First, the studies report that the vast majority of teachers appreciate the quality of EPs' work, although there are frequent complaints about the quantity. Schools therefore want to see more, rather than less, of their EP. Second, headteachers, in particular, value the professionalism, dedication and strength of the personal relationship with their EP. Third, in general, schools would like EPs to have more time to devote to non-statutory work, in particular general advice and support, in-service training (INSET) and direct intervention with children. Fourth, there is frequently a lack of communication between schools and the educational psychology service on the aims and objectives of the service. This can lead to schools expecting a different kind of service from their EP than the one they get. Indeed, Dowling and Leibowitz (1994) conclude, somewhat dramatically perhaps, that 'sensitivity and respect for consumer needs and wants will be essential for survival'.

It is important to consider the findings of educational psychology service evaluations with caution. Most, with the exception of the HMI report and Morgan's 1994 study, were carried out by practising EPs who work for the service which is being evaluated, which could result in a degree of bias creeping into the interpretation of the results. In addition, it should be remembered that schools do not pay for the service. If they did, then they might be considerably more critical than they are at present. Finally, service evaluations tend only to survey the views of teachers. We know little about the opinions of social and health service personnel and of other LEA support services. Similarly, there are few if any surveys which seek the views of parents and children.

Statutory assessment: A poisoned chalice?

Many writers, for example Mittler (1985), have challenged educational psychologists to be clear about the distinctiveness of the profession. One obvious distinctive contribution is the psychologist's involvement in statutory assessment – a role which many perceive as being the core of EPs' work. Lunt and Farrell (1994) suggest that this work has led the profession into a double bind. On the one hand it has resulted in it growing in size and becoming, for the time being, secure within LEA structures. Indeed, educational psychology is the only profession within applied psychology with a statutory function, something of which other applied psychologists might be envious. On the other hand, LEAs, as the employers, may view EPs as being solely employed to carry out this task and not to take on other work. As a result, the statutory function can be perceived as being limited and restricting. Indeed, Williams (1993) describes statutory work as being 'a chain around the neck of psychologists'. Faupel and Norgate (1993) refer to the consequences of the 1981 Act as being the 'single greatest disaster' for educational psychology services as they become reduced to being 'providers' of additional resources. Both the above articles also make the point that statutory work reduces the potential for EPs to work as applied psychologists for the benefit of all children. This point is also taken up forcefully in a wide-ranging article by Maliphant (1994).

At this point, it is worth recording that this problem pre-dates the 1981 Education Act. The DECP survey (Wedell & Lambourne, 1980) and some of the comments which were written about it (e.g. Maliphant, 1980) argued that an excessive amount of EP time was spent in allocating children to special schools. At a seminar held in 1974, Klaus Wedell referred somewhat pessimistically to the problem of EPs being forced to spend too much time taking on the role of 'the educational undertaker!'.

By restricting the role to one of carrying out statutory assessments, EPs are in danger of becoming deskilled, as opportunities to use and develop skills in other areas – for example in INSET, or direct intervention with individuals or groups, or through research and evaluation – are reduced. The Statementing role may therefore lead educational psychology into becoming a second-rate profession in applied psychology. Further questions might also be asked about the need for EPs to undergo such a long period of training (seven years) if they are only needed to undertake statutory work. (See Farrell and Lunt, 1994; Lunt and Farrell, 1994; Maliphant, 1994; Figg, 1994, and Farrell and Lunt, 1995 for a detailed discussion of current issues in the training of educational psychologists.)

What, then, is the solution? If the government were to bring in an amendment to the 1993 Education Act which stated that it was no longer a legal requirement for EPs to be involved in statutory assessments, how would the profession respond? One might suspect that it would be outraged, perhaps because job security would be seen as being threatened since LEAs would no longer be 'legally' required to employ EPs. As we have seen, the growth in statutory work is the main reason why EP services have expanded since the early 1980s, and to remove this aspect of the work could have the reverse effect. Although there does not appear to be any immediate threat of the government removing the requirement for EPs to do statutory work, there is a danger that, by complaining so extensively about this aspect of the role, EPs may appear to be belittling its importance. Articles which refer to problems in this area can give the impression that EPs do not value this work as much as other activities, and that they may even be tempted to cut corners in order to gain more time to do other work, for example INSET or other projects. It is difficult to find articles on the role of EPs which have extolled the value of Statementing. Farrell (1989) argues that it is unfortunate that EPs tend not to write about work they have been doing with individual children, hence reinforcing the impression that this work is of less value.

It is unlikely, however, that parents, pupils, schools and LEAs view the work in this way. They have the right to expect the highest possible quality of statutory work, as EPs are involved in making decisions which have a profound effect on their lives. The vast majority of professionals and parents would agree that arrangements for the assessment of pupils with special educational needs (SENs) should be standardised and placed within a legal framework, as this adds accountability and ensures a degree of consistency to the whole procedure. By definition, such children have complex problems which require a detailed and skilled assessment. EPs are the only group of professionals who are thoroughly trained and experienced in the assessment of children with problems, and therefore should be central to the whole Statementing process.

Indeed, there is an extensive range of skills and knowledge that EPs should possess in order to fulfil the statutory role adequately. These include:

- skills in interviewing and counselling teachers, parents and children and in gaining their confidence
- negotiating skills at meetings and case conferences
- knowledge about normal child development from birth to school-leaving age
- knowledge about various handicapping conditions in children; the causes, prognosis and implications for schooling and teaching techniques
- skills and knowledge in psychological assessment, including the use of norm- and criterion-referenced tests, curriculum-based assessment, observation techniques
- knowledge of relevant government legislation, including the 1993 Education Act, the Code of Practice and associated Circulars
- an awareness of the arguments about the effectiveness of segregated and integrated provision for children with SEN
- detailed knowledge about the services which are available in an LEA, of who the decision-makers are, and about the key meetings at which decisions are made
- knowledge about, and the ability to work with, other agencies, for example LEA support services, health and social services.

The above list of skills and knowledge indicates that, in order to carry out statutory work effectively, EPs need to have a great deal of expertise; to describe the work as 'routine' greatly undervalues its importance.

However, EPs can and should fulfil a much wider function within the LEA by using additional skills and knowledge, for example in planning and delivering INSET courses, in research and evaluation and in direct treatment work with groups and individuals. As Faupel and Norgate (1993) and Maliphant (1994) argue, if EPs are going to be effective in applying psychological skills to children and families in a wide range of educational contexts, their work needs to extend beyond the statutory role. One of the problems in achieving this aim is that LEAs employ EPs to help them fulfil their legal duty to assess and provide for children with SENs. If EPs then plead for more staff to undertake additional activities, LEAs may well reply that they do not have the budget or the obligation to employ extra EPs to to this work.

On a more positive note, despite the pressure to undertake statutory work, there is evidence that some EPs do find the time to become involved in a much wider range of activities. Recently, for example, a number have become interested in the application of Solution-focused Brief Therapy

(Rhodes, 1993), in running Assertive Discipline courses (Moss, 1992), in providing Critical Incident Stress Debriefing in schools (O'Hara et al., 1994) and in running Stress Management courses (Bamford et al., 1990). There continues to be evidence showing that EPs are actively involved in systems work in schools (see e.g. Moore et al., 1993; Gregor, 1994; Leadbetter & Tee, 1991, and Stoker, 1992). EPs also make a substantial contribution in social services departments, and increasing numbers are called to give evidence in court. Therefore, despite pressures from schools and LEAs to concentrate on statutory work, the picture is by no means one of EPs exclusively being driven down this path at the expense of all other work.

In concluding this section on the involvement of EPs in statutory work, it is important to reiterate that it is, and should remain, a vital part of the job. EPs should not undervalue its importance, and at the same time they should continue to develop skills and activities in other areas. It is therefore vital for EPs to convince potential employers of the wider contribution which they can make.

The effect of the Code of Practice on the work of educational psychologists

As the Code of Practice (DfE & WO, 1994) only came into effect in September 1994, it is perhaps too early to draw firm conclusions as to its impact on the future development of EP services. At one level, one could argue that it should bring little or no change, as it reinforces the EP's key statutory role in the Statementing process. However, there are other aspects of EPs' work which may well be affected by the Code.

First, the Code and the 1993 Education Act have resulted in an increase in the number of EP posts being advertised, and LEAs are currently having difficulty in filling vacancies. This is probably explained by the new legal requirement for LEAs to complete Statements within six months, which confirms the suspicion that the main effect of the Code on the role of EPs will be to increase their involvement in statutory work. This is ironic, as the delays in Statementing are primarily due to the lack of LEA administrative personnel, rather than the lack of EPs.

Second, the attempt to draw up tighter criteria for the referral of children for statutory assessments may well result in EPs becoming more consistent in their assessment practices. Surveys of the assessment methods used by EPs during the 1980s (Farrell & Smith, 1982; Farrell et al., 1989) suggest that EPs adopted a variety of different methods, some of which relied heavily on IQ tests, while others only used criterion-referenced measures. The new criteria in the Code may result in a more unified approach to assessment and one which is more psychometric. There is already evidence from a few LEAs that criteria based on the discrepancy between IQ and attainment are being used in the identification of children with specific learning difficulties. It is also possible that IQ scores will become increasingly important criteria when making decisions about placing children into schools for children with moderate learning difficulties.

Third, the Code suggests that schools should use the services of EPs in an advisory and consultative capacity in Stages 2 and 3 of the stage-based assessment procedures. Although EPs have been working in this way for many years, it is encouraging that government documents are urging LEAs to recognise the value of work at this level, and it could help EPs to escape the straitjacket of statutory work.

Fourth, the intention of the stage-based assessment procedures to make schools far more explicit about the actions that they have taken to help a child prior to a referral for a statutory assessment should result in only the more serious cases being referred to EPs. It is clearly logical that EPs should use their limited time working with those children who need the greatest help. One consequence of this development, however, it that the EP will be seen even more as the 'consultant' rather than the 'GP', to use a medical analogy. Children are being screened before they can see an EP in the same way that patients are screened before they see a consultant. This development is not new and may be desirable, but it does have implications for those who believe in the concept of community psychological services. How, for example, do parental referrals link into the way of working implied in the Code? Do parents have a right to a free assessment from their LEA EP? Does this cause problems for the educational psychology service if the school thinks the child in question is only at Stage 2 and that the parent is fussing and overprotective? How does the service prioritise such a referral? After all, the parents may be right, and their child could have serious problems. Organising EPs' work so that it is wholly dependent on school referrals may deny parents and children access to their services. Is it possible to plan service delivery, even within the confines of the Code, so that there is time to take direct referrals from parents or even children?

Fifth, the new Special Education Needs Tribunal, which replaces the old and cumbersome appeals procedures, may make EP services more accountable and dissuade EPs from cutting corners as they plough through statutory assessments.

Finally, the vastly increased role for special educational needs coordinators (SENCOs) has provided EPs with opportunities to develop and expand their INSET role. There are already several examples where EP services, often in collaboration with other support services, have organised training for SENCOs.

The Code of Practice has therefore provided EPs with opportunities to expand their services and range of work. This is likely to be effective, provided, of course, that the intention of the Code to reduce – or at least put a brake on – the number of referrals for statutory assessment is successful. If it is not, then EPs are likely to continue to devote a substantial amount of their time to statutory work.

Who should employ educational psychologists?

Currently, the vast majority of EPs are employed by LEAs, and, as referred to earlier in this chapter, this has brought many benefits in terms of the expansion of the number of EPs and in job security. As LEA employees, EPs are also in a good position to advise officers and elected members on the development and effectiveness of services within the LEA, and can therefore shape LEA policy in a range of areas. At the present time, therefore, there is no ground-swell of opinion in favour of services becoming independent of LEAs. Indeed, the 1988 Education Reform Act, which brought with it the threat of financial delegation and the prospect that EP services might be purchased by schools, had the beneficial effect of encouraging them to focus their thoughts on the whole issue of defining and providing a quality service (see e.g. Gersch et al., 1990; Fox, 1991). This has led to the development of excellent brochures describing the range of services that an educational psychology service can offer within the LEA.

Secure though the profession is within the LEA base, it has been argued (Farrell, 1989) that, through being employed by LEAs, EPs may not be in the most appropriate position to work in the best interests of children and families and to act as advocates on their behalf. As LEA employees, they may sometimes shy away from specifying a child's needs accurately when it is known that the LEA does not have the resources to meet them. Instead, they may describe the child in such a way as to make his or her needs fit the available LEA resources – this is sometimes referred to as 'resource-led Statementing'. Making recommendations for resources which the LEA does not have may highlight the child's needs, but it can also make the EP unpopular with the LEA. As LEA employees, EPs are mindful of the necessity to keep employers happy, even if this may mean that they compromise on their assessments. If they were independent of the LEA, they might feel more able to act as a genuine advocate for the child and family, even if this might 'ruffle the feathers' of the LEA.

If LEAs did not employ EPs, who would? If we believe in the rights of all children to receive the services of a psychologist free of charge, another agency would have to pay. Some voluntary agencies – for example the Barnados organisation or SCOPE – do employ EPs, but only on a limited scale and for a specified client group. The day when we can rely on voluntary organisations to pay for the work of EPs across the country is a long way off, and indeed this position may never be reached. Furthermore, EPs working independently may not be able to exert the influence over LEA policy and development that they can at present. Of course, if LEAs cease to exist – a possibility which seems, for the present, to have receded – the situation would be very different.

Nevertheless, there are possibilities for the partial delegation of EP services which offer potentially exciting opportunities for the future. It is conceivable that LEAs may continue to appoint EPs to undertake all individual casework (including statutory work) and advisory work in schools. However, services could generate additional income by running INSET courses, both within the LEA and elsewhere, and by publishing booklets and other materials which they have developed. In addition, social services departments, the health service and the police might be persuaded to employ more EPs. Indeed, social services departments have employed a considerable number of EPs for many years. Through becoming partly disengaged from LEAs, educational psychology services could have more freedom to develop and expand their range of activities, and therefore offer a more effective psychological service to children and their families. From this development it would be possible to conceive of a psychological service which employed a range of applied psychologists – for example educational, clinical, occupational – who could offer services to industry, education, social and health services. Such a development would bring the various branches of applied psychologists closer together and have implications for training.

It is clear that such a development will not take place in the near future, and indeed there are pressures within the professions of applied psychology to remain separate, rather than unite. For the foreseeable future, therefore, EPs will continue to be employed by LEAs, and it is their responsibility, within this potentially restricting framework, to continually emphasise the important and valuable role that the service can play, not only in implementing the provisions of the 1993 Education Act but in direct intervention, advisory, preventative and in-service work.

Conclusion

This chapter has reviewed the development of the profession of educational psychology over the last twenty years and discussed some of the key issues facing EPs at the present time. Inevitably, some areas have not been included, for example the development of educational and school psychology services overseas (see Lunt, 1991; Lindsay, 1992, and Burden, 1994 for a wide-ranging analysis of international developments). On the whole, there are reasons to be optimistic about the future. The profession continues to expand, reflecting an increasing demand for EP services. The importance of the work is enshrined in legislation, and despite the limitations that this can impose, the range of work in which EPs are involved continues to develop. It is likely that the status of the profession will be further enhanced by forthcoming developments in training which should result in the professional qualification being upgraded to that of a professional doctorate (Farrell & Lunt, 1995). However, it is important for services to keep abreast of international developments and to enhance links with other professions within applied psychology in order to ensure that EPs do not become relegated to the status of a second-rate profession in applied psychology – something which could happen if they allow themselves to be strangled by statutory work and if projected improvements in training do not materialise.

Postscript

I consider myself fortunate to have trained as an educational psychologist at the University of Birmingham during the academic year 1974/5, when Klaus Wedell was the course tutor, and to have been a member of his tutorial group. Throughout this time, I was impressed by the reflective and thoughtful way in which he approached issues and by his willingness to listen to new ideas, always adopting a non-dogmatic but questioning approach which enabled us all to get to the heart of the problem.

At the time, Klaus was keen to expound the virtues of his 'sequential strategy' to the assessment of pupils with learning difficulties, a subject on which he had written an extremely influential article (Wedell, 1970). This had a profound effect on all the trainees, so much so that we decided that it would be an appropriate reflection of the pervasiveness of this aspect of the course for us to enact a small vignette of a tutorial at an end-of-year party. I was cast in the role of Klaus and was faced by a nervous trainee who asked me how to build a brick wall! I, of course, began by saying that I was 'terribly sorry' that I had not explained this adequately in previous seminars and then launched into a long exposition of how, by using the sequential strategy, it would be possible to complete this task. Clearly, our training in assessment had brought generalisable benefits far beyond those of working with children with learning difficulties!

It was not long after I had completed my training that Klaus moved to the Institute of Education, and although my contact with him since then has been intermittent, I have continued to be influenced by his work, and consider myself privileged to have been one of his trainees.

140 *Psychology and Education for Special Needs*

References

Bamford, J., Grange, J. & Jones, P. (1990) 'An experiential stress management course for teachers', *Educational Psychology in Practice*, 6(2), pp.90–6.

Burden, R. (1994) 'Trends and developments in educational psychology', *School Psychology International*, 15 pp.293–347.

Department for Education & Welsh Office (DfE & WO) (1994) *Code of Practice on the Identification of Pupils with Special Educational Needs*, London: HMSO.

Department of Education and Science (DES) (1968) *Psychologists in Education Services* (The Summerfield Report), London: HMSO.

Department of Education & Science (DES) (1978) *Special Educational Needs: Report of the Committee of Inquiry into the Education of Handicapped Children and Young People* (The Warnock Report), Cmnd 7212, London: HMSO.

Department of Education and Science (DES) (1990) *Educational Psychology Services in England: Report of HMI*, London: HMSO.

Dowling, J. & Leibowitz, D. (1994) 'Evaluation of educational psychology services: Past and present', *Educational Psychology in Practice*, 9(4), pp.241–50.

Evans, M.E. & Wright, A.K. (1987) 'The Surrey school psychological service: An evaluation through teacher perceptions', *Educational Psychology in Practice*, 3(3), pp.13–20.

Farrell, P. (1989) 'Educational psychology: Crisis or opportunity?', *The Psychologist*, 12(6), pp.240–1.

Farrell, P. & Lunt, I. (1994) 'Training psychologists for the 21st century', *School Psychology International*, 15, pp.195–208.

Farrell, P. & Lunt, I. (1995) 'The future of professional training in educational psychology', *Educational Psychology in Practice*, 11(1), pp.3–9.

Farrell, P., Dunning, T. & Foley, J. (1989) 'Methods used by educational psychologists to assess children with learning difficulties', *School Psychology International*, 10(1), pp.47–57.

Faupel, A.W. & Norgate, R. (1993) 'Where to educational psychology? Roles, responsibilities in the world of the 1993 Education Act', *Educational Psychology in Practice*, 9(3), pp.131–7.

Figg, J. (ed.) (1994) 'Competent to practise', *Educational and Child Psychology*, 11(1), pp.5–91.

Fox, M. (1991) 'The EPS: A quality service', *Educational Psychology in Practice*, 6(4), pp.229–33.

Gersch, I.S., McCarthy, M., Sigston, A. & Townley, D. (1990) 'Taking educational psychology services into the 1990s', *Educational Psychology in Practice*, 6,(3), pp.123–31.

Gregor, A. (1994) 'When are we going to get an extension Miss? A team approach to meeting the needs of the very able child in mainstream', *Educational Psychology in Practice*, 10(2), pp.93–9.

Her Majesty's Inspectorate (HMI) (1990) *Educational Psychology Services in England*, London: DES.

Leadbetter, J. & Tee, G.A. (1991) 'A consultancy approach to behaviour problems in schools', *Educational Psychology in Practice*, 6(4), pp.203–10.

Lindsay, G. (1991) 'The educational psychologist in the new era', in G. Lindsay and A. Miller (eds) *Psychological Services for Primary Schools*, Harlow: Longman.

Lindsay, G. (1992) 'Educational psychologists and Europe', in S. Wolfendale, T. Bryans, M. Fox, A. Labram and A. Sigston (eds) *The Profession and Practice of Educational Psychology*, London: Cassell.

Lunt, I. (ed.) (1991) 'Educational psychology and Europe', *Educational and Child Psychology*, 8(4), pp.5–83.

Lunt, I. & Farrell, P. (1994) 'Restructuring educational psychology training in the UK', *The Psychologist*, 7(60), pp.268–71.

Maliphant, R. (1980) 'What do we do now?', *Occasional Papers of the Division of Educational and Child Psychology*, 4(2), pp.13–17.

Maliphant, R. (1994) 'School psychology', *The Psychologist*, 7(6), pp.263–7.

Mittler, P. (1985) 'Integration: The shadow and the substance', *Educational and Child Psychology*, 2(3), pp.8–23.

Moore, L., Clarke H., Corfield, S., Edwards, L., Evans, S., Farino, F., Pasternicki, G., Pratten, A., Robertson, J. & Wakefield, D. (1993) 'A school based action research project on truancy', *Educational Psychology in Practice*, 8(4), pp.208–15.

Morgan, A. (1994) 'Which service? Senior teachers' perceptions of educational psychology services to primary schools', unpublished MEd dissertation, University of Manchester, Department of Education.

Moss, G. (1992) 'The right to teach', *Special Children*, June/July, pp.16–19.

O'Hara, D.M., Taylor, R. & Simpson, K. (1994) 'Critical incident stress debriefing: Support in schools – developing a role for an LEA educational psychology service', *Educational Psychology in Practice*, 10(1), pp.27–35.

Rhodes, J. (1993) 'The use of solution focused brief therapy in schools', *Educational Psychology in Practice*, 9(1), pp.27–36.

Stoker, R. (1992) 'Working at the level of the institution and the organisation', *Educational Psychology in Practice*, 8(1), pp.15–25.

Wedell, K. (1970) 'Diagnosing learning difficulties: A sequential strategy', *Journal of Learning Difficulties*, 3(6), pp.23–9.

Wedell, K. & Lambourne, R. (1979) *Psychological services for children in England and Wales*, Social Science Research Council.

Wedell, K. & Lambourne, R. (1980) 'Psychological services for children in England and Wales', *DECP Occasional Papers*, 4(1) and (2), pp.1–84.

Williams, T. (1993) 'Consumer access to psychology', in I. Lunt (ed.) *Whither educational psychology? Challenges and changes for the future of the profession*, Division of Educational and Child Psychology, London: British Psychological Society.

Wright, H.J. & Payne, T.A.N. (1979) *An Evaluation of a Psychological Service: The Portsmouth Pattern*, Winchester: Hampshire County Council.

Part III

Policy, organisation and training

9 Implementing the 1981 Education Act

Jennifer Evans

Introduction

The 1981 Education Act represented the culmination of a series of changes in the conceptualisation of special educational needs (SENs) and provision. Prior to the implementation of the Act, special education had been organised around a number of categories of special educational need and provided, for the most part, in separate segregated institutions which were, themselves, categorised in terms of distinct disabilities. The development of the use of these categories and the system of education which grew up around them has been documented by (among others) Tomlinson (1982) and Norwich (1990). Their creation had been part of the 1944 Education Act, which had established 12 categories of handicap (or 'defects of body or mind') for which provision had to be made. One group, the 'severely sub-normal' were deemed to be the responsibility of the health rather than the education authorities, but, for the rest, provision was to be made in special schools. The categories corresponded to sensory and physical handicaps and intellectual and emotional difficulties. The emphasis in assessment was on deficits within the individual child, and a medical model of diagnosis and treatment.

During the 1960s and 1970s, parents and others interested in the education and welfare of children with disabilities campaigned for a change in approach. There was concern that a significant proportion of children (those deemed to be severely sub-normal) were the responsibility of the health authorities, rather than the education authorities, and were being provided for in 'junior training centres', rather than in schools. This was felt to be unacceptable, and, in 1971, after a long campaign, the responsibility for the education of 'educationally sub-normal (severe)' children was transferred to local education authorities (LEAs). Thus the right of all

145

children to an education was established.

A second concern of many parents, educators and other professionals was the system of categorisation, which appeared to be both rigid and arbitrary, relied upon a medical model in which the emphasis was on a child's deficits, and did not take into account compensating strengths or the interaction between the child and his or her environment in creating or ameliorating educational difficulties. During the 1970s, increasing numbers of children were being placed in special schools, and 'ascertainment' of a child as 'handicapped' became increasingly seen as having the consequence of marginalisation in respect of a child's peers and opportunities within the labour market (Tomlinson, 1982; Coard, 1971). In 1973, the then Minister of Education, Margaret Thatcher, set up a committee, chaired by Mary Warnock, to:

> review educational provision in England, Scotland and Wales for children and young people handicapped by disabilities of body or mind, taking account of the medical aspects of their needs, together with arrangements to prepare them for entry into employment; to consider the most effective use of resources for these purposes; and to make recommendations. (DES, 1978)

The Warnock Report and its implications for SEN policy and practice

The Warnock Committee reported in 1978. Its recommendations, on the face of it, were far-reaching and innovative (at least as far as special education in the UK was concerned). It recommended the abolition of categories of handicap, and their replacement with a single term: 'learning difficulties'. The committee had heard evidence that 1 in 6 children at any one time would require some form of special educational provision, and 1 in 5 would require it at some time during their school career. So the concept of 'learning difficulties' was introduced to include a wider range of children with problems, and, at the same time, to blur the distinction between children categorised as 'educationally sub-normal' (i.e. those in special schools) and those with 'educational difficulties', who were supported by 'remedial services' within mainstream schools. Children with 'severe, complex and long-term disabilities', who were judged, on the basis of a multi-professional assessment of their needs, to require special educational provision, should have those needs recorded. The committee recommended that the 1944 and 1962 Acts be amended to embody a broader concept of special education which related to a child's *individual needs*, rather than his or her disability.

Thus the Warnock Report paved the way for changes in legislation embodied in the 1981 Education Act which introduced the concept of the Statement of Needs and a relative definition of SENs and provision, which, as will be described later, has led to a number of challenges in its implementation.

Other aspects of the Warnock Report which have had a profound impact on special education are its emphasis on the role of parents in decision-making about their child's needs (now greatly enhanced by various Charters), and the emphasis on the *integration* of pupils with SENs within mainstream schools. It saw a key role for advisory and support services and for teacher training in enabling schools to improve their capability to provide for pupils with SENs. The report also stressed the need for collaboration between professionals and services (i.e. education, health and social services) in making provision for children with learning difficulties. It called for inter-professional training and closer coordination in the planning and delivery of services for children and young people with SENs. It was also concerned with improving pre-school provision and with the transition from school into adult life – two areas which still give cause for concern.

It is clear, then, that the Warnock Report reflected the key issues in special educational needs at the time (the late 1970s), in terms of its conceptualisation of the nature of SEN and the policy recommendations which it made about the organisation and delivery of special educational provision. It is interesting to note, however, that these issues are still the subject of debate and controversy, particularly in the years following the 1988 and 1993 Acts and the publication of the Code of Practice (Norwich, 1990, 1992; Lunt & Evans, 1994; House of Commons, Education Select Committee, 1993).

The 1981 Education Act

The 1981 Education Act can be seen as the legislative embodiment of the key recommendations of the Warnock Report. It was described by the Education Minister of the time as the embodiment of good practice (Goacher et al., 1988). It was part of a shift in ideas and policies about special education which was taking place in many other Western countries, including the USA, which passed similar legislation in 1975, and Italy, which brought about a radical change, requiring the integration of all but the most severely handicapped children, through legislation passed in 1971. Many of these legislative changes resulted from a wider political and societal emancipation which embodied ideas about democracy, equity and human rights. The 1981 Act can be seen therefore as 'just one event in the general process of policy and service development' (Goacher et al., 1988) which was subject to many influences both within the UK and beyond.

The particular manifestation of these ideas within the UK context has, however, been the subject of both positive and negative evaluation by commentators. Kirp (1982) described the UK government's response as 'professional-centred', in contrast to the US approach, which he described as 'rights-centred'. US welfare legislation stresses 'individual entitlement to governmentally subsidised benefits' and a perception of clients as active participants in decisions about their needs and the services they require. The UK system, by contrast, is seen by Kirp as 'enabling professionals, by the exercise of benign discretion, to offer the highest level of service on the least stigmatising terms possible, given available social resources' (Kirp, 1982, p.173). Kirp acknowledged, however, that the new emphasis on parental choice within the Warnock Report and the 1980 White Paper (DES, 1980), and greater control over local expenditure by central government, might challenge the professional hegemony.

Fulcher (1989) has observed that the widening of the definition of special educational needs to include 20 per cent of the school population was an attempt to de-stigmatise the notion of handicap. However, what it has succeeded in doing, in her view, is to legitimate the notion that up to 20 per cent of the school population has needs which are outside the facilities which ordinary schools generally provide.

More positive evaluations of the 1981 Act see it as 'empowering parents' (Russell, 1986), providing a means for open decision-making and accountability for the use of resources (Wedell, 1990), providing a stimulus to the development of a wide range of support for pupils with learning difficulties (Lunt & Evans, 1994), and opening the way to greater integration of pupils with SENs into mainstream schools (Bennett & Cass, 1989). However, these positive evaluations of the policy and practice implications of the Act have been tempered as examples of its implementation in LEAs have emerged.

A major DES-funded evaluation of the 1981 Act was set up in 1983, the year in which the Act was implemented (Goacher et al., 1988). It was directed by Klaus Wedell and John Welton, and located at the Institute of Education, London University. This three-year project carried out a survey of changes in English and Welsh LEAs' provision for SEN following the 1981 Act. It also carried out case studies in five LEAs to examine the *process* of implementation, to investigate in more detail the variety of forms which implementation took within England.

Key findings from this 1981 Act research project can be summarised under six main headings:

- The definition of special educational needs
- Statutory assessment and Statements

- Parental involvement
- Integration
- Inter-service cooperation
- Planning and resource allocation

The definition of special educational needs

The research found that the abolition of categories of handicap and their replacement with a more general concept of 'special educational needs' was generally welcomed by those working in the field. There was a recognition that the old system of categories did not adequately reflect the complexity of children's needs. However, there were difficulties for practitioners in moving away from categorisation towards considering each child's needs individually. There were several aspects to this.

Those writing advice for Statements tended to concentrate on describing children's difficulties, rather than on considering the child's 'strengths and weaknesses and his or her relationship to the environment, at home and at school', as suggested in the Circular which accompanied the implementation of the Act (DES, 1983). The result was that, in the early years of the 1981 Act, the designation of a child as having SENs requiring a Statement nearly always resulted in the child being place in a special school, rather than extra resources being made available in the mainstream. As will be discussed later, a widening of the use of the term, and of the use of Statements, has meant that this is no longer the case.

There was, and continues to be (see Audit Commission/HMI, 1992), a wide variation between LEAs in the proportions of children given Statements and the types of need which were considered eligible for a Statement. These differences stem from the definition of eligibility contained in the 1981 Act, which defined special educational provision as that which was 'additional to or otherwise different from' provision made generally in schools in the LEA. A Statement was to be provided for those children for whom the LEA was 'to determine' the provision. These two aspects of the definition of SENs have caused wide discrepancies in practice in LEAs across the UK. Since the 1981 Act, wide differences in statement rates have emerged. There have been calls for national criteria for the threshold of need which would require a Statement (Audit Commission/HMI, 1992), but, given the further fragmentation of responsibilities for educational provision, this would seem to be impossible to accomplish.

Another finding, which still has resonance today, was that the concentration of resources on children with Statements had diverted attention away from children with SENs who did not have Statements (see Evans & Lunt, 1994. LEAs had begun to build up expertise among teachers and advisers for SEN during the 1980s, and these were offering support to some children without Statements. But increasingly, as education budgets were squeezed during the 1980s, and particularly more recently after the introduction of Local Management of Schools (LMS), special needs resources became tied to Statements.

In the early 1980s, before LMS and the close monitoring of resources which that entailed, LEAs were finding planning for special educational provision difficult. 'Needs' is an open-ended concept, and estimating the size of demand was problematic. In practice, LEAs tended to be reactive rather than proactive, and this led to major difficulties in controlling expenditure and in rationalising resource allocation. Even with the current, more detailed awareness of the impact of resource allocation decisions, LEAs are finding it difficult to control SEN expenditure (Lunt & Evans, 1994).

Statutory assessment and Statements

The statutory assessment procedures of the 1981 Act were designed to ensure an open and accountable form of multi-disciplinary decision-making which would also allow parental involvement. In practice, they became a source of excessive bureaucracy, delays and distress for parents. There were a number of reasons for this.

LEAs tended to become very concerned about the resource implications of Statements, and therefore wary of committing the LEA to make particular forms of provision over the long term. Statements, therefore, tended to be very bland documents, which gave rather vague assessments of needs and provision. This led to a great deal of frustration for parents, who expected Statements to give a clear indication of their child's needs and of the provision which would be made. The vagueness of the descriptions of need in Statements tended to mask any discrepancies between the needs and the provision offered, so there was no way of estimating the shortfall or of making a case for extra resourcing.

An emphasis of the legalistic aspects of the assessment led to delays in the completion of assessments and the writing of Statements. Writers of assessments did not draw on their existing knowledge and records of children, but conducted a new round of assessment once the procedures had started, thus slowing down the completion of assessments. Many Statements were taking over a year to complete. The University of London Institute of Education research (Goacher et al., 1988) found that an average time varied between 12 weeks in some LEAs to 56 weeks in others. The situation had not improved by the time the Audit Commission/HMI (1992) carried out their study. They found that the median time for completing Statements was 12 months. The Audit Commission/HMI concluded that delays were due to factors within LEAs' control, such as the administrative procedures they had set up for processing the assessments, rather than inherent difficulties. However, in the current climate of resource restrictions, it seems unlikely that LEAs will find it easy to become more flexible in their approach to the statutory assessment procedures.

As discussed in the previous section, the relative definition of special educational needs and provision and the different histories, cultures and contexts of LEAs at the time the 1981 Act was implemented led to wide divergence among LEAs in the proportion of children given Statements and the criteria by which Statements are issued. Statement rates in the 1980s varied between 1 and 3 per cent of the school population in different LEAs. As the decade progressed, the average Statement rate for the country increased from 1.8 per cent in 1985 to 2.2 per cent in 1993. The Audit Commission/HMI (1992) found a variation between less than 1 per cent to over 3 per cent in the 12 LEAs in their sample. They found no correlation between social deprivation and number of Statements issued. Evans et al. (1989) concluded that there appeared to be no direct relationship between prevalence of need, availability of provision and the proportion of Statements issued in LEAs.

Annual reviews of Statements were part of the system put in place by the 1981 Act to ensure that children's needs were being met. These reviews were to be carried out by the school in which the child was placed, and could involve a number of professionals and parents. In practice, annual reviews were often cursory, particularly those carried out in mainstream schools. Special schools found it easier to gather together the views of professionals and to encourage parental participation. The Audit Commission/HMI found that, in 25 per cent of cases, annual reviews were not regularly carried out. They recommended that LEAs should be involved in all annual reviews, and that an educational professional from the LEA, preferably an educational psychologist, should attend the annual review of a child with a Statement at least every two years. The Code of Practice has provided a more detailed framework and requirements (see Chapter 4).

The 1981 Act set up a system of appeals for parents who were not satisfied with LEA decisions about their child's needs. There were two routes for appeals. One was to a local appeal committee set up in accordance with the 1980 Act, which consisted of members of the LEA. This was used when parents were appealing against the provision specified in the Statement. The other was an appeal to the Secretary of State for Education, which could be used in the case where an LEA refused to make a Statement or where a local appeal had failed. Parents were, on the whole, not successful at appeal. In the mid-1980s, some 73 per cent of local appeals were decided in favour of the LEA, as were 75 per cent of appeals to the Secretary of State. During the 1980s, parents increasingly used other routes to challenge LEA decisions. A number of key judgments were made as a result of judicial reviews of LEA decisions (Lunt, 1992; Denman & Lunt, 1993), and it became obvious that a more independent and authoritative system was needed.

Parental involvement

The Warnock Report had placed a great deal of emphasis on the importance of the role of parents in decision-making about their children's needs. It contains a chapter entitled 'Parents as Partners'. However, the translation of parents' rights, as envisaged by the Warnock Report, into the legislative framework of the 1981 Act produced some problems in guaranteeing their full partnership. In the first instance, the right to choose a school, given to parents under the 1980 Act, was withdrawn from parents of children with Statements of Special Educational Needs. In their case, the final decision on placement would be made by the LEA. Secondly, the very bureaucratic interpretation of the 1981 Act produced by many LEAs inhibited parents from full participation. The ULIE research (Goacher et al., 1988) found that information booklets produced by LEAs were not 'user-friendly' and did not encourage parents to become active participants in the decision-making process. This finding was confirmed by Rogers (1986), who undertook a study for the Centre for Studies in Integration in Education (CSIE). The time taken to complete assessments, and the lack of support given to parents to help them through the process, combined to make parents feel isolated and powerless. A number of LEAs had tried to make the process less intimidating, but parents were still in a relatively powerless position *vis-à-vis* the professionals involved.

Integration

The inclusion of pupils with SENs within mainstream education was a growing feature of a more comprehensive conceptualisation of education current in the late 1970s. This conceptualisation has been under threat since the 1980s, and the inclusion of pupils with SENs has not shown a marked increase since the implementation of the 1981 Act (Swann, 1991). The 1981 Act was seen by many as promoting inclusion, since it stipulated that LEAs had a duty to ensure that children with SENs, including those with Statements, were educated in ordinary schools, if this is what their parents wanted. There were three provisos attached to this: that the child received the special education he or she required; that it was compatible with the efficient education of other children in the school, and that it was an efficient use of resources. In practice, this meant that the proportion of children being educated in special schools dropped by only 12.5 per cent between 1983 and 1991 (Audit Commission/HMI, 1992). In some LEAs, the proportion of pupils in special schools had increased (Swann, 1991). The proportion of children with Statements in mainstream schools has also increased, but this is due, in most LEAs, to the overall increase in children with Statements in the school population. So the 1981 Act did not provide the basis for a revolution in the ways in which children with SENs were educated.

Inter-service cooperation

The effective operation of the 1981 Act required cooperation between LEAs, social services departments and health authorities in assessment and provision. The Circular which accompanied the Act (DES, 1983) was a joint Circular issued by the education department (DES) and the health and social services department (DHSS). Such cooperation appeared, in many instances, to be difficult to achieve. This was due to a number of factors. First, the three services had differing organisational and political structures at local level; second, they had different priorities and funding arrangements; and third, the professionals within the services had few opportunities to work collaboratively across their professional domains. This led to a number of difficulties in implementing the 1981 Act effectively. The ULIE research (Goacher et al., 1988) found that there had been very little joint planning for the initial implementation of the 1981 Act at the local level. This led to confusion and lack of coordination. This lack of coordination affected every level of the services, from policy-making and planning of resource allocation to service delivery to individual children and families. Concern over these aspects led the DES to fund a project which developed an inter-service training package which attempted to provide training materials for managers and practitioners within education, health and social services to address these problems of management of change across different services (Evans et al., 1989).

Planning and resource allocation

This final theme is inter-related with a number of preceding ones, as has already been indicated. Following the 1981 Act, the majority of authorities increased their spending on services for children with SENs. However, the wider definition of SENs and the greater awareness of special needs among parents and teachers meant that demand for services also grew. The result has been that LEAs especially, but also health and social services, have faced growing pressure on resources for children with special needs. However, the efficient and cost-effective use of resources has been inhibited by lack of joint planning and coordination among services. Among other factors, this was made difficult by the lack of clarity inherent in the relative definition of SENs and provision which faced LEAs and other services with growing demands on behalf of a population whose size was difficult to estimate. The fact that much of this demand remained hidden because of policies to restrict costs has meant that, since the implementation of the Act, there has been a perceived crisis in the resourcing of special education (Lunt & Evans, 1994).

Despite the many problems associated with the 1981 Education Act, it marked an important step forward in the conceptualisation of SENs and the move towards a more inclusive system of education. It gave important (albeit qualified) rights to parents to be involved in decision-making about their child's education, and it encouraged a full multi-professional assessment of children's needs and a written commitment from LEAs to make provision. As Welton and Evans have remarked (1986) the 1981 Act's 'principles were formed in a climate of educational thinking and government policies very different from those which prevailed at the time of its implementation'. As the 1990s have progressed, the climate for education has become even more difficult. We have seen the introduction of a National Curriculum, Local Management of Schools, open enrolment and the publication of league tables. These, together with a diminution in the role of LEAs as advisers and planners, have led to renewed concern about the education of children with special needs.

Recent developments in special education policy

Special education was virtually ignored by the policy-makers framing the 1988 Education Act. It was not until that Act was in place that the government turned its attention to special education. It ordered a review by the Audit Commission/HMI of the operation of the 1981 Act. This review, published in 1992, indicated that many of the initial problems of implementation were still prevalent. These were summarised by one of the authors of the report as: 'a lack of clarity, accountability and incentives' (Vevers, 1992). In the same article, Paul Vevers writes:

> this lack of clarity has several consequences: Firstly, parents are unclear when they are entitled to extra help for their child. Secondly, the respective roles of schools and LEAs have not been defined, leaving room for conflict over who is responsible in any given case. Thirdly, LEAs have an open-ended commitment to an ill-defined group at a time when their resources are limited. (p.89)

This was an acknowledgement that the new organisation and governance of the education system had caused severe problems for the provision of special education.

The report made a number of recommendations. At a national level, these included:

- DFE guidance as to the level of need which should 'trigger' a formal assessment – i.e. the threshold of need which constitutes the prima facie case for full assessment
- a framework for defining the responsibilities of ordinary schools – i.e. the generally available provision
- a new type of statement, specifying objectives and resources
- time limits to complete statements
- the use of special needs performance indicators at school level
- consideration of the use of financial incentives to implement the 1981 Act and publication of indicators of LEA performance in special needs.

At a local level, the report recommended a clear distinction between the role of the purchaser of services (the LEA) and provider of services (usually the school). Greater financial delegation by LEAs is clearly a step in this direction. Thus special education began to be discussed in the new language of the market.

The White Paper *Choice and Diversity* and the 1993 Education Act

The White Paper (DfE, 1992) was written around five themes: quality, diversity, increased parental choice, greater autonomy of schools and greater accountability. There were two further themes hidden in or implied by the White Paper: selection and specialisation in schools. Chapter 9 of the White Paper ('Pupils with special educational needs') was introduced with the statement: 'the Education Act 1981 is one of the most important landmarks of education legislation this century. The Government remains firmly committed to the general principles enshrined in that Act.' The government has incorporated much of the 1981 Act into the 1993 legislation. It is difficult to see, nevertheless, how the principles of integration and entitlement fit into other provisions of the 1993 Act which stress competition and selection.

However, the 1993 Act did introduce some measures to improve the accountability of LEAs and schools to parents of children with SENs. These were:

- to give parents of children with Statements a right to 'express a preference' for a school for their child, which the LEA would have to comply with unless certain provisos were not met
- to lay down strict time limits for making assessments of SENs
- to make parents' rights of appeal more coherent and to extend those rights
- to set up an independent tribunal which would replace both the Secretary of State and the local appeals panels.

Alongside the new arrangements under the 1993 Act, the government has issued the *Code of Practice on the Identification and Assessment of Pupils with Special Educational Needs* (DfE & WO, 1994). This is described in detail in Chapter 4, but it is interesting to note here that, as in the 1981 Act, the emphasis is on procedures, rather than on provision, and that elaborate procedures have been devised for *all* pupils with SENs, not just those who may require a Statement.

Reflections on the legacy of the 1981 Act

The influence of the 1981 Act on the conceptualisation of SENs appears to remain strong, even after the immense changes in the structure and governance of education which have taken place since 1988. Despite the difficulties with a relative definition of SENs and provision, these have been incorporated into a new system which stresses *national* norms of attainment and standards of provision. The difficulties and inconsistencies resulting from this have been acknowledged (e.g. in the Audit Commission/HMI 1992 report) but, aside from exhortations to government and LEAs to provide clear and unambiguous criteria for deciding that a child has SENs no solutions to these difficulties have been proposed.

The broad definition of SENs which the Warnock Report introduced has been applied to a growing proportion of the school population, with the result, as Fulcher (1989) has commented, that teachers have seen themselves as responsible for a diminishing proportion of pupils – those *without* special educational needs. Research on the effects of Local Management of Schools on special education (Evans & Lunt, 1994) have indicated that more children are being given Statements and more children are being excluded from school since the implementation of LMS and the introduction of grant-maintained schools. Skrtic (1991) has suggested that the 'traditional bureaucratic configuration of schools is as a performance organisation, an inherently non-adaptable form that must screen out diversity by forcing students with special educational needs out of the system'. He maintains that students with SENs are 'artifacts of the traditional curriculum'. Given the pressure to traditionalise and normalise the National Curriculum in the UK and the devolution of responsibilities for provision for special education to schools who have a huge range of other responsibilities, it is likely that the lack of criteria for deciding on SENs will result in more pupils being included within this group.

The extended rights given to parents of pupils with SENs under the 1981 and 1993 Acts reflect the broader entitlements for parents given by the 1980 and 1988 Acts, and the Parent's Charters. However, rights for parents of children with SENs are still somewhat circumscribed, and partnership in terms of consultation and involvement in decision-making still seems to be limited. Indeed, one could argue that over-subscribed schools now have more power to select pupils and to reject those with SENs.

The 1981 Act, which was conceived in a time of a broadly-based commitment to a comprehensive, inclusive system of education, with a thrust towards social justice and equality of opportunity, has been superseded by legislation which places education within a market framework in which individual parents compete to claim the 'best' education for their child. Under such a system, it is difficult to envisage how the broad principles of the 1981 Act – which were to offer children with special needs the same range of opportunities as those without special educational needs – can be realised.

Postscript

I first came to work with Klaus on the DES-funded evaluation of the implementation of the 1981 Education Act. This project was directed by Klaus and John Welton, and was an example of inter-disciplinary research – Educational Psychology and Policy Studies. The research project was a reflection of Klaus's commitment to the education of children with SENs and his influence on policy development in the UK. Klaus was a consultant to the follow-up project, which developed a training strategy for managers in education, health and social services. I later worked with Klaus on the 'Clusters' project, in which we explored the possibilities of collaboration between schools for enhancing special educational provision. This, too, reflected Klaus's interest in the organisation of services so that they could better meet the needs of children.

I feel very privileged to have worked with Klaus and have been inspired by his commitment, creativity and energy. Like so many people who have come into contact with Klaus, I feel that my life has been enhanced by knowing him.

References

Audit Commission/HMI (1992) *Getting in on the Act: Provision for Pupils with Special Educational Needs,* London: HMSO.

Bennett, N. & Cass, A. (1989) *From Special to Ordinary Schools,* London: Cassell.

Coard, B. (1971) *How the West Indian Child is Made Educationally Subnormal in the British School System: The Scandal of the Black Child in Schools in Britain,* London: Beacon Press.

Denman, R. & Lunt, I. (1993) 'Getting Your Act Together: Some implications for EPs of judicial review', *Educational Psychology in Practice,* 9(1), pp.9–15.

Department of Education & Science (DES) (1978) *Special Educational Needs: Report of the Committee of Inquiry into the Education of Handicapped Children and Young People* (The Warnock Report), Cmnd 7212, London: HMSO.

Department of Education and Science (DES) (1980) *Special Needs in Education,* Cmnd 7996, London: HMSO.

Department of Education and Science (DES) (1983) *Assessments and Statements of Special Educational Needs,* Circular 1/83, London: DES/DHSS.

Department for Education (DfE) (1992) *Choice and Diversity,* White Paper, London: HMSO.

Department for Education & Welsh Office (DfE & WO) (1994) *Code of Practice on the Identification and Assessment of Pupils with Special Educational Needs,* London: HMSO.

Evans, J. & Lunt, I. (1994) *Markets, Competition and Vulnerability: Some Effects of Recent Legislation on Children with Special Educational Needs,* London: Institute of Education/Tufnell Press.

Evans, J., Everard, K., Friend, J., Glaser, A. & Norwich, B. (1989) *Decision-making for Special Needs: An Inter-service Resource Pack,* London: Institute of Education.

Fulcher, G. (1989) *Disabling Policies: A Comparative Approach to Education Policy and Disability,* London: Falmer Press.

Goacher, B., Evans, J., Welton, J. & Wedell, K. (1988) *Policy and Provision for Special Educational Needs,* London: Cassell.

House of Commons, Education Select Committee (1993) *Meeting Special Educational Needs: Statements of Needs and Provision,* London: HMSO.

Kirp, D. (1982) 'Professionalism as policy choice: British special education in comparative perspective', *World Politics,* 34(2), pp.137–74.

Lunt, I. (1992) 'Recent judgements and their implications for educational psychologists', *Newsletter of Division of Educational and Child Psychology,* 52.

Lunt, I. & Evans, J. (1994) *Allocating Resources for Special Educational Needs Provision,* Stafford: NASEN.

Norwich, B. (1990) *Reappraising Special Needs Education,* London: Cassell.

Norwich, B. (1992) *Time to Change the 1981 Education Act: The London File,* Institute of Education, University of London.

Rogers, R. (1986) *Caught in the Act. What LEAs Tell Parents Under the 1981 Education Act,* London: Centre for Studies in Integration in Education.

Russell, P. (1986) 'The Education Act 1981', in A. Cohen and L. Cohen (eds) *Special Educational Needs in the Ordinary School: A Sourcebook for Teachers,* London: Harper and Row.

Skrtic, T.M. (1991) 'Students with special educational needs: Artifacts of the traditional curriculum', in M. Ainscow (ed.) *Effective Schools for All,* London: David Fulton.

Swann, W. (1991) *Variations Between LEAs in Levels of Segregation in Special Schools*

1982–90: Preliminary Report, London: Centre for Studies in Integration in Education.

Tomlinson, S. (1982) *A Sociology of Special Education,* London: Routledge and Kegan Paul.

Vevers, P. (1992) 'Getting in on the Act', *British Journal of Special Education,* 19(3), pp.88–92.

Wedell, K. (1990) 'The 1988 Act and current principles of special educational needs', in H. Daniels and J. Ware (eds) *Special Educational Needs and the National Curriculum,* London: Institute of Education/Kogan Page.

Welton, J. & Evans, J. (1986) 'The development and implementation of special education policy: Where did the 1981 Act fit in?', *Public Administration,* 64, pp.209–27.

10 Clusters: Inter-school collaboration for special educational needs

Brahm Norwich and Ingrid Lunt

Introduction

In this chapter, we intend first to review some of the thinking and practice behind the idea of 'clusters' over the past decade, then to describe some research findings from a project which looked at clusters for special educational needs (SENs). We will then look at some of the models of clusters which have been put forward, and finally consider some practical ways forward in the present legislative and policy climate in the field of SENs.

A decade of clustering

The implementation of the 1981 Education Act in 1983 has been followed by a decade of change and developments in provision for SENs. In 1985, reviewing provision for pupils with SENs in the former Inner London Education Authority (ILEA), the Fish Committee recommended that secondary schools and their feeder primary schools in an area should group together to form 'clusters' to collaborate and share their concern and responsibility for the pupils with special needs in that community or geographical area (ILEA, 1985). The functions of the 'cluster' were envisaged to include sharing responsibility for SENs in a community, providing a continuity of concern by facilitating links between under-fives, primary, secondary and tertiary educational provision, providing a focus of service delivery for health, education and social services professionals, and

161

achieving some cost-effectiveness and economies of scale. The 'cluster' of the Fish Committee implied some sharing or pooling of resources and the organisation of different professionals to work around the cluster in order to provide continuity and coordinated multi-professional support for SENs. In the decade following the Fish Report, when one could expect that its recommendations would be put into practice, there have been considerable changes in how provision for SENs is made (in particular because of the changes in legislation in this area), and the context of SENs provision has altered dramatically. Nevertheless, over that decade, several Local Education Authorities (LEAs) have adopted some form of 'cluster'-type arrangements, responding in different ways to the challenge of meeting SENs in the years following the 1981 Education Act.

There are various forms of inter-school collaboration described in the literature and found in practice. In the literature, the concept of 'clusters' falls somewhere between two other distinct forms of inter-organisational collaboration: 'networks' and 'federations'. 'Networks' are generally understood to be fairly loose and informal links between schools, often for sharing of information, mutual support, or exchange of ideas and practice. They are characterised by their informality, often being created for a specific task or tasks, and their fluid and flexible membership. 'Federations', on the other hand, are more formalised and permanent groupings of schools, often set up in rural areas, where a number of schools may be grouped together under one headteacher, offering 'an exciting balance between individuality and the strengths of cooperation' (Benford, 1988). Between these two extremes are groups of schools which have been variously referred to as 'clusters', 'partnerships', 'pyramids', 'consortia', 'family groups', 'academic councils' and other names; these usually have some formality of membership and structure but are much less formalised and permanent than federations, though more formalised than networks. As their names imply, such groupings of schools vary considerably in their nature, size, purposes, scope, organisation and management and resourcing aspects.

LEA versus school interests in clusters?

The idea of cluster groupings and collaboration between schools may be considered either from an LEA or from a school perspective, and indeed clusters differ as to how far they are 'bottom-up' (originating from and/or managed by the schools) or 'top-down' (initiated by and/or managed by the LEA) in their origins and management. From an LEA perspective, clusters might form a convenient administrative arrangement for developing policies for the integration of pupils with SENs, for allocating resources to pupils with SEN and for achieving economies of scale. It if were possible to coordinate support services (e.g. education, health and social services) around a cluster group of schools, this could vastly improve communication and decision-making in an area well known for difficulties in collaboration. The allocation of some resources (e.g. a support teacher) to a group of schools has attractions both professionally and administratively, and the introduction of a 'tier' of responsibility between the LEA and the individual school would also appear to have benefits. From the point of view of schools, collaboration has been widely assumed to be a good thing almost in and of itself, and for many schools, collaboration has produced benefits such as the sharing of expertise and specialist resources and mutual support. Nevertheless, the current educational context has sharpened the need for schools to carry out the cost–benefit analysis and to consider how far the effort required to collaborate with other schools is matched by the benefits to individual schools, their teachers and pupils. As Hudson has observed:

> From an agency's viewpoint, collaborative activity raises two main difficulties. First, it loses some of its freedom to act independently, when it would prefer to maintain control over its domain and affairs. Second, it must invest scarce resources and energy in developing and maintaining relationships with other organisations, when the potential returns on this investment are often unclear and intangible. Hence it could be posited that an agency prefers not to become involved in inter-organisational relationships unless it is compelled to do so and that simple appeals to client well-being may constitute insufficient motivation. (Hudson, 1987, p.175)

It is this tension between the benefits to be derived from collaboration and the costs of maintaining the collaboration which is highlighted in the current educational context in the UK, where a potential for competition between schools has been introduced by the recent government legislation for a more market-oriented education system.

Recent developments

In spite of some of the tensions brought about by recent legislation, there has been growing interest in inter-school collaboration from many quarters in the wake of the introduction of the National Curriculum, Local Management of Schools and grant-maintained schools. This has been one of the main responses to the introduction of more autonomous schools and the resulting reduction in LEA services for SENs. This response can be seen as partly reflecting the attempt to seek practical ways of maintaining the economy of scale lost by devolving resources and management responsibilities to schools. The intention is to retain the means to maintain quality staffing and materials. The response can also be seen to reflect a value position which fears the negative effects of setting up a quasi-market system on schools' willingness and competence to provide for the diversity of pupil need. It is in this context that the educational and special needs literature has shown an interest in practical instances of school clustering and forward-looking ideas and analyses of what is involved in inter-school collaboration.

A special edition on collaboration in the journal *Support for Learning* (Gains, 1994) illustrates that this area is seen by many practitioners and academic commentators as important for development in the special needs education field. Some of these articles outline in some detail what has been involved in examples of inter-school collaboration. For example, Cade and Caffyn describe the cluster centring around one comprehensive and six primary schools in Nottinghamshire, the King Edward VI family (Cade & Caffyn, 1994). This description, like others in the special edition of the journal, provides interesting and useful details, such as the LEA context, the local coordination of support services, how a contract was agreed between the cluster of schools and the LEA, and the entry requirements for joining the family cluster. Clusters like this one were included in the analysis of kinds of clusters reported in the Economic and Social Research Council (ESRC) project which is described in the next section. The fact that such case descriptions are now available in professional journals is an indication that the cluster concept has become a practical option for schools.

That the cluster concept and inter-school collaboration has reached a certain central status within the special needs education field is also shown by their incorporation into the wider prescriptive and theoretical schemes of higher education commentators on the field. So, for example, Dyson has tried to incorporate cluster collaborative notions into a framework which switches the focus of special needs education from individual difficulties to the curriculum and system of schooling to 'effective schools for all' (Ainscow, 1991; Dyson, 1994). What is behind this shift is an attempt to present a new and alternative conception of the special needs task, which seeks to reorganise school practices and norms in response to the challenges presented by diversity. However, Dyson recognises that schools are themselves shaped by the local and national system of school governance, and that special needs education has traditionally been the domain of LEAs within a national legislative framework.

So the current interest in clusters is linked with the debate about the future of LEAs. In this debate, there are those who see little positive future for LEAs (Moore, 1991; Thomas, 1992), while others believe that some agency like an LEA is needed to protect the interests of children with difficulties (Housden, 1993). Dyson's views are presented in terms of the idea of schools as 'autonomous problem-solvers' within an 'enabling framework'. The enabling framework, which is not a traditional LEA, would do more than simply administer the system. Yet Dyson recognises that LEAs have had a crucial developmental role in special needs provision over recent years by adopting a different conceptualisation of their role. This has involved them in:

- delegating resources and responsibility over and above what legislation required
- involving schools in management and policy issues traditionally the domain of LEAs
- promoting inter-school collaboration over joint management of delegated resources, joint formulation of policy and review of special needs across schools.

Despite this recognition, Dyson and Gains (1993) envisage that the management of special needs provision is possible without LEAs. This is where the supposed function and role of clusters is deployed to take over some of the functions covered by LEAs: achieving economies of scale by sharing resources, facilitation of problem-solving and critical evaluation of individual school practice through interchange with other cluster schools. As Dyson says: 'At their best, clusters may be able to re-invent the characteristics of the best LEAs' (Dyson, 1994, p.58). How Dyson and Gains envisage such a system to work will be discussed more fully under the heading 'Ways forward', later in this chapter.

Research considering clusters

An ESRC-funded research project[1] carried out by Klaus Wedell and colleagues at the Institute of Education looked at clusters as a form of organisation for meeting SENs (Lunt et al., 1994). The research team carried out case studies in 4 LEAs which had some form of cluster organisation and sampled the views of another 12 LEAs through focus-group discussions. It became clear at the start of the project in 1991, first, that examples of 'cluster groupings' in the sense of the definition of the Fish Report (ILEA, 1985) would be hard to find, and second, that there was an enormous array of different collaborative arrangements across the country, some of these focused on SENs, others with a different focus, for example the Technical and Vocational Education Initiative, National Curriculum and in-service training (INSET). The detailed case studies enabled the team to focus on the processes involved in setting up and running clusters, while the focus-group

[1]   ESRC project R-000-23-2571. The support of the ESRC is gratefully acknowledged.

discussions led to a consideration of the wider context in which LEAs were developing provision, including forms of school collaboration.

Interviews carried out in the four LEAs where clusters were studied in detail enabled the research team to identify some emerging themes concerning the dynamics of clusters (Evans et al., 1994). The focus of the interviews was to elicit:

- factors which had led to the formation of the clusters (antecedent factors
- factors concerning the operation and functioning of the cluster (process factors)
- factors concerning outcomes of the clusters (outcome factors).

The research revealed two main types of cluster: one concerned with aspects of transition between primary and secondary schools (e.g. a 'pyramid'), and another concerned with sharing or allocation of resources. Emerging themes included: *size*: there appeared to be an optimum size of between 6–8 schools for effective collaboration; *complexity*: a simple or single focus appeared to be easier to maintain; *initiation*: the existence of a catalyst or a key person (for initiation and coordination) appeared to be important; *ownership*: the schools required a sense of ownership and involvement for effective functioning; *task focus*: the involvement in a specific task or project, and *pay-off*: schools need some kind of pay-off to compensate for the time and effort involved, as mentioned above. The more actively-functioning clusters usually involved a key 'player' for whom the cluster was an important element of provision and who had both been able to act as some kind of catalyst in the formation of the cluster and play a central role in its maintenance and functioning.

The 12 LEAs involved in the focus-group discussions had been identified during the course of the first phase of the research and through the project's growing network of contacts. The representatives of the LEAs described a wide variety of arrangements intended to serve a range of different purposes which enabled the research team to develop a taxonomy of different cluster or collaborative arrangements. These included groups of small rural primary schools aimed at pooling resources, including those for SENs; schools grouped together through the allocation by LEAs of additional staff; 'pyramids' of secondary and feeder primary schools which bid for LEA funding for SEN, and geographical groups determined by LEAs for delegation under LMS schemes. This phase of the research coincided with a time when LEAs were just beginning to implement LMS and were being required to devolve budgets to school level. The discussions therefore raised questions of responsibility for SENs and the resourcing of provision, both for non-Statemented and for Statemented pupils, and the tensions and pressures between schools collaborating and competing in the developing context of open enrolment and pupil-led funding. Several representatives in the groups expressed fears that the turbulence of the political climate in education at the time might undermine collaborative efforts, and anxiety about the future in relation to initiatives of this nature. In the next section we consider possible ways forward and some of the ideas which have been described in the current literature.

Ways forward

Ideas and schemes for the future

One rich source of ideas about clustering for the future comes from experience of inter-school collaboration in the Technical and Vocational Education Initiative (TVEI). Drawing on studies of this experience, Wallace and Hall (1994) propose that inter-school collaboration is a way of subverting recent government educational policy. Government policy, according to them, assumes that increased rivalry through schools competing for parental custom will increase the quality of education for all – a quasi-market strategy. This is evident in what they call the 'little business kit' of open enrolment, Local Management of Schools based on pupil-led funding, greater diversity of schools, league tables of attainments and truancy rates, and increased powers to school governors. Wallace and Hall, like others, see collaboration, which they define as 'joint work for joint purposes', as an alternative to a competitive strategy for educational policy. This is based on a typology of working relationships in which there is a continuum from collaboration to conflict (Hall & Oldroyd, 1992). As Figure 10.1 shows, the typology can be understood in terms of two dimensions: whether the relationship is positive or negative, and whether the strategy is conflict-resolution or problem-solving.

In this model, what distinguishes collaboration from cooperation is the amount of shared effort, pooling of resources and commitment. Also, collaboration is about joint working for specific goals; it does not mean working together for *all* goals. This makes it possible that schools might collaborate in some areas but compete in others. It is also possible that collaboration among a cluster of schools may be in order to compete with other clusters or individual schools. Collaboration in this model is also a *voluntary* partnership, as distinct from relationships of dominance and compliance.

Gains and Smith (1994) have identified a range of different kinds of collaborative networks between schools which have special relevance to special needs provision. These include pooling resources to acquire

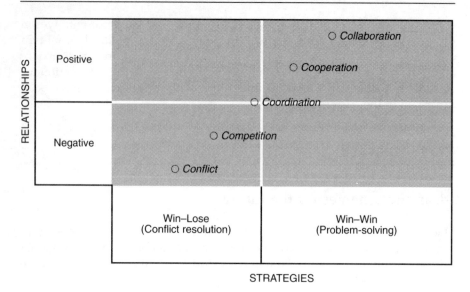

Figure 10.1   A continuum of ways of working
Source: Wallace and Hall (1994)

materials and staffing, information exchange, skill exchange, specialist input, specialist input on a rota, the resource base that attracts pupils to it, and specialist equipment and materials which rotate around the schools. These kinds of working relationships are called 'micro-models', because they focus on the specific types of collaboration between schools. In addition, Dyson and Gains (1993) have proposed a larger-scale macro-collaborative model for special educational provision (Figure 10.2).

In this macro-model, schools are seen as autonomous but working together for specific purposes in clusters. Clusters of schools are then seen as working together as consortia to share even more specialised services. These groupings within groupings are seen to function within an enabling structure, as described above. This is an interesting scheme, as much for the alternative it promotes as for what it shows about assumptions about the nature of special needs education. It is therefore worth discussing the ideas underlying this complex model in more detail.

Dyson and Gains propose that there is a basic shift taking place in thinking about special needs and the nature of educational organisations. It is not clear, however, whether they believe that this is actually taking place or whether they mostly wish it to happen. They identify the traditional approach to organising special provision as one of structuring provision in advance and where problems are dealt with by placement into these

ENABLING STRUCTURE
Strategic Management Decisions

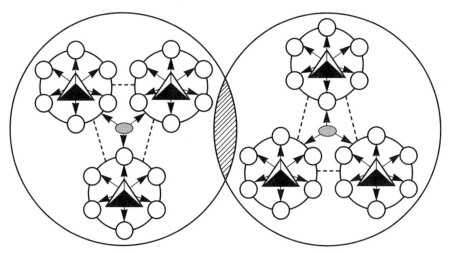

Key: Regional responsibility for securing and monitoring the delivery of services

O   Individual schools/institutions internally providing support

     A cluster of schools/institutions with mutually agreed arrangements and contracts

     Skills interchange:

     1.   Support services

     2.   Special school resource base

     3.   Training and staff development facilities

     Consortium – a collection of clusters

     Core services e.g. SPS serving a consortium

- - - - Informal arrangements

———▶ Direct connections/services

     Spheres of cooperation between consortia

Notes
The figure is diagrammatic, and it is not meant to indicate:
*   a particular scale of activity
*   a necessary geographical distribution of elements
*   the strength or intensity of arrangements within a cluster or consortium.

Figure 10.2   A collaborative model for the provision of services to students with special needs
Source: Dyson and Gains (1993)

structures. This has depended on a hierarchical system which is centrally managed, one which contrasts with Dyson and Gains's preferred system of a devolved system of management based on networks which enable flexible problem-solving. This emerging system is defined in starkly contrasting terms to the traditional one, with the implication that educational systems are either one thing or another: either structure-focused or process-focused, either centralised or devolved. What is questionable about this kind of scheme is its use of simple dichotomies and the exclusive opting for one alternative. It is much more likely that organisations can be characterised by the balance between their focus on structure and on process. So, if it is the case that educational organisations are becoming more process-focused, this is consistent with structuring playing a significant part.

What seems to underlie the Dyson and Gains perspective is a wish for a radical departure from the past, a break in continuity from what they see as problematic traditional practices. In pursuing this wish, they are willing to interpret the organisational and management changes brought about by quasi-market educational policies as having potential for inter-school collaboration, despite the government's intention to promote competition. As outlined above, their model of an educational system includes not only the *autonomous providers* (the schools) and *networks and interactions* between the schools (the clusters), but some *strategic control* which sets the parameters of the problems to be solved, devolves responsibilities and resources and monitors outcomes. The central issue about the viability of this kind of system is the relationship between the enabling structure, with its strategic control, and the autonomous schools. It is in this area that the Dyson and Gains scheme holds out expectations which seem to have little grounding.

The role of the enabling structure in their scheme is to create conditions under which mainstream schools can make effective provision. Part of this would involve a transfer to mainstream schools of responsibility and resources which have been exercised traditionally by LEAs. The change proposed here is clear: mainstream schools would become 'self-managing securers of effective learning for virtually all students' (Dyson & Gains, 1994, p.168). Yet they at once introduce two provisos which seem to leave significant responsibilities with the enabling structure. Firstly, they do not envisage schools having to provide education for virtually all pupils from their own teaching resources, but to 'secure education by deploying its financial resources'. Secondly, they see the enabling structure still retaining responsibility for a 'small number of highly atypical students'. What is not clear in their scheme, therefore, is whether there is a radical departure from the emerging role which LEAs are currently adopting. They assert that their model does not need a Statementing procedure in its current form, but they do not explain how atypical pupils will be defined and who will identify them. Nor is there any account of how financial delegation to schools for additional needs will be arranged without some externally-moderated scheme for assessing schools' additional resource needs. Again there is a role for an LEA-like enabling structure.

It is very useful to consider a model of educational provision, like the Dyson and Gains one, where schools assume more responsibilities, take on more resources, and form links with other schools and services to discharge their responsibilities. But, if more mainstream school-based provision for special needs is to come about, there is a need to consider major changes in educational legislation. This would involve the current duty to secure provision for pupils with special needs placed on LEAs by the 1993 Education Act being extended to the governors of schools. This would be a change of major significance for the school system and special needs provision, but it is unlikely that such a switch would place unconditional duties on school governing bodies. Certain conditions would need to be placed on the kinds of provision which mainstream schools would be expected to secure, as discussed in Norwich (1992). As argued above, this would still leave an important role for an LEA-like enabling structure, or to use the Dyson and Gains term, for an 'agency with strategic management functions'.

This discussion shows that the part which inter-school collaboration plays as a strategy for enhancing special needs provision depends critically on more basic questions. These concern the respective roles and relationships between schools and local and national strategic management agencies and the *location of responsibility* for special provision. A change in the role of mainstream schools as the providers and securers of special provision would entail considerable changes in the culture, orientations and practices of many schools, in particular how they regard and cope with pupil diversity. Much as such changes may be welcomed, it seems unlikely that they can be expected without some wider national commitment, additional resourcing and development work aiming to include more pupils with severe difficulties into mainstream schools. The impetus for this change needs to come mainly from people and agencies which have a broader focus of interest than individual mainstream schools.

With parental preferences now playing a more powerful role in special provision decision-making, the legal status of provision managed by clusters also becomes an important matter. The ESRC project referred to above found that most examples of clusters covered non-Statemented provision – that is, provision for less significant difficulties. Currently, LEAs may be able to devolve funds for Statemented provision to individual schools and clusters, but in doing this, they are still legally responsible for securing such provision. Were there to be a switch of legal responsibility for securing this provision to mainstream schools, these schools would have to assume some of the formal roles and relationships with parents which LEAs currently do.

How schools, especially primary schools, might respond to taking on these functions is worth considering. So despite the apparent radical change offered by the Dyson and Gains model, caution is needed in believing that the introduction of more autonomous schools, which was for purposes of competition, can be readily transformed into clusters and consortia of collaborating schools.

Practical strategies

The implication of this analysis is that clusters have an important but dependent role in enhancing special provision. Although Wallace and Hall (1994) do not deal with these more basic considerations, they are encouraging about the prospects for collaboration within the existing legal framework of schooling. They see inter-school collaboration as voluntary partnerships, and therefore ones into which unwilling schools will not enter. This leads them to seeing clustering as dependent on teachers and heads who still wish to express professional service values. The advice they offer about 'going collaborative' is based on the view that such schemes require the gradual development of mutual trust. They suggest that current levels of collaboration be assessed, consideration be given to the purpose and feasibility of increasing collaboration and that a small number of priority joint tasks be undertaken. Assessing readiness, trust and commitment are emphasised, as is the importance of wider consultation with those whose support is needed. Much of the advice also pertains to other kinds of organisational and school developments – careful consideration and design of procedures and resource-allocation systems and establishing realistic ground-rules and safeguards against things going wrong. Another approach to developing clusters is proposed by Gains and Smith (1994), who point out the importance of taking account of the various stages in forming a cluster – the role of the catalyst, establishing a joint philosophy, forming rules, disseminating information, auditing resources and increased interaction.

The approach to developing clusters taken in the book based on the ESRC 'Clusters' project (Lunt et al., 1994) is one which looks for the benefits which clustering offers different groups in the education service. This is a practical approach which considers the perspectives of headteachers and governors, SEN teachers and coordinators in schools, LEA officers and inspectors and support services such as educational psychology services. The development approaches which are recommended are those which link into school development planning principles and practices. The last chapter of Lunt et al.'s book discusses some of these models and presents some practical methods for organising the development activities. Included among these are some practical questions about clustering which were derived from the

ESRC research findings. These cover questions about initiators, consultation, goals of collaboration, activities included in collaboration schemes, different kinds of collaborative activities, the size and membership of clusters, the origin and use of shared resources and the role and functions of a cluster management group.

Concluding comments

As this chapter shows, inter-school collaboration has moved over the last decade from the realm of good ideas into viable organisational developments. Few would have anticipated at the time of the Fish Report in 1985 that there would be a major restructuring of the educational system over the following decade. Nor was it predictable that national changes intended to promote inter-school competition would become useful conditions which would enable schools to opt for collaborative strategies. The experience of clustering in the context of wider organisational and management changes in special educational provision has also enabled us to understand better the place of clustering in the wider system of provision. It has shown that the potential contribution of clustering in promoting quality in special education provision depends critically on the responsibilities of schools in relation to those of strategic management agencies, such as LEAs.

Experience of inter-school collaboration and ideas drawn from organisational theories and analyses of such arrangements have also pointed to some principles which have practical relevance to those interested in clustering. Inter-school collaboration involves collaboration between organisations which themselves have to deal with issues of internal collaboration between different sections and areas of work. The size and phase of the school is clearly a significant factor in the nature and extent of intra-school collaboration. As regards special educational provision, the development of a school's SENs policy and whole-school practices depends on internal collaboration between different sections of the school's staff. This is an important consideration, as external links need to be justified partly in terms of how much they support an individual school's overall provision for those with SENs. This implies that efforts to develop inter-school collaboration over special educational provision need to be balanced with efforts to promote better intra-school collaboration. This is where the time costs of collaboration become a consideration. Managing time plays a critical part in determining the priorities between inter- and intra-school collaboration and the extent of such collaboration.

As Wallace and Hall (1994) indicate, collaborative strategies have some compatibility with competitive ones. It is possible for schools to have competitive relationships in some areas while still being able to collaborate in other areas. This might seem strange to some people for whom collaboration is an alternative strategy to competition, and who look to collaborative arrangements as a substitute to the national move to a more competitive school system. Yet collaboration could develop in a competitive context when schools adopt a broad and differentiated conception of their tasks and identify a range of approaches which could be suited to these tasks. From this perspective, and for individual schools, inter-school collaboration can be used as a means to the end of enhancing their special provision. But collaboration is also valued as a good thing in itself, and not just as a means to an end. When it is seen in these terms, this is usually from a cross-school perspective which sees benefits deriving from joint work and contacts across schools. It may be useful to distinguish here between schools working jointly and working separately in a collaborative atmosphere. The economies of time might lead individual schools to put more efforts into internal school collaborative SEN work and less into inter-school work. In such a case, separate working could, nevertheless, be undertaken in a collaborative manner.

Postscript

We have come to write this chapter through our involvement with Klaus Wedell in the ESRC 'Clusters Project'. Klaus has had a long-standing interest in clusters from the time of his membership of the ILEA Fish Committee on special educational needs. His interest and influence were felt in this and other parts of the Fish Report. Since then, Klaus was involved as a consultant to the DES/DoH Management Development Project on an inter-service approach to decision-making for special needs. In this project, management-of-change ideas and practices were applied to the workings of the 1981 Education Act. This involved some work on developing clusters as one strategy, which was reported in the resource pack produced by this project. From this work derived the idea of the ESRC 'Clusters Project' which is referred to in this chapter. There is currently a follow-up 'Clusters Project'. We hope this chapter illustrates Klaus's commitment to the principles of joint working informed by a collaborative ethos. This area of his work also shows his keen sensitivity to new and viable ideas for developing special educational provision.

References

Ainscow, M. (ed.) (1991) *Effective Schools For All*, London: David Fulton.
Benford, M. (1988) 'Beyond clustering', *Education*, 23 September, pp.294–5.

Cade, L. & Caffyn, R. (1994) 'The King Edward VI family: An example of clustering in Nottinghamshire', *Support for Learning*, 9(2), pp.83–8.

Dyson, A. (1994) 'Towards a collaborative, learning model for responding to student diversity', *Support for Learning*, 9(2), pp.53–60.

Dyson, A. & Gains, C. (1993) 'Special needs and effective learning: Towards a collaborative model for the year 2000', in A. Dyson and C. Gains (eds) *Rethinking Special Needs Education in Mainstream Schools: Towards the Year 2000*, London: David Fulton.

Evans, J., Lunt, I., Norwich, B., Steedman, J. & Wedell, K. (1994) 'Clusters: A collaborative approach to meeting special educational needs', in S. Riddell and S. Brown (eds) *Special Educational Needs Policy in the 1990s: Warnock in the Market Place*, London: Routledge.

Gains, C. (1994) Editorial, *Support for Learning*, 9(2), p.50.

Gains, C. & Smith, C.J. (1994) 'Cluster models', *Support for Learning*, 9(2), pp.94–8.

Hall, V. & Oldroyd, D. (1992) *Development Activities for Managers of Collaboration*, University of Bristol, National Development Centre for Education Management and Policy.

Housden, P. (1993) *Bucking the Market: LEAs and Special Needs*, Policy Options for Special Needs Paper, Stafford: NASEN.

Hudson, B. (1987) 'Collaboration in social welfare: A framework for analysis', *Policy and Politics*, 15(3), pp.175–82.

Inner London Education Authority (ILEA) (1985) *Educational Opportunities for All? The Fish Report*, London: ILEA.

Lunt, I., Evans, J., Norwich, B. & Wedell, K. (1994) *Working Together: Inter-school Collaboration for Special Needs*. London: David Fulton.

Moore, J. (1991) 'Local education authority restructuring under ERA: Meeting or creating special educational needs', *Support for Learning*, 6(1), pp.16–21.

Norwich, B. (1992) *Time to Change the 1981 Education Act*, London: London File/Tufnell Press.

Thomas, G. (1992) 'Local authorities, special needs and the status quo', *Support for Learning*, 7(1), pp.36–40.

Wallace, M. & Hall, V. (1994) 'Go collaborative! Subvert reform for the sake of the children', *Support for Learning*, 9(2), pp.68–72.

11 International aspects of special education

Peter Evans

Introduction

The globalisation of the world economy has inevitably led to increasing interest in international comparisons of statistics and practices in order to inform social and educational policy. A particular feature of these developments has been growing concern for social justice and equity – issues which are at the heart of the special education movement. It is not an exaggeration to claim that Klaus Wedell has had a significant influence on the educational implications of this trend through his involvement with two international organisations which together serve to influence educational policy and practice in almost every country of the world. They are the Organisation for Economic Co-operation and Development (OECD)[1] and the United Nations Educational, Social and Cultural Organisation (UNESCO).[2] This is not to say that his interest and impact have been insignificant elsewhere. He has, for example, enjoyed a long-term relationship with the Spanish government and made a significant contribution to the reform of education policy that has taken place in Spain over the past decade. Many other examples of international work could be

[1] The OECD comprises 25 nations: Australia, Austria, Belgium, Canada, Denmark, Finland, France, Germany, Greece, Iceland, Ireland, Italy, Japan, Luxemburg, Mexico, the Netherlands, New Zealand, Norway, Portugal, Spain, Sweden, Switzerland, Turkey, United Kingdom, United States of America. It is concerned with the development of policy in a wide range of areas that concern the development of the economies of its Member countries including education, health and social policy.
[2] UNESCO is part of the United Nations. It is concerned with the educational, social and cultural development of its many Member states that come from all of the world's regions. In special education much of its work has focused on the development of practical assistance to many of these nations.

quoted, such as the collaboration in special education between UK and Indian universities in the early 1980s. However, the major involvement has been with the OECD in particular, and to a lesser extent with UNESCO.

One of the central ideas that has influenced thinking and helped to link pedagogical practice to management and policy reform has been that of compensatory interaction (Wedell, 1980). This model locates the educational growth of children in the complex interaction between the child and the school which develops over time, and stresses the important role that the school can play in promoting either success or failure in the child. Three studies which have been strongly influenced by this core idea will be described.

The contribution to UNESCO

The UNESCO study on teacher training

This UNESCO study on teacher training and special educational needs (SEN) was published in 1985 and involved countries in the five world regions of Arabia, Latin America, Africa, Asia and Oceania, and Europe. The study was concerned with teacher training within the general context of the integration of disabled children into mainstream schools, which continues, a decade later, to be the significant international issue in special education. The systemic nature of this work is reflected in its formulation – an approach central to Klaus's thinking. It looks to means of overcoming features of the system which may of themselves be contributing to the presence of learning difficulties, and of marshalling all available practical resources to overcome such obstacles in the support of children with SEN.

In the context of the mainly developing countries studied in the report, the questions to be considered are very basic. Is ordinary education likely to be accessible to children throughout a country? Are there economic and social reasons preventing children from attending school? Are there policies to provide universal education? In what kinds of schools is education made available, and for what age range? What scope do teachers have for modifying the curriculum and methods to meet the needs of those with special needs? How are children's disabilities identified and assessed? What resources are available to meet the ascertained needs? Is the training of teachers appropriate? Do teachers think that those children with disabilities should be in their classes? If not, where should they be? What priorities do countries give to various measures which are likely to facilitate the integration of handicapped pupils? All of these questions, even a decade later, still have a familiar ring to them.

These questions are grouped into four areas identified as in need of development. They are:

- estimating the demand for education
- specifying the educational services required for integration
- specifying the knowledge and skills required of teachers and others, such as advisors and psychologists, in these services
- subsequently, specifying the forms of training required.

The need for a wide base to the training is also recognised, which should include managers, consultants, teachers' aides, technicians and parents. The need for interdisciplinarity in the training courses on offer is also promoted, and the significant role that other pupils may play in peer group tutoring is not forgotten.

The contribution to the OECD

The socio-economic background

The OECD is essentially an economic organisation. However, within its charter and recently-expressed medium-term strategic objectives (OECD, 1992), it emphasises the need to develop and make the 'best possible use, in a context of rapid technological change, of our countries' prime asset, namely their human resources', while paying close attention to the 'numerous social problems besetting our countries, problems which, if we are not careful, could in the long run jeopardise economic development and even political and social cohesion'. The work that is carried out by the OECD is selected following discussions between the Member countries and the Secretariat. It is intended to support and inform policy-making in the Member countries in areas of agreed concern, and is unlike the recommendations made in the European Union (EU), which often carry the force of law.

From a methodological point of view, there is considerable variation in the ways in which the research is carried out, although the case study approach to understanding good practice is widely used. The frameworks for the gathering of data are discussed and agreed with policy-makers and researchers, and much of the data is then gathered by the countries themselves. Typically, the work is synthesised into reports and the policy implications abstracted. These reports are discussed at a high level within ministries and often presented to ministers.

The work on disability and children and youth at risk has been carried out in the context of changes in the demands of the labour market for ever more skilled workers who can operate effectively and competitively in the increasingly complex conditions of the workplace. Involvement of these groups in post-compulsory education is now a clear and important trend. In addition, workers must increasingly show a preparedness to continue to develop and expand their skills; attitudes which must also be allied to flexibility and a willingness to consider alternative forms of employment throughout the cycle of working life.

These factors need to be set against a backdrop of substantial changes in the structure of the population in many Member countries. The birth rate is declining, the composition of family structures is changing, and the number of citizens available to support and maintain many economies at their present levels is reduced. Countries simply cannot afford to waste their citizens. The financial implications of these developments, though not easy to assess, are likely to be of staggering proportions. Gerry (1992), for instance, has estimated (conservatively) that the cost of maintaining disabled people under the age of 30 in the USA on passive, lifelong total dependency programmes is in excess of $1,000,000,000,000.

High levels of unemployment, leading to decreases in revenues and increases in passive benefits, allied to increasing costs of health care of the growing aged population, are but a few of the challenging implications which are leading to wide-ranging reviews of many of the accepted services in our societies. Education has not escaped scrutiny. Perhaps in most countries, education has come under more scrutiny than other sectors, but it is now widely accepted that far too many children fail at school, with social and personally tragic consequences.

These issues of failure and disability are as high now on the political agenda as they have ever been, and Klaus Wedell has been as influential as anybody in formulating the questions that have underpinned the research described here in a way that is relevant to policy.

Two areas in particular have been of central concern. These are firstly, the study on the integration of the disabled into mainstream schools, and secondly the study on children and youth at risk. Taken together, these two areas of work cover the whole range of special educational needs, and more, given the large estimates made by countries of those said to be 'at risk'. More will be said of this later.

Integration of disabled children into mainstream schools

For most of the Member countries of the OECD, the integration of disabled children into mainstream schools is the major policy issue in special education, and this has been reflected in changes in the relevant legal and policy frameworks (OECD, 1995). An inspection of basic statistical data gathered from participating countries immediately reveals two major issues. First, the data show the wide variation that exists in the definitions of the concepts of SEN and disability, which together make the task of comparison fraught with difficulty. Second, they reveal substantial differences in scope for increasing the involvement of disabled children in mainstream schools.

Table 11.1 brings together some fundamental data. The first column shows the proportion of pupils for whom special provision is made. This varies substantially from country to country, ranging for 0.74 per cent in Turkey to 17.8 per cent in Finland. Such figures are difficult to interpret, since they appear to reflect a complex interaction of definitional, resourcing and placement issues in the context of countries' different legal and policy frameworks. In attempting to estimate proportions of children integrated, the method adopted was to identify those who are outside regular education and compare this total with that of the overall total for whom provision is made, as indicated in column one. Thus columns two, three and four identify proportions outside education, in special schools and units and in special classes. Column five provides an estimate of those outside the mainstream by summing columns two, three and four.

It is clear from this analysis that there are several different ways in which countries are operating. First, there are those who accept the broader notion of SEN, as described in the Warnock Report (DES, 1978) (i.e. that on average between 16 and 20 per cent of children will need special education at some time in their school lives) and provide generously for these children – see, for example, Canada (New Brunswick), Denmark, Finland and Iceland. Second, there are those countries who define their disabled populations more restrictively and equate them with those being educated in some form of segregated provision – examples are Austria, Belgium and the Netherlands. Third, there are countries with relatively low levels of provision – such as Greece, Ireland, Japan, Sweden, and England and Wales.

The variations in these figures reflect, in part, administrative categorisation, and it is important not to conclude, especially for those countries with low estimates, that other provision is not made. In many countries, for example the Netherlands, such provision *is* made, and it can be quite generous, but it falls under a different budget heading. However, the figures do show quite clearly substantial differences in proportions of children educated in special schools.

Further analysis of the data reveals this and other variations quite clearly. Table 11.2 shows a breakdown of data for children with motor impairment in countries where the data were available. This table shows in column two the wide variation in proportions of children said to have motor impairment – for example Spain (0.15 per cent), France (0.27 per cent) – and also the differences in the proportions integrated; 87 per cent are in special schools in Belgium, but only 20 per cent in Sweden. These findings are not restricted to

Table 11.1   Proportion of children with SEN for whom provision is made: In special schools and units, special classes and outside the education system

	% of Pupils with SEN for Whom Provision is Made	Outside Education	In Special School and Unit	In Special Class	Total Outside Mainstream
Australia	5.22	nil	0.63	0.92	1.55
Austria	2.55	<0.1	2.55	<0.1	2.55
Belgium	3.08	<0.1	3.08	n/a	3.08
Canada (New Brunswick)	10.79[1]	nil	n/a	n/a	n/a
Denmark	13.03	nil	0.65	0.98	1.63
Finland	17.08	0.14	1.85	0.83	2.82
France	3.54	1.38[2]	1.26	0.64	3.28
Germany[3]	7.00	nil	3.69	n/a	3.69
Greece	0.86	0.18	0.20	0.48[4]	0.38
Iceland	15.71	nil	0.58	0.71[4]	1.29
Ireland	1.45	0.22	1.04	0.41	1.67
Italy	1.27	n/a	n/a	n/a	n/a
Japan[5]	0.89	nil	0.37	0.52	0.89
Netherlands	3.63	<0.1	3.63	nil	3.63
Norway[6]	6.00	<0.1	0.6 (schools and classes)		<0.7
Spain	2.03	n/a	0.80	0.23	1.03
Sweden	1.60	nil	1.03	⟶	1.03
Switzerland	4.90	nil	4.90 (schools and classes)		4.90
Turkey[7]	0.74	n/a	0.28	0.33	0.61
United Kingdom[8]	1.85	nil	1.3	n/a	1.3
United States	7.00	nil	n/a	n/a	2.90[9]

Notes:

n/a = not available

1   This figure includes gifted students.
2   Children in establishments provided by the Ministry of Social Security. A proportion of these are educated in ordinary schools.
3   Former Federal Republic of Germany only (1989). The 7% figure is an estimate.
4   Part-time only; otherwise, in ordinary class.
5   Column 1 covers those children of compulsory school age.
6   Many more than the 6% quoted have individualised help for minor disabilities.
7   An estimated 14% of children between 0 and 18 years are handicapped.
8   England and Wales only.
9   This figure was derived by adding together children who were receiving a good to fair proportion of their education outside the mainstream, as described in the detailed notes on the USA in the text.

Table 11.2   Placement of children with motor impairment

	No. of Children	% of Total School Population	No. in Special School or Class	% in Special School or Class	No. in Mainstream	% in Mainstream
Belgium	3,279	0.16	2,853	87	426	13
Finland	1,168	0.21	921	79	247	21
France	26,686	0.27	20,695	78	5,991	22
Spain[1]	2,986	0.15	1,930	65	1,056	35
Sweden	1,800	0.20	360	20	1,440	80

1   6–14-year-olds only, in an area managed by the Ministry of Education and Science which covers approximately 45% of the school population of Spain.

motor impairments; they apply also to hearing and visual disabilities (OECD, 1995). The differences in proportions of children estimated to fall into these categories are not easy to explain, but it seems unlikely that they reflect absolute differences between countries in the prevalence of these types of disability. It is much more likely that a large proportion of the variance is accounted for by differences in definition, policy, educational practice and funding arrangements.

In general, the data that have been gathered show wide variation in definitions, in the categories used, in the provision made, in the extent of integration – indeed in almost every measurement made. This of itself argues for considerable review of the policies and practices that countries use to define their 'disabled' populations of children.

In accordance with the work carried out for UNESCO, the study on integration completed at the OECD reveals the importance of the need for reform and development at a number of levels of the political and education systems studied. From a synthesis of work from 21 countries and 64 case studies on aspects of integration, considered alongside an international literature review (Evans, 1993; OECD, 1995), the following issues can be abstracted that are relevant to anyone wishing to integrate disabled children more effectively.

Policy development and implementation

Policies at government, regional district and school levels must constantly affirm that children with SEN are educated in ordinary schools. The implementation of these policies should be monitored and evaluated on a regular basis. Efforts to promote and sustain positive attitudes towards those with SENs on the part of all concerned should regularly be made.

The role of the school

In ordinary schools, children should not have to repeat a year in order to reach a certain standard before moving on to the next year group. Teachers need to assess continually the progress of their children with SENs and review periodically their provision. Both social adjustment and academic achievement should be assessed, leading, where necessary, to programmes intended to reduce social isolation and increase self-esteem. When those children with SENs require additional educational support to follow the ordinary school curriculum, this should normally occur in the regular classroom, rather than through small-group withdrawal or placement in a special class. Teachers and support teachers need to be given time to consult, assess and plan as well as to teach and develop the necessary resources, which need to be stored systematically in a common base.

The role of the special school

The transition of children from special schools to ordinary schools involves considerable preparation. This may include briefing special-school children on the ways of ordinary schools; providing opportunities for ordinary-school and special-school class teachers to see one another at work as well as to discuss the children, and running sessions with teachers, children and parents in ordinary schools to help them understand and develop positive attitudes towards children with SENs. Where special schools are shifting from direct provision for children to the provision of advisory and training services to ordinary schools, they must maintain a balance of staffing to ensure that both kinds of provision continue to be effective.

Developing access to the curriculum

Access to the curriculum is, of course, a key issue. Buildings must ensure that children with sensory and motor disabilities have the same access as other children to the school premises, and equipment needs to be modified appropriately – for example for those with sensory or motor disabilities. Curriculum planning at the school level should be a whole-school policy which ensures a balanced curriculum for all. Finally, access through funding must be considered. Funding arrangements, which are becoming more and more important in educational organisations, can facilitate or impede integration. In the UK, the Statementing procedure can ensure that children with SENs can be given the necessary support for them to be effectively integrated. In other countries, however, the process of tying funding specifically to disabilities can serve to label children and steer them towards segregated special schooling. Other elements of national policy, while not directly concerned with either curriculum access or integration, may nevertheless have an impact on both. In the UK, recent legislation introduced funding for schools based largely on the number of pupils enrolled. It is likely that this type of funding arrangement, working together with the policy of encouraging parental choice between schools based on published academic achievement scores, may well put pressure on headteachers to pass less able children on to special schools.

Pedagogy and classroom organisation

In each classroom, the teacher should develop a range of strategies that will take account of different abilities – for instance, allowing children to complete the same work at different rates, or in a simplified form, and from time to time setting different group or individual work for different children. The implied flexibility in these classroom arrangements requires a continuum of support from increasingly specialised teachers and external support staff. If children do need to be taken out of the class for some reason, it is important that the teacher continues to ensure that the balance of the curriculum for those children is not unduly disturbed or that any crucial element is missed.

Parental and community development

Parents should be as widely involved at as many levels of decision-making as possible. At a national level, this includes parent organisations, but at district and school levels, individual parents and communities will need to be consulted. Parents' views need to be taken seriously, and they should be seen as partners who can help in classrooms, work on governing bodies as well as acquiring teaching skills to help their own children at home.

Support services

It is important that district-level support services act to monitor the progress and review the provision of children with disabilities. When formal assessment is necessary, the appropriate specialists must be consulted and parents involved. Staff of external services need to develop advisory and support skills and negotiate, with schools and other advisors, the coherence and relevance of educational arrangements and learning targets. In addition, these staff should also monitor transition-to-work arrangements.

Training

The training of teachers and other professionals is a pivot of success. Courses need to be offered at all levels – pre-service, postgraduate and in-service – to a wide variety of persons. The collaboration between schools and teacher training establishments, as well as those professionals in external services, is essential to ensure both complementarity and full coverage of course content. Courses need to emphasise the pedagogic and class organisation skills necessary to teach children with SENs in regular classrooms. In addition, there is a need to develop training in all aspects of special education, including research, innovation, inspectorial, administrative, managerial advisory and teacher training roles.

Resources

It is essential that teacher supply and training arrangements are adequate, at national level, for implementing a policy of integration. The distribution of educational resources should not encourage regional and district authorities to place children with SENs in special schools, rather than ordinary ones. In allocating resources, a realistic appraisal should be made of the different expenditures needed to provide adequate education for children of differing abilities. Incentives for teachers in ordinary schools to provide for children with SENs in ordinary classes should be planned. Resources need to reflect likely increased costs during initiation and at early stages of implementation, and also take account of the costs of monitoring and evaluating progress. Within schools, banks of teaching materials and associated technical equipment which are developed or acquired will need to be maintained, to enable class teachers to differentiate their work to cater for children with SENs, and to ensure that children with sensory or motor disabilities have full access to the curriculum. Some of these resources may be developed and stored on an across-schools basis.

Concluding comment

The account given above of the recent work at the OECD on integration is based on a great deal of information gathered with the help of Member countries, supplemented by a literature review. All of the evidence that has been gathered strongly supports the view that, if the right school organisation and contextual and social supports are made available, many disabled children can be integrated successfully into mainstream schools, with positive benefits in terms of academic standards not only for the disabled but also for non-disabled students. But one word of caution: there is evidence that disabled children, when integrated, may become socially isolated if schools do not take care to prevent this possibility.

Children and youth at risk

The second study which has been carried out at the OECD concerning special education, and with which Klaus has been involved is that on *Children and Youth at Risk* (OECD, 1994). The term 'at risk', which is in common use in the USA, is becoming widely used in many countries. As defined in the OECD study, children and youth 'at risk' are 'those who are failing at school and who are unsuccessful in making the transition to work and adult life and as a consequence are unlikely to be able to make a full contribution to adult life'. The idea of 'at riskness' is forward-looking and stresses prevention – this is one of the strengths of the term. Natriello et al. (1990), for instance, describe 'at risk' students as those who 'have certain characteristics that make it possible to identify them, but that these characteristics become problematic only in conjunction with events and conditions that have yet to unfold'.

However, this notion can be broadened and its nuances enhanced if other countries' concerns are taken into account. Three aspects of poverty were identified. In schools with high concentrations of poverty, there tends to be low academic performance and a high drop-out rate. In poor families, there is a tendency for low achievement, and in families where there has been poverty over a long – in contrast to a short – period, children also show low achievement.

In many OECD countries, students from ethnic minorities are more likely to show low school achievement. However, this statement must be qualified by recognising that there are many different minority groups, such as travellers, Gypsies and circus families, whose children may not attend school regularly. In addition, different minority groups show different characteristics. In the inner-city areas of the UK, children from some Asian countries show higher school achievement than indigenous UK groups. It is also true that girls often do better than boys, and second- and third-generation immigrants also tend to achieve higher standards.

Family variations are also implicated. Children from one-parent families tend to show lower achievement than those from two-parent families, as do children from families of low-achieving parents. The breakdown of relations between the home and the school, poor housing and experience of abuse are all associated with low levels of attainment.

Other factors that many countries identified as predicting 'at risk' status included: the type of school attended (e.g. government, independent or denominational), its location (urban or rural), a lack of community support, the non-availability or non-use of leisure facilities, and lack of a political voice.

It is clear from this list that a whole range of issues that lead to marginalisation from the mainstream of society are associated with low achievement and a consequent, intended or unintended, functional exclusion from the social aspirations that the majority aim to achieve. These are seen operationally as failure in school, low attainment, low self-esteem, lack of participation, truancy, school refusal, drop-out, behaviour problems and delinquency. The social correlates have been identified as health problems, substance abuse, psycho-somatic illness, early pregnancy, inability to integrate into the workplace, with consequences of unemployment, poverty and inclinations to crime.

Some countries considered gender a risk factor. In Australia, for example, although girls stayed at school longer than boys, there was little evidence that this experience widened their opportunities in any real way. In Germany, two-thirds of the applicants for vocational training were women, and the majority were oriented towards a small spectrum of poorly-paid jobs. In that country there has been a tradition for a social network to operate for boys, helping to find them opportunities in the labour market – an arrangement that has not traditionally functioned for girls. On the other hand, for some countries – for example Sweden – there was substantial concern over the educational and adaptational difficulties faced by boys, often associated with aggression and crime.

Prevalence

It is difficult to estimate the true size of the 'at risk' population, since there are no hard and fast definitions, and few statistics are kept. However, some can be quoted which are indicative. In Australia, estimates were given of 'at risk' youth between the ages of 15 and 19. In 1983, 20.3 per cent of this group were estimated to be 'at risk'. This figure had declined dramatically by 1989, to 11 per cent.

In Belgium, where statistics were not readily available, other studies have shown that 34 per cent of 5-year-olds were 'at risk' of experiencing substantial difficulties of adapting to the first year of primary school; 25 per cent subsequently had difficulties during the first year.

In France, in the Zones d'Education Prioritaires (ZEPs) – areas where there are perceived to be particular concentrations of disadvantaged families and where there is special action supported by additional central government funds – 15 per cent are considered 'at risk'.

In the Netherlands, 47 per cent of primary-aged children are considered 'at risk' and attract additional funding in education priority areas weighted according to a scale of 'at riskness'. However, only 5 per cent leave school with no form of certification.

In the UK, by contrast, despite the early development of educational priority areas (EPAs), there is no straightforward definition of 'at risk'. Over recent years, 10 per cent have left school with no qualifications.

In the USA, around 30 per cent of children under the age of 18 are considered to be 'at risk' of educational failure. This figure is based on four demographic factors: poverty; race and ethnic minority status; living in a one-parent family, and poor English proficiency. If all of these factors are considered together, then a group of between 6–8 per cent emerges which is seriously 'at risk' – a group which trebled in size between 1970 and 1980.

As implied above, combining 'at risk' factors should decrease the false positives identified from a simpler single-factor model. This view is supported by work of Rutter (1980), who found that children suffering from one risk factor were as likely to experience serious consequences as those with no risk factors. However, if two or three risk factors were present, the chances of an unfavourable outcome increased fourfold. With four risk factors, the chances of a negative outcome increased tenfold. This is an area for substantial further research, with considerable policy implications.

Intervention strategies

The work on 'at risk' children and youth – which also looked independently at intervention strategies in the pre-school, school-age and transition-to-work periods – is too extensive to summarise in this chapter. One example, focusing on school development will be described briefly.

Australia has developed a clear, integrated approach to tackling the problems presented by those who are failing at school. The Disadvantaged School Programme (DSP), which was set up in 1975, serves schools with concentrations of students from disadvantaged socio-economic circumstances – those 'at risk'. The idea is to provide effective learning through more rewarding and relevant schooling and improved interaction between schools and communities. It emphasises whole-school and community approaches, and depends on joint participation of community groups, members of the school community and the education authorities.

Local committees, which must include parents and community representatives, review school objectives and draw up proposals for improving learning outcomes in schools. Funding is allocated on the basis of need and the likely effectiveness of the proposals, rather than on a per capita basis, by supporting planned whole-school change intended:

- to promote school-based curriculum development, to broaden life experiences, to increase self-confidence and to improve basic educational skills
- to improve economic, political, organisational and technical knowledge for pupils to function effectively in society
- to develop school – community liaison and participation of parents in

the development and implementation of curriculum programmes
- to involve pupils in expressive arts
- to support schools in documenting, evaluating and disseminating outcomes – an approach coordinated and supported by systems at the national level.

Evaluation is a key component in ensuring that programme goals are implemented, and future support is contingent on acceptable evaluations. The programme has been shown to increase fundamental skills, especially in basic educational attainments, improved attitudes to school, attendance and discipline problems and parent and community involvement.

The Australian example given above is operating within a more general framework of educational goals for the twenty-first century in which education has an important role to play in attaining social justice. The scope of the task is tremendous, and the following outline serves both to give some ideas of the nature of the reforms that are required and to conclude this section.

In Australia, there are five federal programmes covering:

1   poverty and disadvantage
2   geographic isolation
3   ethnicity and English as a second language
4   Aboriginality
5   gender

These complement state and territory initiatives to develop a student management discipline code which involves:

- student participation
- student enterprise
- peer tutoring
- pastoral care
- self-protective behaviours (e.g. versus abuse)
- literacy and numeracy skills
- parental participation
- school–industry links
- labour market awareness
- post-compulsory education
- school, technical college and further educational cooperation
- the use of alternative educational settings
- school-linked accommodation programmes

Effective schools link the issues together in a whole-school approach, 'which integrates all groups in the school, students, staff, parents and community and recognises and values each group in the process of participation, negotiation, decision-making and co-operation'.

Final comment

The work on children and youth at risk complements the work carried out on the integration of the disabled, and gives a flavour of the style of work carried out by the OECD and UNESCO in education by using case studies of good practice gathered in many countries to influence policy-making and reform efforts. The work on disability and 'at riskness' points in the same direction. It reveals the need for reforms in curriculum and pedagogy, in school management and in overall system support if schools are to meet the needs of *all* children in the next millennium.

Note

The views expressed in this article are the author's, and they cannot be interpreted as representing the views of the OECD or its member countries.

Postscript

I first met Klaus Wedell when he was appointed as Professor of Educational Psychology (Special Educational Needs) to the London Institute of Education in 1979. Klaus Wedell revealed his passion for work by organising, it seems within hours of his arrival, a seminar on a Saturday morning on parental involvement in supporting children with learning difficulties. His work rate never abated: if anything it increased and expanded into direct involvement with the development of policy and legal frameworks relating to the new provision for special education. If Klaus Wedell takes on a task, it is always with at least 200 per cent commitment. Somehow he manages to combine a tenacious belief in equity and social justice and intellectual honesty with great modesty, humour and charisma when fighting against substantial odds. This demeanour has won him tremendous respect all over the world. The ability to be concerned and practically skilled in promoting the individual educational progress of any single child, along with the capacity to operate at a systemic and policy level and communicate the ideas straightforwardly, at essentially one and the same time, is remarkable. All of these skills he brought to the OECD work – which is so very much richer for them.

References

Department of Education & Science (DES) (1978) *Special Educational Needs: Report of the Committee of Inquiry into the Education of Handicapped Children and Young People* (The Warnock Report), Cmnd 7212, London: HMSO.

Evans, P.L.C. (ed.) (1993) *European Journal of Special Needs Education* (special issue on integration), (3), whole issue.

Gerry, M. (1992) 'Economic consequences', in M.J. McLaughlin, L. Florian, D. Neubert, G. Boyd-Kjellen and L. Friedsen (eds) *Transitions to Employment: Proceedings of the 1990 International Symposium of Persons with Disabilities,* University of Maryland at College Park.

Natriello, G., McDill, E.L. & Pallas, A.M. (1990) *Schooling Disadvantaged Children: Racing Against Catastrophe,* New York: Teachers College Press.

OECD (1992) *Medium-term Strategic Objectives,* C(92)6/FINAL, Paris: OECD.

OECD (1994) *Children and Youth at Risk,* CERI/CD(94)1, Paris: OECD.

OECD (1995) *Integrating Students with Special Needs into Mainstream Schools,* Paris: OECD.

Rutter, M. (1980) *Changing Youth in a Changing Society: Patterns of Adolescent Development and Disorder,* Cambridge, Mass.: Harvard University Press.

UNESCO (1985) *Helping Handicapped Pupils in Ordinary Schools: Strategies for Teacher Training,* Paris: UNESCO.

Wedell, K. (1980) 'Early identification and compensatory interaction', in R.M. Knights and D.J. Bakker (eds) *Treatment of Hyperactive and Learning Disordered Children: Current Research,* Baltimore University Park Press.

12 Lobbying for special education

Margaret Peter

Pressure groups in general

When Clement Attlee claimed, half a century ago, 'Pressure groups? We don't have them in this country', he was discounting centuries of campaigning which go back to the craftsmen's guilds of the Middle Ages. Had he confined his denial to pressure groups for special educational needs (SENs), he would have been nearer the truth, but, even then, at least sixty years behind his time. Pritchard (1963) describes how, after earlier action, headteachers and representatives of governing bodies and school boards educating the deaf met at Manchester Town Hall in 1889 to urge the government to adopt the report of the Royal Commission on the blind and deaf. Similar pressure on the government of the day came from teachers and others critical of education provided for the blind.

In his denial, Attlee was no doubt thinking of US-style pressure groups: highly-organised, highly-financed businessmen who wore their dollars on their sleeves. Although Attlee was a Labour Prime Minister, the first since the early 1930s, he did not, apparently, define pressure groups as including the trade unions that had helped to bring him to power, let alone any of the other organisations attempting to influence government policy. Fifty years later, perhaps, his awareness might have been closer to that of the Conservative Minister, Michael Portillo, quoted recently in *The Sunday Times* (Baxter, 1994): 'All you have to do is set up a pressure group, print up some headed paper, put out a press release – preferably findings of some spurious survey – and you've got a spot on every news programme.'

Defining the term

Definitions of 'pressure group' still vary. Sometimes 'pressure group', 'interest group' and 'lobby' are used interchangeably. Other writers make fine and scholarly distinctions between terms, arguing that 'pressure' implies capitulation, which, often, it does not. 'Interest group' is broader and most open to challenge as synonym for the other two. 'Lobby' and 'pressure group' will be used in the following pages to refer to action by two or more individuals to bring changes in the law, but excluding groups closely associated with the party in power.

Writers also tend to subdivide pressure groups into 'sectional' groups which protect the interests of those who support them and 'promotional' ones which promote specific causes and may even spring up like mushrooms overnight to fight for a cause (Kimber & Richardson, 1974). Sectional groups might include such unlikely-sounding alliances as the Amalgamated Association of Beamers, Twisters and Drawers, as well as the more familiar Confederation of British Industry. Promotional groups could include the Noise Abatement Society, Friends of the Earth and those concerned with SENs. But the division between the two is not clear-cut, and many groups contain both sectional and promotional elements.

The growth of pressure groups

The spread of pressure groups concerned with SENs is part of a rapid and recent growth in the number of ideologically-based groups in the post-war years. The *Guardian Directory of Pressure Groups* (quoted in Marsh, 1983) found that over half of the 184 groups which it listed, and which gave their age, had come into being after 1960. The majority had reformist and liberal causes to pursue, rather than business interests to promote. Pre-1900, according to Shipley (1979), quoted by Rush (1990a), there were 109; between 1960 and 1979 the number had jumped sixfold, to 628. *The Media Guide 1993* (Peak, 1992) lists over 450, and, two years later, the 1995 edition contains 8 per cent more (Peak, 1994), but these lists do not claim to be comprehensive. Reliable figures are elusive when definitions vary, and no one yet seems to have counted the rise in relation to groups representing SENs. What does seem beyond dispute is that pressure groups in general are a growth industry, although not one which endears itself to the Treasury. Its members have an awkward habit of asking for extra government money, rather than offering to ease the balance of payments deficit.

Causes of growth

Why have pressure groups grown so rapidly since the 1960s? Governments, you can argue, have only themselves to blame. Simultaneously, they have encouraged rising expectations among the electorate and imposed central controls over aspects of daily life where few or none existed at the beginning of this century (Marsh, 1993). Government interventions in economic and industrial policy, as Marsh points out, provoked lobbies like the Trade Union Congress into defending their interests against legislative intrusion; changes in social policy have provoked similar reactions. According to Miller (1987), the volume of legislation, reckoned in pages, rose from around 200 in 1900 to 2,000 in 1986. The startling increase in Acts and Regulations on education since the Conservatives took office in 1979 is just one example of this 'Gothic monstrosity of legislation', as it has been called.

As the range and volume of law-making expand, sections of the electorate feel threatened by acts of aggression and blows from Statutory Instruments. The more control from Whitehall, the more legislation, the louder and more numerous will be the voices of dissent. Government action creates a momentum for pressure groups to form.

The process, however, is not one-way. To claim that governments meddle, and pressure groups bristle, is misleading. Laws are not created in a vacuum; they may be drafted in response to lobbyists' pleas. Two examples from special education and disability are the 1981 Education Act, prompted by the Warnock Report's (DES, 1978) agenda for change, and the 1986 Disabled Persons Act, a private member's bill introduced by the Labour MP Tom Clarke and encouraged by disability organisations. Government intervention, which writers like Rush (1990a) and Marsh (1983) see as causing pressure groups to form, may be the consequence instead. Pressure groups of all kinds may help to create legislation which, in turn, may incite new pressure groups to arise in order to oppose or improve its measures.

The rise in the number of quangos in recent years is another reason for the spread of pressure groups. As more and more powers are wrested from locally-elected authorities and vested in faceless bodies, miles away, questions about accountability multiply. There is clamour for safeguards against neglect and exploitation, and protests sometimes pay off. During the passage of the bill on teacher training, which became law in 1994, lobbyists won an amendment to ensure that knowledge and understanding of SENs would be represented on the new Teacher Training Agency.

When government delegates powers to quango members, who are non-elected, it also seeks to retain control overall through wodges of prescriptive and detailed legislation designed to reduce, if not remove, the risk that the quangos will bite the hand that feeds them. The surge of primary and secondary legislation, Circulars and official guidance is inevitable. So is the incitement to further action by lobbyists.

At the same time, government encourages the trend for groups to respond. In a democracy, it is politically expedient for leaders to consult widely. They must be seen to be listening to the electorate's views (even if close examination reveals leaders to be selectively deaf). In deserving and relatively uncontroversial activities like special education – in contrast, say, with the privatising of the water industry – government is well disposed to take notice of consumers' views, at least on the detail of policy. Being seen on the side of the angels is a chance that no politician dare miss.

However, more laws and more quangos do not add up inevitably to more pressure groups. Individuals have always raised their voices for or against new laws. The difference is that more of them have to come to realise that together they can achieve greater results than in ones, twos or threes. Collective action may not guarantee success, but strength of numbers, good organisation and coherent strategies make failure less likely. Success, in turn, breeds further growth. Victories over officialdom and bureaucracy win headlines for lobbies like Greenpeace and the International Fund for Animal Welfare. Achievements by groups in the USA inspire others to follow suit; even failure can spur new attempts to do better. Triumphs, when they occur, may owe something to the 'Disgusted, Tunbridge Wells' factor. Rush (1990a) refers to disillusion with the main political parties. More and more individuals, he suggests, are tending to fight causes through pressure groups, rather than through the machinery of traditional politics. Membership of the major parties is now much lower than it was in the 1950s. Pursuing a single cause through a pressure group in a beguiling option to having its merits weighed against a range of competing priorities within the wider agenda of a large political party. The procedures can be tedious and slow.

Pressure groups for special educational needs

Pressure groups for children and adults with SENs reflect some of these general trends. They, too, appear to have grown in response to the volume and content of legislation, the threat of quangos, government's need to consult and the success of collective action. Their members have lobbied both actively and reactively over the past century: they have been active in bringing specialised legislation to the statute book, and reactive in opposing the broader legislation representing the main thrust of government policy when they felt threatened by it.

Early developments

The first legislation in England and Wales on the education of children with special needs, the 1893 Elementary Education (Blind and Deaf Children) Act and the Elementary Education (Defective and Epileptic Children) Act six years later were brought to the statute book through lobbying by doctors, teachers and other campaigners, as Pritchard (1963) describes. It had been the neglect of such children in the earlier legislation, the Elementary Education Acts of 1870 and 1876, that fuelled the demand for these specialised laws of the 1890s.

The first half of the twentieth century saw the birth of more organisations (and thus of potential pressure groups) committed to helping those with disabilities and learning difficulties. Many were founded as charities to provide education and other services to those in need. Some may have been inhibited – as several still are – from widening their role and lobbying overtly. Charity law on this matter is complex and confusing, although what one body avoids as 'political', others take by the horns. The Royal National Institute for the Deaf (founded in 1911), for instance, followed a number of charities founded in the nineteenth century, like Dr Barnardo's (1866) and the Royal National Institute for the Blind (1868), in bringing influence to bear on government policy from time to time.

Developments since the 1960s

The greatest expansion in organisations acting wholly or partly as pressure groups for SENs mirrors the general trend already noted. A few active campaigners, like The Spastics Society (1952), now renamed SCOPE, and the National Society for Mentally Handicapped Children (1955), now MENCAP, were founded a few years earlier, but most began around the 1960s, when, according to Harold Macmillan, the electorate had 'never had it so good'. The new arrivals covered a wide range: from the Association for Spina Bifida and Hydrocephalus (1966) and the Association for All Speech Impaired Children (AFASIC) (1968) to the National Association for Gifted Children (1966) and the British Dyslexia Association (1972), but the impression that post-1960 growth has been dominated by charities campaigning for special needs is misleading. *Charities Digest* (1994) also lists such unlikely-sounding enterprises as the Dark Horse Venture (1989), which encourages people of 55 and over 'into discovering exciting new challenges' (a 'window of opportunity', perhaps, for several contributors to the present book).

In the 1960s, there was mounting pressure on the government to change the law on special education. Section 57 of the 1944 Education Act excluded children with severe learning difficulties from education. This was the stimulus for the launching of the campaign to bring pupils out of the junior training centres and into the schools. Parents whose children were excluded from school joined forces as early as 1946 to fight for change. They lobbied MPs in the Labour government and wrote to the Ministers for Health and Education. Early in the campaign, the then Minister of Education rebuffed them with the response that the proposal to bring such children into the education system 'cannot be entertained because it is not in accordance with the law'. The parents (who seem to have had a sounder grasp of constitutional democracy than the Minister) replied: 'But Parliament exists to change laws which are not in accordance with the interests of the people' (Fryd, 1969).

Subsequent pressure from campaigners brought a debate in the House of Commons in February 1966, in which the Minister of Health remained steadfastly unconvinced of the need for change. It took two more years before Harold Wilson, then Prime Minister, announced the transfer, and two more before the Education (Handicapped Children) Bill became law. The efforts of the various pressure groups to achieve the 1970 Act were not, however, closely coordinated. Collective lobbying was still in its infancy, and, as the Act focused exclusively on children with severe learning difficulties, the special education organisations in the front line of battle were few.

Victory in 1970 spurred campaigners to press for a national inquiry into special educational provision for children and young people with disabilities and learning difficulties. This paved the way for the 1981 Education Act. It was around this time, in 1976, that Klaus Wedell gained an early opportunity to influence policy, when he led a delegation from the Division of Educational and Child Psychology of the British Psychological Society to give evidence to the Warnock Committee.

Developments since the 1980s

Success in persuading the government to set up the Warnock Committee encouraged further action. The 1981 Education Bill marked a new phase in the development of pressure groups for SENs. As lobbying began to be seen as more important than previously, societies like MENCAP and SCOPE followed the 1977 lead of the Royal Association for Disability and Rehabilitation (RADAR) in appointing a paid and full-time parliamentary officer who, when the need arose, could haunt Westminster's corridors of power to brief and bend the ears of MPs willing to table new clauses and amendments on the charity's behalf. Other bodies followed suit. Some of the unions, including the National Union of Teachers, made similar appointments, but their officers were not exclusively concerned with SENs.

Like the Act passed eleven years earlier, the 1981 Education Act was an example of specialised legislation springing from the roots of special education – professionals and parents taking initiatives in pushing for improvements in the law and focusing wholly on SENs. The major Acts which followed, those of 1988 and 1993 in particular, generated more heat and were much wider in scope: cornerstones of the Conservative government's strategy to change the face of education as a whole. The difference in contexts is important, suggests Butler (1983): 'An act which deals exclusively with special education would seem less likely to be dealt with in Parliament in a context of partisan antagonism than an act which also contains politically contentious topics such as an assisted places scheme.'

The 1988 Education Act could be described as an Act designed to 'privatise' schools through the nationalising of the curriculum, leaving children with SENs on the margin. The threats to this and other minorities rallied scores of pressure groups, and brought many together in united opposition to a centrally-imposed curriculum, the fear of league tables based on national testing, opting out, open competition between schools and the dilution of the powers of local education authorities (LEAs). It was probably this Act, more than any before it, that kindled awareness of the need for collective action. Alliances were formed and joint representations were made to government Ministers and civil servants. By the time the bill received royal assent, many more references to SENs appeared in it, but the concessions came nowhere close to the core of government policy.

Encouraged by modest successes, a number of individuals and groups who had singly or in handfuls tried to influence the clauses of the 1988 Education Bill came together to respond to the bill which became the 1992 Further and Higher Education Act. Under the aegis of SKILL, the National Bureau for Students with Disabilities, the disability consortium succeeded in making the Further Education Funding Council responsible for providing further education up to the age of 25 for disabled students needing to receive it in non-maintained provision (Corlett, 1992).

This trend for collective action was intensified when the White Paper *Choice and Diversity* (DfE, 1992) was published in July 1992. There is nothing like disaster for bringing consensus, as someone remarked at the time. A consortium was formed, the Special Education Consortium (SEC), through the initiative of the Council for Disabled Children (CDC), and support exceeded expectations. Over fifty organisations and many individuals gave their strength to a combined authority that no previous group had been able to muster and which Davie (1995) emphasises in his recently-published account of the SEC's activities. The steering group met weekly during the passage of the bill to prepare briefs and take action. Its large consultative forum fed in information and opinions about the government's proposals, and included bodies ranging from Barnardos and the British Association of Social Workers to the Cystic Fibrosis Trust and the Aga Khan Education Board. Its smaller policy group to guide policy gave it an unprecedented 'level of legitimacy', as Paul Ennals, Chairman of the SEC, expressed it. Here again, Klaus Wedell made a major contribution, together with Paul Ennals, Philippa Russell, Director of the CDC, and Philippa Stobbs, CDC's Senior Development Officer. Others described Klaus Wedell's role on the SEC as that of an 'academic and thinker'. He himself described it – disarmingly self-deprecating as usual – as that of a 'backroom boy', who reminded those members negotiating with Ministers and civil servants of the principles to which the SEC must hold firm.

The coordinated, three-tier structure of the SEC and the efforts of other groups paid dividends. In 1993, the changes to the bill were numerous, and some were substantial. A paper summarising the concessions wrung from the government by mid-June was circulated by the CDC shortly before the bill received royal assent. It listed 17 changes, which included the duty of schools to make public their policies for SENs, the mandatory exception of educational psychology and education welfare services from LEA money delegated to schools, the abolition of indefinite exclusions from school and LEAs' duty to provide education otherwise than at school for excluded pupils. The extent of the revisions, though largely on the detail of the bill, exceeded the expectations of many lobbyists.

When the education bill on teacher training was introduced by the government some months later, the recently-formed Special Educational Needs Training Consortium acted as a pressure group to try to make the clauses more responsive to special training needs. Together with other organisations, the consortium succeeded in ensuring, as mentioned earlier, that SENs would be represented on the new Teacher Training Agency. The change was similar to one relating to the composition of the Funding Agency for Schools in the 1993 Education Act, prised out of the government with force of argument. This time the government did not resist – once beaten twice shy, a principle established, or merely ministerial whim?

Styles and methods of lobbying

Over recent years, pressure groups for special needs have become more professional, lobbyists more astute. At least four styles of lobbying have been used to influence recent bills, Regulations, Circulars and other guidance. They can be distinguished broadly as:

- consultative
- confrontational
- media-centred
- unconventional.

In practice, pressure groups may resort to all or most of the four to varying degrees.

The consultative

The SEC, in working through civil servants and Ministers rather than, primarily, through MPs and peers, followed the consultative approach advocated by Charles Miller in *Lobbying Government* (Miller, 1987). His shrewd, do-it-yourself guide to the ungentle art of lobbying advises groups to pick their targets carefully, identifying who wields power to make any particular decision related to government policy and legislation in hand. This can range from the full cabinet and the departmental Minister concerned down to the civil servants at assistant secretary or principle level.

Although SEC members may not have read Miller, and identified some of their targets by trial and error, they were largely successful in gaining access to Sanctuary Buildings at the right level – one floor from the top for the Minister of State, five floors lower for assistant secretaries – in order to influence the content of the bill. Arguments were prepared, briefs written and jiggery-pokery scrupulously avoided. The core group of the SEC always made sure that senior officials were informed in advance of any amendments which were being fed to parliament through MPs and peers, were advised of the lines being taken in any discussions with Ministers, and given copies of briefs being distributed to members of both Houses. The consortium also had the advantage of being unsullied by any significant political bias.

Compared, for instance, with the Child Poverty Action Group, whose lobbying efforts were handicapped by an image reeking of the politically contentious issue of family poverty (McCarthy, 1983), the consortium was the acceptable face of lobbying. For these and other reasons, it was able to work within the system. Whether or not the risks of being too closely associated with the Establishment were wholly avoided is not clear.

The confrontational

At the same time, other pressure groups were hacking away at the system, working more frequently through the parliamentary opposition instead. Because of their perceived left-wing bias, their access to members of the government and civil service was more difficult. Organisations like the National Union of Teachers (NUT) and the Association of Metropolitan Authorities (AMA) were likely to lobby opposition MPs and peers and to aid and abet tactics like ambushes in the House of Lords, as the AMA did during the passage of the 1993 Education Bill. The influence of MPs over what goes into bills and what passes into law is more limited than might be thought. Rush (1990b), in his 1986 survey of organisations seeking to influence public policy through parliament, discovered that Ministers and civil servants came top as targets to influence, while parliament rated a poor fourth.

Both the NUT and the AMA, nevertheless, had their moments of triumph, fleeting or otherwise. The NUT succeeded in adding Section 21(3) to the Act, giving the Secretary of State powers to secure information on SEN provision from both the Funding Agency for Schools and LEAs. The AMA helped to contrive an ambush in the Lords, which, until its reversal in the Commons a few days later – *sic transit gloria AMAndi* – gave a heady victory over the powers of the Funding Agency for Schools. Had the amendment survived, LEAs would have had a duty to submit strategic plans for the comprehensive development of educational provision in their area to the Secretary of State for approval. Both special educational provision and grant-maintained schools would have been included.

Members of parliament and peers were also targeted by IPSEA, the Independent Panel for Special Education Advice. Although much smaller than the NUT and AMA, it succeeded, either on its own or working through the SEC, in writing into the 1993 Act (or the subsequent Code of Practice) parents' rights to request a formal assessment of their child, and to have their child's non-educational needs set out in the Statement, and also the right of the child or young person to express his or her views when being assessed. An account of IPSEA's lobbying appears in the Open University reader *Equality and Diversity in Education* (Wright, 1994).

The media-centred

The media-centred approach to lobbying has probably been exploited less often as a primary strategy than the consultative and confrontational ones. Rush's survey (1990b) placed the media third in rank order of sources used to influence public policy. Special educational needs are not usually headline-seizers in the mass media – no 'sex appeal', as David Tench (1994) would put it. But where practice appears to flout civil rights, national publicity in the press and on television can create or accelerate change. Stanley Segal, when editor, frequently used the pages of *Forward Trends* in the 1960s as part of the campaign that hit the national press and led to the 1970 Education Act and the Warnock Inquiry into special education. Margaret Stirling's widely-publicised research into pupil's exclusions from school strongly influenced the government's decision to abolish indefinite exclusions through Section 261 of the 1993 Education Act (see e.g. Stirling, 1992). Recently, in a wider context, disabled people have achieved national media coverage for the introduction of a civil rights bill.

A further example in which media exposure was crucial related to the 1992 Education (Schools) Act and its associated guidance from the Office for Standards in Education (OFSTED), the *Framework for the Inspection of Schools* (OFSTED, 1994a). A statement in the December issue of the *British Journal of Special Education* (Chorley, 1993) that OFSTED could not guarantee that all schools with designated units for pupils with SENs would have that provision inspected made front-page headlines in *The Times Educational Supplement* (Pyke, 1993). It excited widespread concern and criticism, and it led to new guidance being issued to school inspection teams three months later, tightening the inspection arrangements and emphasising that all these units should be inspected in future (OFSTED, 1994b).

The unconventional

Miller's view that lobbying 'as a professional technique falls between the law and public relations' is not at odds with the approaches described so far (Miller, 1987). But how would he describe the tactics of a former teacher from Hertfordshire who, almost single-handedly at first, hacked at the system in order to get Section 17 added to the 1988 Education Act? As the mother of a son with dyslexia, for whom learning a foreign language compulsorily seemed, at best, an irrelevance, Ann Brereton regularly attended the sittings of the Commons committee on the bill. She passed home-produced briefing papers to MPs and plied committee members during coffee breaks with chit-chat, reasoned arguments and the occasional Penguin biscuit (only the merest crumb of 'sleaze'). Relying on what she described as the 'Miss Marple' approach, but one which was far from amateur in anyone's book, she was a major influence in getting Section 17 – disapplying the National Curriculum in exceptional circumstances – into the law.

How successful has the lobbying been?

Both active and reactive lobbying can claim their successes, but strategies, time scales and targets are likely to vary from one type of lobbying to the other. Success in active lobbying usually shows in primary legislation; success in reactive lobbying is more likely to be reflected in secondary legislation and related guidance.

Lobbying in the 1960s and 1970s was characterised by action, rather than reaction. Tireless campaigners like Stanley Segal were ready to challenge prevailing opinion and to pursue the unattainable (see Mittler & Sinason, in press). When, with Peter Mittler, Jack Tizard and others, he first demanded that children with severe learning difficulties should be transferred from junior training centres into schools, the notion was heresy to the educational Establishment. Likewise, the demand for a national inquiry into special educational provision seemed a pipedream in the 1960s. It took sustained lobbying over one to two decades to achieve the goals. The impossible, as everyone knows, takes a little longer.

In contrast, lobbying for SENs has been more reactive than active since the

204 Psychology and Education for Special Needs

passing of the 1981 Education Act. The government has set the agenda, and pressure groups have responded. The relentless flow of bills, Draft Regulations and Circulars has left them breathless in the wake of the DfE, and has taxed their resources sorely. So far, success in influencing policy, though encouraging, has fallen short of hopes.

Although recent exercises in reactive lobbying have raised public awareness of SENs in both government and the public at large, the inner fortress of Conservative education policy has not been breached. Pressure groups have avoided 'banging away at the unattainable' when dealing with primary legislation, and have concentrated on 'areas for manoeuvre round the periphery', as Tench (1994) puts it. While the amendment to the 1993 bill obliging governors to publish details of their schools' policies on SENs was seen as 'significant' (Morris et al., 1993), pressure groups acknowledged that their attempts to introduce other key amendments met with failure or weak compromise. Section 159 on the planning role of LEAs in relation to the Funding Agency for Schools and other schools in the area was so diluted that it imposed no duties at all. However, what begins as a minor amendment on the periphery of legislation can conceivably, through a series of subsequent laws, worm its way closer to the centre of government policy. Some observers see access for the disabled as an example of this process.

It was – as Klaus Wedell has observed – in the secondary legislation, in the Code of Practice and in Circulars that pressure groups were able to leave their footprints recently. The repeated emphasis on consultation among schools in Circular 6/94 (DfE, 1994) and the Code of Practice (DfE & WO, 1994) might otherwise have been missing. Revisions to the Draft Code ensuring, for instance, that the burden on teachers at Stage 1 of the school-based assessment was lightened were made as a result of responses to the DfE's consultation on the Code.

Some possible consequences of successful lobbying

The willingness of government to concede more in secondary legislation and Circulars than on the face of an Act ('face-saving exercise' differently defined?), noted by Miller (1987), can give rise to contradictions in governmental policies. The stress in Circular 6/94 on consultation and, by implication, collaboration (Wedell, 1994) and in Circular 7/91 (DfE, 1991) on the coordinating role of LEAs and on school funding is at odds with the market-forces thrust of the primary legislation. Similarly, the costs of implementing an ambitious Code of Practice, without extra funding, are already causing certain schools to switch some of their resources to the servicing of the Code from the National Curriculum which is one of the central pillars of Conservative educational reforms (Peter, 1994; see also

Forth, 1995). More widely, despite the government's mounting efforts since 1979 to erode the powers of the LEAs with a battering ram of Acts and Regulations, the Education Acts of 1988 and 1993, between them, add a number of new duties for LEAs, especially towards special educational provision. Other examples of contradiction concern LEA funding for support services and coherent and cost-effective planning of special educational provision (Wedell, 1994). Some contradictions are not, of course, to be sniffed at; they can be used creatively. They can also, inadvertently, add to confusion and uncertainty.

Successful lobbying, when it occurs, raises another problem. The greater awareness of special needs issues which the SEC and others have recently succeeded in cultivating in Ministers and senior civil servants may have been at the expense of other deserving minorities and the pressure groups representing them. The difficulty in general is raised by McKenzie (1974): 'There remains,' he writes, 'the problem of the ill organised (or even unorganisable) sections of the community. Is there not a danger that they will be either ignored or trampled upon by the really powerful interest groups?' He sees the ballot box and public opinion polls as safeguards against such dangers, but, in relation to minority groups, neither is likely to be the answer.

The tendency for more powerful pressure groups to win changes in the law, official recognition and resources, at the expense of other deserving minorities, is disturbing. Those representing ethnic minorities, and unsuccessful in winning certain amendments to the 1993 Education Act, have cause to look with envy at the successes of the special needs lobbies. There has also been resentment among organisations run by disabled people at the presumption of others who claim to speak on their behalf. The influence on government policy of associations run by people with no personal experience of having a disability can give rise to hostility, as Oliver (1990) implies. What makes it worse, writes Drake (1994), is that agencies run *by* the disabled have much less funding than those run *for* them. Conversely, ill feelings have arisen among special needs supporters about the success of the dyslexia lobby in gaining what many have seen as a disproportionate share of scarce resources for children with specific learning difficulties. The somewhat closer links which have begun to develop between bodies run by disabled people and those run on their behalf, and between the dyslexia and other special needs organisations, point the way to the cooperation and coordination which will be essential if pressure groups are to become a force to be reckoned with. The Integration Alliance, formed in 1990, is one example of a pressure group which is controlled by disabled people (they constitute just over half of its council of management) but includes member organisations run on behalf of the disabled, like the Centre for Studies in Inclusive Education, and Elfrida Rathbone. In future, active and reactive lobbying will need to be *interactive* too.

Future trends?

Rising expectations – fuelled by such innovations as the Code of Practice, Special Needs Tribunals to deal with parents' extended rights of appeal, and the publication of schools' policies for special educational provision – may contribute to another outbreak of pressure groups. Is it likely, for instance, as Robinson (1994) suggests, that parents' annual meetings with their school governors will turn out to be a breeding ground for new groups dissatisfied with their schools' special provision?

More widely, pressure groups run for and by disabled people appear to be growing in number and activity. The British Council of Disabled People indicates the likely trend. It now has 103 member organisations, compared with only 6 when it was formed in 1981. It echoes the wider, national trend for pressure groups in general to form umbrella organisations (Rush, 1990b). At this very moment, no doubt, a newly-unfurled brolly group is waiting to put its spokes in.

Other causes of the growth of the 'fifth estate', as it has been called, are still potent. Quangos seem set to continue and multiply, unless, of course, Lord Nolan's recent committee of inquiry into standards of conduct among holders of public office persuades the government to practise birth control. At the same time, secondary legislation gathers its own momentum, and a rising generation of civil servants reared under sixteen years of Conservative and interventionist rule are becoming addicted to administering regular fixes. The impact of European Union law is also likely to make itself felt in future. Harmonisation between the way in which children with learning difficulties are dealt with in the UK and their treatment in the courts elsewhere in Europe may be required in future years. There are, for instance, disparities in how France and the UK deal with matters to do with integration (Rabinowicz, 1994) which could become a focus for those campaigning for inclusive education and other civil rights for the disabled. At a world-wide level, exchange of information by pressure groups using Internet will be influential.

Reactive lobbying may soon enter a new phase. As new laws begin to grip and a legislative lull descends – one hopes – upon the education system, many pressure groups are likely to change their role for the time being. They will be monitoring the ways in which the new laws and the Code of Practice are being translated into action, rather than barking at draft legislation and guidance. Act Now, formed to monitor the implementation of the 1986 Disabled Persons Act soon after it was enacted, is an example of a group with this kind of role.

The initiative for active lobbying is likely to pass to disabled people themselves in the immediate future, and to include further direct action. More than ten years ago, Marsh (1983) surmised that direct action could increase as ideologically-based pressure groups in general became disillusioned with their ability to influence policy by more conventional means. The direct action days organised last year by the Integration Alliance, Rights Now, Direct Action Network and others confirm that this trend has already begun to spread to children and adults with disabilities and learning difficulties.

Much will depend on the continuing willingness of people like Klaus Wedell to give their time and energy to pursuing the cause of children with SENs, and on individuals and organisations to provide the financial resources. Successful lobbying does not usually come cheaply. The SEC spent £15,000 on tackling the 1993 Education Bill, through the generosity of the Royal National Institute for the Blind, and IPSEA spent £5,000 on printing, postage and related costs in running its campaign, excluding staff time (Wright, 1994). Neither figure takes account of the many hours given spontaneously, without payment.

Marsh's suggestion that, among pressure groups in general, direct action was likely to increase is becoming a reality. Should it spread even further, London University's outgoing Professor of Educational Psychology and Special Educational Needs may yet be seen taking up a unilateral position on the pavement of Woburn Square. If so, his action may be related only marginally to Section 168 of the 1993 Education Act, but – and not for the first time – he will be making a Statement.

Acknowledgement

The author would like to thank John Fowler, of the Association of Metropolitan Authorities, for his comments on sections of this chapter.

Postscript

I have known Klaus Wedell since 1966 through his contributions to *Special Education* and, subsequently, to the *British Journal of Special Education*, for which he was Chairman of the Editorial Board in 1992–3. We have worked together as members of the monitoring group of SENNAC, the Special Educational Needs National Advisory Council, responding to draft legislation and guidance on special educational provision.

References

Baxter, S. (1994) 'The secret powers of the new persuaders', *The Sunday Times*, 18 September.

Butler, P. (1983) *Politics and Law Making in Special Education*, Discussion Paper 10, Exeter University Research Group.

Charities Digest (1994) London: Family Welfare Association.

Chorley, D. (1993) 'OFSTED prepares for special inspections', *British Journal of Special Education*, 20(4), pp.127–8.

Corlett, S. (1992) 'SKILL: National Bureau for Students with Disabilities', *Contact*, Autumn, pp.23–4.

Davie, R. (1995) 'A consortium for children: Analysis of the dialogue with policy makers leading to the 1993 Education Act and the 1994 Code of Practice', *Therapeutic Care and Education*, 3(3), pp.206–17.

Department for Education (DfE) (1991) *Local Management of Schools: Further Guidance*, Circular 7/91, London: DfE.

Department for Education (DfE) (1992) *Choice and Diversity*, White Paper, London: HMSO.

Department for Education (DfE) (1994) *The Organisation of Special Educational Provision*, Circular 6/94, London: DfE.

Department for Education & Welsh Office (DfE & WO) (1994) *Code of Practice on the Identification and Assessment of Pupils with Special Educational Needs*, London: HMSO.

Department of Education & Science (DES) (1978) *Special Educational Needs: Report of the Committee of Inquiry into the Education of Handicapped Children and Young People* (The Warnock Report), Cmnd 7212, London: HMSO.

Drake, R.F. (1994) 'The exclusion of disabled people from positions of power in British voluntary organisations', *Disability and Society*, 9(4), pp.463–82.

Forth, E. (1995) 'A view from the top', *Special*, 4(1).

Fryd, J. (1969) 'The transfer from health to education service', *Forward Trends*, 13(3), pp.80–4.

Kimber, R. and Richardson, J.J. (1974) 'Introduction', in R. Kimber and J.J. Richardson (eds) *Pressure Groups in Britain*, London: Dent.

Marsh, D. (1983) 'Introduction: Interest groups in Britain, their access and power', in D. Marsh (ed.) *Pressure Politics: Interest Groups in Britain*, London: Junction Books.

McCarthy, M. (1983) 'Child Poverty Action Group: Poor and powerless?', in D. Marsh (ed.) *Pressure Politics: Interest Groups in Britain*, London: Junction Books.

McKenzie, R.T. (1974) 'Parties, pressure groups and the British political process', in R. Kimber and J.J. Richardson (eds) *Pressure Groups in Britain*, London: Dent.

Miller, C . (1987) *Lobbying Government: Understanding and Influencing the Corridors of Power* (1st edn), Oxford: Blackwell.

Mittler, P. & Sinason, V. (eds) (in press) *Changing Policy and Practice for People with Learning Difficulties*, London: Cassell.

Morris, R., Reid, E. & Fowler, J. (1993) *Education Act 93: A Critical Guide*, London: Association of Metropolitan Authorities.

Office for Standards in Education (OFSTED) (1994a) *Framework for the Inspection of Schools*, (amended May 1994), London: HMSO.

Office for Standards in Education (OFSTED) (1994b) *Special units and inspection: Update* (7the issue), March, p.7.

Oliver, M. (1990) *The Politics of Disablement*. Basingstoke: Macmillan.

Peak, S. (ed.) (1992) *The Media Guide, 1993*, London: Guardian Books/Fourth Estate.

Peak, S. (ed.) (1994) *The Media Guide, 1995*, London: Guardian Books/Fourth Estate.

Peter, M. (1994) 'Hazy days for the code breakers', *TES Extra*, 22 October.

Pritchard, D.G. (1963) *Education and the Handicapped*, London: Routledge and Kegan Paul.

Pyke, N. (1993) 'Inspection pledge broken', *The Times Educational Supplement*, 24 December.

Rabinowicz, J. (1994) personal communication.

Robinson, J. (1994) 'The legal framework for SEN provision', unpublished paper delivered at NFER-Nelson training seminar on special needs, held in London.

Rush, M. (1990a) 'Pressure politics', in M. Rush (ed.) *Parliament and Pressure Politics*, Oxford: Clarendon Press.

Rush, M. (1990b) 'Parliament and pressure groups: An overview', in M. Rush (ed.) *Parliament and Pressure Politics*, Oxford; Clarendon Press.

Shipley, P. (1979) *Directory of Pressure Groups and Representative Organisations* (2nd edn), Sevenoaks: Bowker.

Stirling, M. (1992) 'How many pupils are being excluded?', *British Journal of Special Education*, 19(4), pp.129–30.

Tench, D. (1994) unpublished paper delivered at the annual meeting of the Educational Law Association in London, 16 September.

Wedell, K. (1994) 'Conclusions', in I. Lunt and J. Evans (eds) *Allocating Resources for Special Educational Needs Provision*, Stafford: NASEN Enterprises.

Wright, J. (1994) 'From Bill to Act: The passing of the 1993 Education Bill', in P. Potts, F. Armstrong and M. Masterton (eds) *Equality and Diversity in Education 2: National and International Contexts*, London: Routledge.

13 Professional development for special needs education

Peter Mittler

Introduction

The definition of special educational needs (SENs) in the United Kingdom applies to an average of 20 per cent of all children, and is far broader than the 1.5 per cent of children in special schools. More than half of all children who are thought to require 'additional provision' and are given Statements of SEN under the 1981 and 1993 Education Acts are now in ordinary schools.

Since every teacher is likely to be working with pupils with SENs, it follows that the training and education of all teachers must include an introduction to the needs of such pupils and ways in which they may be met in ordinary schools.

The needs of children with SENs overlap with those of an even larger group of 'low-achieving' or 'under-achieving' children, most of whom come from socially and economically disadvantaged backgrounds. The relationship between social disadvantage and educational attainment seems to have become almost a taboo subject not discussed in polite educational circles. But it represents a major challenge for educational planning, classroom practice and teacher education (Mittler, 1993a). At the international level, UNESCO recognises that special needs education is an integral element of the Education for All initiative and of the United Nations Convention on the Rights of Children (UNESCO, 1994).

Implications of new legislation for training

The new *Code of Practice on the Assessment and Identification of Pupils with Special Educational Needs* (DfE & WO, 1994) sets out clear expectations of ways in which all ordinary schools are expected to identify, assess and meet the needs of pupils with learning or behavioural difficulties. Every school is required to develop a clear special needs policy statement, to appoint a special needs coordinator, and to 'have regard to' the guidelines in the Code of Practice on procedures for early identification and intervention.

The implications of the Code of Practice for teacher training are that all teachers must have basic competencies in special needs education, and that those with designated responsibilities for working with pupils with SENs will need additional skills. This includes all school SEN coordinators (SENCOs), members of learning support teams within schools, as well as peripatetic teams of support teachers employed by the Local Education Authority (LEA) or other agencies. It also includes all teachers working in special schools and in special classes and units in ordinary schools.

The Code of Practice has been well received because, for the first time, detailed guidance is given on ways in which ordinary schools should not only identify but seek to meet special needs at an early stage. But their implications for teacher education have so far not been adequately recognised by the government. If children who require 'additional provision beyond that which is generally available' are eligible for additional resources, those who teach them should also have access to additional training to equip and support them in this task. This calls for a radical reappraisal of the whole of initial and post-experience training for all teachers, but particularly those with specific responsibilities for working with pupils with SENs.

Initial teacher education

All courses of initial teacher education (ITE) have for some time been required to include a SEN element to ensure that all new teachers have some degree of awareness of how children with SENs can be identified and supported in gaining access to the curriculum. Training institutions were inspected by Her Majesty's Inspectorate (HMI) to ensure compliance with these requirements. A summary of these requirements and an account of the difficulties experienced in implementing them has been published elsewhere (Mittler, 1992, 1993b) and discussed in greater detail, but these accounts have now been overtaken by new legislation and new challenges.

The Education Act which was approved in 1994, after much debate inside and outside parliament, removed the control and funding of all initial teacher training courses from the Higher Education Funding Council and vested it in a new Teacher Training Agency (TTA) established in September 1994.

In addition, the government has made it clear that it would like to increase the proportion of time which teacher training students spend in schools from the present norm of around 67 per cent in secondary training to as much as 100 per cent in some cases. Schools are being encouraged to set up consortia in order to accept full responsibility for initial teacher training and will be provided with the fees which would normally go to the training institution. They are allowed to offer such training without the support of higher education, if that is their choice. But they can also contract with higher education to provide certain elements of training.

The new proposals differ radically from existing practice which is based on a real partnership between schools and higher education, with a much greater role being played by schools in the selection of students and in training in classroom and pedagogic skills than in the past.

How will universities or schools (with or without university input) be able to provide an adequate SEN element in future, now that an increasing proportion of training will be school-based? It is not enough to observe 'good SEN practice' in schools, even where it exists (and HMI reports suggest that good practice is not all that common). Students need opportunities to read and think critically about what constitutes good practice, and to be exposed to staff with interests and experience in this area.

It is not clear how the time can be found for universities to continue to provide a special needs element in initial training, or how schools can do so on their own. Students undertaking their training in schools will be entirely dependent on the quality of special needs provision in those schools. Since HMI and research reports are critical of the quality of such provision at the present time, it is hard to have confidence in the new arrangements. It also remains to be seen whether the new Teacher Training Agency will ensure that all training courses develop a special needs element.

At Manchester University, a *Special Needs Resource Pack* has been written as an exercise in a version of 'distance education' for secondary students who will have only limited courses with their tutors in a 36-week course, only 12 of which will be spent in the university (Farrell, 1993). The pack includes specific tasks and exercises for them to carry out in the university, in schools and in private study, as well as introductory notes and materials. In addition, all students are still required to spend two weeks in a special needs placement.

Three complementary approaches to providing the SEN element in initial teacher training have been identified (Mittler, 1992):

- *permeation* – in which a special needs element is included as an integral element of all theoretical and practical courses and experiences
- *focused* – in which attention is concentrated on special needs issues during a course of lectures, seminars or practical experiences
- *optional* – in which students have an opportunity to study aspects of

special needs practice in greater depth.

An early evaluation by HMI (1990) drew attention to the problems of relying too greatly on the 'permeation' approach delivered by mainstream ITE tutors and stressed the need for both 'focused' and 'optional' elements provided by specialist tutors. A detailed report and guidelines were also prepared by the Council for National Academic Awards (CNAA, 1991) which validated all teacher education courses in the public sector, but which has since been abolished.

Despite these courses, the HMI surveys of the *New Teacher in School* (e.g. OFSTED, 1993b) regularly report that new teachers feel inadequately prepared to teach low-achieving children.

Continuing Professional Development

Given the problems of providing an adequate SEN element to ITE students, what are the prospects of doing so within the framework of Continuing Professional Development (CPD)?

Induction

With the abolition of the probationary period, it is more than ever important that the process of induction, whether provided by schools or LEAs, should pay particular attention to ways of supporting new teachers in working with pupils with SENs. A report on induction by HMI (1992a) suggests that this is not receiving enough attention. Now that universities are becoming more involved in supporting induction, there is an opportunity to ensure that SEN issues are addressed.

Government grants for in-service training

Up to the 1980s, government funding for post-experience training was provided from a central pool of funds. In 1983, special needs was one of only four initial priorities identified by the Department of Education and Science (DES) in its scheme of earmarked in-service funding, then totalling around £7 million. The total sum available for 1993/4 is now £320 million, of which 60 per cent is provided by the Department for Education (DfE), with the balance to be found by LEAs. £10 million is available for all SEN training, compared with £180 million for training on National Curriculum, assessment and information technology.

During the early 1980s, SEN training funds were allocated to specific national SEN priorities. These included one-term courses for designated teachers in ordinary schools (the SENIOS course); post-experience qualifying courses for teachers of hearing-impaired and visually-impaired children (for which there is still a mandatory requirement), and courses for teachers of children with severe learning difficulties, as well as professional training for educational psychologists. Other areas were regarded as 'local priorities' for which LEAs had to assume a greater share of the costs.

At first, the earmarking of training funds and the setting of national and local priorities had a beneficial effect, since it was designed to encourage a planned approach to the identification of staff development needs at the level of the LEA, the school and individual members of staff. From the mid-1980s, however, what started as a promising government initiative has disintegrated in response to lack of LEA resources, both human and financial.

Furthermore, the policy of delegating budgets to schools, while welcome in some respects, has left little or no money for staff development. Certainly, the sums available make it impossible for schools to second a staff member for advanced courses, even on a part-time basis. In addition to the cost of fees, schools still have to find the replacement costs of teachers absent from school on training courses, even for one day.

The DfE has since exacerbated the problem by providing only a lump sum for all SEN training, and abolishing funding for local priorities altogether, leaving LEAs and schools to determine their own priorities. As a result, many of one-term SENIOS courses, as well as full-time and part-time courses for specialist teachers of sensorily and intellectually-impaired children, are under-subscribed and becoming unviable. The only exception is a small sum earmarked for courses of teachers of 'deaf/blind' children – an exception almost certainly due to persistent lobbying by the appropriate voluntary organisation.

We now have a major crisis of teacher supply on our hands, which the government has until now steadfastly refused to acknowledge. This arises in large measure from the decision made in 1985 to phase out specialist initial training courses for students wishing to work with children with sensory or intellectual impairments.

An HMI (1992b) national report shows that, in 1986, over 200 new teachers from 11 four-year full-time BEd courses qualified to work with pupils with severe learning difficulties. By 1991, only 35 new entrants qualified by an in-service route, and it was estimated that only 15 teachers would gain a specialist qualification in this field in 1994. Similarly, only 101 teachers obtained a specialist qualification in the education of hearing-impaired children in 1992, compared to the officially estimated target of between 140 and 160 needed to replace normal losses.

The same survey provides information on virtually all the specialist award-bearing courses available in the field of hearing impairment (HI), visual impairment (VI) and severe learning difficulties (HMI, 1992b). It includes the following conclusions:

- All HI and VI and three-quarters of severe learning difficulty courses provided satisfactory or better training and preparation. The standard of teaching was generally good.
- All VI courses had recruited their full numbers, but recruitment to HI courses had fallen by 20 per cent in two years.
- Eight of the 12 severe learning difficulty courses were under-subscribed, and most of their course members were already teaching in severe learning difficulty schools. The majority of students were over 35, with over ten years' previous teaching experience.

A separate national review of all government-supported training carried out by HMI between April 1991 and April 1992 specifically noted the low priority given in ordinary schools to training in the field of SENs (OFSTED, 1993a).

Opportunities for more experienced teachers

As initial teacher education moves increasingly out of higher education and into schools, opportunities for CPD for all teachers become even more important.

The story of the gradual attrition of opportunities for teachers to study for award-bearing courses is too well known to require retelling. What has not emerged, however, is a coherent policy for staff development for teachers. Long courses have been replaced by a large number of short one-day training events, mostly based in schools and delivered by other teachers and by advisers. A large number of training days have been directly targeted on the National Curriculum and the assessment arrangements. These include the five days a year 'non-contact days' which can be devoted to training, usually within the school.

At the same time, the advent of modularisation has further eroded opportunities for specialisation. Most Diplomas and MEd degree courses are now 'generic', rather than categorical. While this has undoubted advantages in laying broader foundations in special needs issues 'across the board', the advent of modular courses makes it difficult to assess the extent to which teachers have made a detailed and in-depth study of one or more areas of special needs provision.

In the past, proposals for new award-bearing courses had to be approved by the DES, who usually sought the advice of HMI, who in turn provided helpful and constructive advice – for example on the content of the course, the balance between theory and practice, aims, objectives and methods. Such quality control is no longer available, partly because the size of the inspectorate has been drastically reduced, and partly because those who are left are largely concerned with school inspection.

Distance education

Another response of universities to the gradual disappearance of one-year full-time courses has taken the form of the production of distance education courses. Potts (in press) describes the well-established and highly successful work of the Open University, which as been active in this field for over twenty years. Other universities are also producing distance education versions of their existing Diploma and MEd modules. Some of these distance courses are designed for use within the UK itself, particularly for teachers working with visually- and hearing-impaired pupils and those with severe learning difficulties. Others are designed for students working overseas, particularly those in developing countries.

Training designated teachers in ordinary schools

A welcome and successful initiative took the form of one-term courses specifically for 'teachers with designated responsibilities for pupils with SENs in ordinary schools'. With the aim of helping experienced teachers to become agents of change in their own school, course members typically spent three days in higher education and two days back in their schools. By 1986, 25 such courses were running, and even in 1988, the DES was expecting all teachers with designated SEN responsibilities to undergo such training eventually. The planning and delivery of the courses provided opportunities for a distinctive partnership between higher education, an LEA adviser, the headteacher and the seconded teacher. The students were supported in the development of a whole-school approach and in the management of change.

An independent evaluation by the National Foundation for Educational Research (Hegarty & Hodgson, 1988) of these 25 one-term SENIOS courses suggested that they had a considerable impact on schools, particularly where the headteachers were already committed to change and where management of change was well planned and resourced. The report provides many examples of innovations which could be directly attributed to the courses.

Given this promising start, it is a great pity that these courses are now withering on the vine, largely due to the inability of LEAs to fund their share of the costs. Some of the courses are now taught on the basis of one half-day or evening a week, but with greatly depleted numbers. The partnership with LEAs has eroded with the disappearance of specialist advisers and the demands of inspection.

Opportunities for support teachers

One of the distinctive features of special needs practice in the UK can be found in the work of peripatetic teams of teachers who visit groups of schools in order to support teachers working with pupils with SENs. Learning support teams have until now been based on and funded by LEAs; some areas of specialisation have been developed, such as support of children with sensory or physical impairments, those with specific learning difficulties, or pupils with emotional or behavioural difficulties. Their work complements that of teachers in mainstream schools with designated responsibilities for pupils with SEN.

With the devolution of funding to schools and a reduced role for LEAs, there are uncertainties about how support services are to be funded in the future and the extent to which schools will wish to pay for their services. But if support services are to remain an LEA responsibility, how and from whom will they receive further training? What should be the content of courses?

It is obviously vital that support teachers should have access to courses which are related to their distinctive needs over and above those available to all teachers. In particular, they need preparation and support in respect of their consultancy and negotiation roles, and in the skills involved in working with other adults, including those in senior management positions whose support for their work is vital.

A detailed report by Blythman (1985) documents the development of a nation-wide Diploma in Learning Difficulties in Scotland; 40 per cent of the course content was specifically concerned with preparation for such consultancy and support work in ordinary schools.

Staff of special schools

Staff working in special schools include not only teachers but nursery nurses and classroom assistants, now collectively known as 'special support assistants'. In addition, there is a need for joint courses with speech therapists, physiotherapists and other health practitioners such as doctors and nurses, as well as educational psychologists, educational social workers, careers officers and specialist advisory teachers and curriculum specialists. There is a strong argument for much more joint training, not only with other professionals but also with governors and parents. Traditionally, teachers in special schools had access to a wide range of full-time Diploma and MEd courses, or their part-time equivalents. Some of these provided mandatory qualifications. But recruitment to these courses dropped by two-thirds in a single year, as a direct result of the funding changes introduced by the government around 1986. The training imperatives introduced by the 1988 Education Reform Act, the introduction of the 'non-contact' days and the need for short school-based and skill-based courses marked the demise of the long course in its traditional form. As a result, hardly any teachers now have the opportunity to undertake an advanced course leading to a Diploma or MEd or research degree, even on a part-time basis. As a nation, we are failing to provide advanced courses of professional development and research training for the next generation of teachers.

In addition to training in all aspects of the National Curriculum, assessment arrangements, individual planning, financial management, and so on, teachers in special schools also require support in working with colleagues in ordinary schools and in promoting, managing and, above all, in sustaining change in both special and ordinary schools. They have much to contribute to their colleagues in ordinary schools in relation to curriculum planning and modification, devising a small-steps approach to helping pupils access the programmes of study and attainment targets of the National Curriculum assessment and record-keeping, individual educational planning, behavioural methods and management, aspects of microtechnology and working with parents. They also have much to teach each other about ways of supporting integration, the obstacles encountered, and how they might be overcome. At the same time, they themselves will need support in adult learning, consultancy and negotiating skills, and in familiarising themselves with the many changes which are taking place in primary and secondary schools.

Evaluation of Diploma courses

Although it is unlikely that such courses will be reinstated, it is worth noting the results of a national evaluation of all specialist Diploma courses being provided by higher education in 1984/5, carried out by the National Foundation for Educational Research (NFER), the last year in which such courses were provided in their traditional form.

This is provided in a full report by Dust (1988). The study involved 46 training institutions providing 37 full-time and 37 part-time courses for a total of 636 students, of whom half were from special and half from ordinary schools. Fifty-nine courses were generic, covering several areas of specific SENs, including those encountered in ordinary schools. Data were obtained from 102 tutors, 99 of whom had experience of teaching in ordinary as well as special schools and were also involved in initial teacher education in higher education.

Dust's evaluation provides a detailed analysis of the content of the courses, including theory and practice and the extent to which they sought to prepare students to manage and sustain change in their own schools. Most students have placement experiences in a range of schools other than their own. Unfortunately, no information is provided on the extent to which what was learned on the course had an impact on the teachers, the schools or the pupils they taught.

Contexts for change

Despite this sad catalogue of failed initiatives and missed opportunities, there are nevertheless a number of sources of positive pressures for change which could result in more clearly-articulated demands for staff development. We can consider these under a number of headings.

National contexts

- The 1993 Education Act includes an amendment which will make it mandatory for every ordinary school to develop, implement and publicise its special needs policy and practice. This will also need to list the names of all staff with responsibilities for pupils with SEN. Parents and prospective parents, governors and LEA and other advisers will wish to enquire about the opportunities for professional development available to all staff in the school, particularly the SENCOs and what qualifications for work with pupils with SEN are available to staff.
- Inspections of SEN provision in both ordinary and special schools by OFSTED, which has replaced HMI as the new inspectorate, will also include an assessment of the extent to which schools plan and provide for staff development. These and other inspections will, in turn, identify staff development needs and generate demand for relevant courses.

'Recognised' and 'mandatory' qualifications

The recommendation for a mandatory qualification for all teachers with a 'defined responsibility for children with SEN' was made as long ago as 1954, but is still far from implementation, except in the case of teachers working in schools and units for children with sensory impairments, who must gain a relevant specialist qualification within three years.

For all other teachers, a decision in principle needs to be taken about the definition and status of 'recognised qualifications' in special needs education. Clearly, there is a strong case that all teachers with significant responsibilities for pupils with SENs should have an 'appropriate' qualification.

For most teachers, this will, in practice, consist of a number of modules concerned with special needs education, and may lead to an award which reflects the emphasis of the course of study as a whole on SENs. But in many cases, teachers may be studying for a general dipEd or MEd course which provides a wide range of student choice of modules, including one or two in special needs. It is a moot point whether such generic courses with only a small special needs component can be regarded as a 'recognised qualification in special educational needs', unless, for example, a dissertation or other evidence of specialisation in this area is also included.

Research

Research in special needs has not been well-supported since the mid-1980s, when the government funded three major projects in SEN provision from the NFER and the Universities of London and Manchester. One of these (Robson et al., 1988) and part of a second (Hegarty & Moses, 1988) were specifically concerned with teacher education. These projects developed a range of approaches for evaluating the effectiveness of courses, including case studies, interviews and questionnaires. Brief reference has also been made to evaluations of staff development initiatives; a useful summary has recently been edited by Upton (1991), updating an earlier compendium by Sayer and Jones (1985).

Despite the lack of interest in funding, disseminating or using research, universities can still make a significant contribution by providing support and supervision to teachers and students who wish to undertake their own investigations (Vulliamy & Webb, 1992; O'Hanlon, 1992). By this means, the tradition of critical evaluation and impartial enquiry may be kept alive at a time when it appears to be under threat.

Content of training

The time has now come to try to reach a national consensus on the nature and scope of the knowledge, skills, understanding and attitudes that would constitute an acceptable advanced qualification for staff with significant responsibilities for pupils with SENs. This task is now being attempted by the Special Needs Training Consortium, under the chairmanship of Klaus Wedell. What follows are some preliminary considerations which might inform such a task.

The concept of competencies

We can broaden the concept of *competencies* to include:

- knowledge
- understanding
- skills.

In addition, *attitudes* may be considered to be an additional component of competency. Although attitudes cannot be 'taught or trained', they need to be addressed because attitudes are critical in affecting training outcomes for teachers and therefore for pupils and parents.

How effective is training?

A distinction needs to be drawn between *competence* and *performance*, or between the *content* of a course and the *use* to which it is put in practice. This implies assessment in the workplace, perhaps through the process of teacher appraisal or follow-up by the course-providers, where this is not the school or service itself.

This in turn raises questions about the mode and place of delivery of courses. One advantage of school-based courses is that implementation issues are usually considered from the outset, and the framework for evaluation of course effectiveness already exists. Nevertheless, there are not many published examples of such course evaluations. This suggests a need for teachers to become more skilled and more confident in the evaluation of course effectiveness.

Difficulty or failure in applying what has been learned is not always the fault of the individual. Its origins can often be sought in the organisation itself or in the obstacles to implementation created by individuals in the organisation. For this reason, 'management of change' and an understanding of institutional resistance to change are essential elements of any staff development programme.

Training 'beyond that which is generally available'?

The existing lists of initial competencies derived from CATE and from DfE Circular 9/92 are usefully grouped under a series of headings, but they are vague and non-specific where SEN competencies are concerned. For example, Circular 9/92 (DfE, 1992) refers only to the ability to *identify* SENs, while the accompanying CATE Circular (1992) makes no direct reference to SENs at all.

With the demise of CATE and the still unknown role of the Teacher Training Agency in this field, it seems necessary to make a fresh start by seeking to define a series of competencies and content areas which all teachers will need in delivering high-quality teaching to all pupils, and to those with SENs in particular.

We can draw on earlier attempts to define areas of knowledge and skill required at different levels of responsibility. But it will probably be necessary to redefine these in the light of recent and developing practice and legislation.

The appendix (p. 227) summarises an extract from some detailed *Guidelines Leading to Awards at Level 2 (Diploma in Special Educational Needs)*, published by the Scottish Committee for Staff Development in Education (SCOSDE, 1990). These distinguish between core learning outcomes and specialist pathways for specific needs, such as visual impairment, hearing impairment, severe learning difficulties, moderate learning disabilities, emotional and behavioural disorders, etc.

Training needs of SENCOs

How relevant is the core component of the SCOSDE Guidelines to SENCOs? In what respect do SENCOs have different and distinctive training needs from those of external learning support teams?

In view of the key role to be played by SENCOs and members of learning support teams, we should particularly seek to define the distinctive training needs of these groups and come to some agreement on competencies which are regarded as essential to their roles and functions.

A distinction might be drawn between reactions to the list in principle and the practical constraints of finding the human, financial and time resources to teach it. If it seems ambitious in today's context, can the essential elements of such a prescription be extracted?

Training needs of specialist teachers

Although the training needs of SENCOs and learning support teams will probably be seen to be a high priority by government, LEAs and funding agencies, the needs of teachers in special schools, classes and units are equally pressing. Fortunately, these needs are now being addressed by the monitoring groups.

Conclusions

It is essential that all professional staff with a responsibility for meeting the needs of pupils with SENs should have access to opportunities to update their knowledge, skills and experience. The argument of this chapter has been that such opportunities have been undermined, rather than enhanced, and that such training as has been available has been *ad hoc* and short-term. Nevertheless, despite problems of funding and the reduced role of LEAs, there is a more urgent need than ever to develop a strategic approach to staff development in special schools, classes and support services. This can be achieved through clusters of schools working together and sharing ideas and resources.

The implementation of the Code of Practice and the 1993 Education Act, as well as other legislation such as the 1989 Children Act, requires a massive programme of staff development. This needs to provide relevant and appropriate courses for all levels of staff, from newly-qualified teachers to all teachers in the system, including headteachers of all our schools, principals and senior staff of colleges of further education, members of support services, educational psychologists, school governors, staff of health and social service departments and voluntary organisations. The first priority should be the SENCOs which are required in every school (Mittler, 1994).

There is now a lively debate on the nature and level of the knowledge, skills and understanding required of all teachers in the system, but especially those with clearly-designated and sometimes specific responsibilities for pupils with SENs. At the time of writing, it is not clear whether the government itself will provide leadership in this area – for example by setting up a staff development study group which will make recommendations to the field – or whether it will commission others to do so.

The matter is too urgent and the crisis of teacher education too acute to justify further delay. The time is ripe for action.

Acknowledgements

This chapter is a shortened and updated version of a longer discussion paper, *Teacher Education for Special Educational Needs*, prepared for the series Policy Options for Special Educational Needs in the 1990s, published in 1993 by the National Association for Special Educational Needs, and an adapted version of a chapter prepared for P. Mittler and P. Daunt (eds) *Teacher Education for Special Needs in Europe*, published by Cassell Educational Ltd in 1995.

Postscript

Klaus Wedell and I were two of only six undergraduates completing the Psychology course at Cambridge University in 1953. Both of us were 'European refugees' who had grown up in England during the war.

Oliver Zangwill had just taken over the chair vacated by the legendary Sir Frederic Bartlett and gave a series of lectures on psychology and individual differences, during the course of which he never established eye contact with anyone, but which must have influenced both of us. I then trained as a clinical psychologist in Oxford, and again encountered Oliver Zangwill as a clinician at the National Hospital Queen Square, where his skills as a diagnostician were the envy of many neurologists, though I never learnt the secret of how he could locate a brain lesion by studying the patient's drawing of a bicycle. Klaus began to study visual perceptual skills of children with cerebral palsy at the very time when I became the father of such a child.

Our next series of encounters was on the British Psychological Society (BPS) working party which was established to give evidence to the Warnock Committee. Klaus was a key member of that group, and his characteristic voice and views can be clearly traced in the BPS report and in the documents which followed the endless consultation process and the early drafts of the legislation.

It was clear that we had a joint interest in the process of policy formulation and implementation and both enjoyed lobbying civil servants and Ministers. In the 1970s, I concentrated on the Department of Health in relation to my interest in learning disabilities, while Klaus focused with great effect on the then DES.

Klaus has never confined himself to advocacy and lobbying, but has always based his arguments on research findings, either his own or those of others. He co-directed a series of policy-related research studies on the operation and implementation of the 1981 Education Act; these led straight to the two influential Audit Commission reports, and from there to Part 3 of the 1993 Education Act.

The full extent of Klaus's influence on that Act and on the *Code of Practice on the Identification and Assessment of Pupils with Special Educational Needs* can probably never be precisely established, because he was a member of several groups and teams that worked closely with an exceptionally able and receptive group of officials. But there can be no doubt about the major impact of his persuasive arguments, backed by data and underpinned by his knowledge of day-to-day practice in the field and by his skills in informed advocacy.

It was Klaus's conviction that new initiatives in policy must be matched by a new approach to staff development that brought us together on the Special Educational Needs Training Consortium, a mixed group of providers and consumers of training, chaired by Klaus. This group has now received a small grant from the DfE to examine the training needs of teachers working with pupils with SENs; I am chairing a representative working group which will prepare a report which, we hope, will contribute to the development of more coherent national and local strategies for staff development.

References

Blythman, M. (1985) 'National Initiatives: The Scottish Experience', in J. Sayer and N. Jones (eds) *Teacher Training and Special Educational Needs*, London: Croom Helm.

Council for the Accreditation of Teacher Education (CATE) (1992) *The Accreditation of Initial Teacher Training under Circular 9/92*, London: CATE.

Council for National Academic Awards (CNAA) (1991) *Review of Special Educational Needs in Initial and Inservice Teacher Education Courses*, London: CNAA.

Department for Education (DfE) (1992) *Initial Teacher Training (Secondary Phase) Circular 9/92*, London: DfE.

Department for Education & Welsh Office (DfE & WO) (1994) *Code of Practice on the Identification and Assessment of Special Educational Needs*, London: HMSO.

Dust, K. (1988) 'The Diploma Courses', in S. Hegarty and D. Moses (eds) *Developing Expertise: Inset for Special Educational Needs*, Windsor: NFER-Nelson.

Farrell, P. (1993) 'A Special Needs Resource Pack for Secondary PGCE Students', School of Education, University of Manchester (unpublished).

Hegarty, S. & Hodgson, A. (1988) 'The One Term Courses', in S. Hegarty and D. Moses (eds) *Developing Expertise: Inset for Special Educational Needs*, Windsor: NFER-Nelson.

Hegarty, S. & Moses, D. (eds) (1988) *Developing Expertise: Inset for Special Educational Needs*, Windsor: NFER-Nelson.

Her Majesty's Inspectorate (HMI) (1990) *Special Educational Needs in Initial Teacher Training*, London: DES.

Her Majesty's Inspectorate (HMI) (1992a) *The Induction and Probation of New Teachers*, London: DES.

Her Majesty's Inspectorate (HMI) (1992b) *Survey Inspections of Specialist Training Courses in England and Wales for Teachers Intending to Teach Hearing-impaired Pupils, Visually-Impaired Pupils and Pupils with Severe Learning Difficulties (1990–1991)*, London: DES.

Mittler, P. (1992) 'Preparing all initial teacher training students to teach children with special educational needs: A case study from England', *European Journal of Special Needs Education*, 7, pp.1–10.

Mittler, P. (1993a) 'Children with special educational needs', in G. Verma and P. Pumfrey (eds), *Cross-curricular Contexts: Themes and Dimensions in Secondary Schools*, London: Falmer Press.

Mittler, P. (1993b) *Teacher Education for Special Educational Needs*, Policy Options Paper 3, Stafford: National Association for Special Educational Needs.

Mittler, P. (1994) 'A post-code address',*The Times Educational Supplement*, 13 May.

O'Hanlon, C. (1992) 'Action research in special education', *European Journal of Special Needs Education*, 7, pp.204–18.

Office for Standards in Education (OFSTED) (1993a) *The New Teacher in School: 1992*, London: OFSTED.

Office for Standards in·Education (OFSTED) (1993b) *The Management and Provision of Inservice Training Funded by the Grant for Education and Support*, London: OFSTED.

Potts, P. (in press) 'Inclusive teacher education in Europe: An open learning approach', in P. Mittler and P. Daunt (eds) *Special Needs Teacher Education in Europe*, London: Cassell.

Robson, C., Sebba, J., Mittler, P. & Davies, G. (1988) *Inservice Training and Special Educational Needs: Running Short, School-focused Courses*, Manchester University Press.

Sayer, J. & Jones, N. (eds) (1985) *Teacher Training and Special Educational Needs*,

London: Croom Helm.

UNESCO (1994) *The Salamanca Statement and Framework for Action*, Paris: UNESCO.

Upton, G. (1991) 'Issues and trends in staff training', in G. Upton (ed.) *Teacher Training and Special Educational Needs*, London: David Fulton.

Vulliamy, G. & Webb, R. (eds) (1992) *Teacher Research and Special Educational Needs*, London: David Fulton.

Scottish Committee for Staff Development in Education (SCOSDE) (1990) Guidelines for Awards at Level 2, Edinburgh: Scottish Education Department.

Appendix

Extract from Scottish Committee for Staff Development in Education *Guidelines Leading to Awards at Level 2 (Diploma in Special Educational Needs* (SCOSDE, 1990)

Four thirty-hour modules are envisaged for the core, involving the following areas of knowledge and skill (abbreviated).

Knowledge

a) Evolving concept of special educational needs and the historical, legal and contemporary framework in which it operates;
b) curriculum principles;
c) educational systems and how they can affect opportunities for learning;
d) barriers to learning – curricular, psychological and sociological factors;
e) cooperation with parents, colleagues, school boards and the wider community.

Skills

Demonstrate the beginnings of competence in:

a) analysis of curriculum delivery and learning situations;
b) applying principles of assessment to learning situations;
c) identifying and developing appropriate strategies for planning, implementing and evaluating curricular responses either through effecting change in the attitudes and practices of individuals and institutions or in direct teaching arrangements;
d) collaborative approaches to supporting effective learning;
e) establishing good relationships with parents and the wider community.

Attitudes that reflect:

a) a commitment to the belief that the aims of education are the same for all learners;
b) a willingness to view the whole range of special educational needs within its wider context;
c) an acceptance of corporate responsibility in formulating and implementing adequate responses to meeting special needs;
d) an understanding of the needs of parents and other carers.

14 Klaus Wedell: An appreciation

Ingrid Lunt and Brahm Norwich

Introduction

Klaus Wedell has held a place of national and international importance in the field of special educational needs (SENs) and professional psychology for many years. He exemplifies what many of those of us working in the field aspire towards – a substantial, coherent and lasting impact on policy, and hence a contribution to the benefit of individuals. He draws on a powerful combination of qualities of intellectual rigour, humanity and integrity with political shrewdness and untiring industry.

Klaus has made a substantial and positive impact on services and practice for children with special needs, including professional psychological services and teachers and other professionals in the field. This he achieves through powerful and well-founded conceptual analysis and an ability to get to the heart of problems and issues. His influence on many colleagues with whom he has worked continues to be strong, deriving as it does from an encouraging and positive approach, combined with a modest and self-effacing manner, and a respect and valuing of others' views and contributions. His qualities of energy, idealism and moral commitment have inspired many, and the field of special needs has benefited enormously from his leadership.

Background, career interests and chapter contributions

Klaus was born in Düsseldorf, Germany, and came with his mother and three siblings to England when he was 7 years old. The family moved around frequently during the early years in England, and Klaus finally went to King's College, Cambridge, where he studied Psychology from 1950 to 1953. At Cambridge, he was able to combine study in the disciplines of philosophy and psychology; these disciplines have informed his work over the past forty years in the fields of applied psychology and SEN.

He moved to Bristol in 1955, where he carried out research for his doctorate on the perceptuo-motor problems of children with cerebral palsy. Following his PhD, Klaus worked as a research psychologist in a psychiatric hospital near Bristol. His PhD and the work carried out over the next few years led to his book *Learning and Perceptuo-motor Disabilities in Children*, which was published in 1973 (Wedell, 1973). This work led to Klaus's lifelong interest in and commitment to the field of SENs, initially through a detailed interest in the factors within children which led to difficulties in learning, and the ways in which these could be remedied. Chapter 3 by Sheila Henderson describes the contribution of this early work, discusses subsequent work and considers some of the issues facing this field of work today. Klaus has also had a long-standing interest in the area of specific learning difficulties. Peter Pumfrey's Chapter 4 presents the situation faced by pupils with specific learning difficulties and the challenges that these children pose to those who make provision for SEN.

Klaus moved in 1959 to become an educational psychologist, initially in Bristol until 1964. While there he set up a unit for hearing-impaired children which is still going strong. He was also involved in setting up a unit for children with language impairment, a point made by Jannet Wright in Chapter 5. During this period, Klaus was concerned to make provision for children with disabilities and to ensure that attempts were made to remedy these difficulties, or to compensate for their areas of deficit. In 1964, Klaus moved to Hull to become a senior educational psychologist, and from there to Birmingham, eventually to take up the post of Course Director to the Professional Educational Psychology training course at Birmingham University.

Two of Klaus's past trainee educational psychologists contribute to this book. In Chapter 8 by Peter Farrell we can trace Klaus's influence on the profession of educational psychology. As Chair of the Division of Educational and Child Psychology of the British Psychological Society, Klaus gave evidence to the Warnock Committee and co-authored a report on psychological services for children (Wedell & Lambourne, 1980). During his time in Birmingham, Klaus was involved in the training of over a hundred educational psychologists, and substantially influenced the educational psychology practice, particularly in the psychological services of the Midlands. It was at this time that Klaus became interested in the application of behavioural psychology, and in particular in strategies of task analysis and individual programme planning in order to enable children with SEN to make progress. The course for educational psychologists at Birmingham University became renowned for the development of curriculum-based assessment and strategies based on the application of principles of behavioural psychology to improve children's learning. A parallel interest at this time in screening and early identification is described in Chapter 2 by Geoff Lindsay, with whom Klaus worked and whose PhD on this theme he supervised. At that time, Klaus's interest in the problems of identification and prediction encouraged the development of screening tests in order to pick up children with learning difficulties as early as possible, and to devise learning programmes for them.

The move to London in 1979 to the newly-established professorial chair in Educational Psychology (Children with Special Educational Needs) coincided with developments in policy and provision in relation to SEN with the publication of the Warnock Report (DES, 1978) and the work towards the new legislation of the 1981 Education Act. This coincided, too, with Klaus's move away from his more psychological interests towards a growing interest in SEN policy and curriculum.

Following the implementation of the legislation in 1983, Klaus was commissioned by the DES to lead and co-direct a major research project evaluating the implementation of the 1981 Act. This work led to the book *Policy and Provision for Special Educational Needs* (Goacher et al., 1988). Jennifer Evans, the research officer from that project, describes some of its work in Chapter 9. This research project was followed by a further DES-funded research and development project looking at dissemination of good practice, which led to a widely-used resource and training pack, *Decision Making for Special Educational Needs* (Evans et al., 1989). At about this time, the government made available additional resources for the training of teachers of SEN through its one-term in-service courses set up under DES Circular 3/83 (DES, 1983). Klaus's interest in teacher training led him to set up a successful programme of these courses at the Institute of Education, and this interest in teacher training persists to this day through his contribution both to the PGCE courses and to other in-service courses, both in local educational authorities and at the Institute. Peter Mittler picks up these very important issues in Chapter 13, where he considers the future of teacher training in relation to SEN.

Following the implementation of the 1981 Act, the Inner London Education Authority reviewed its provision for pupils with SEN and set up a committee chaired by John Fish, of which Klaus was a member (ILEA, 1985). One of the key recommendations of the Fish Report was the formation of 'cluster' groups of schools which would serve the SEN of pupils in a local community and which would coordinate services and work towards continuity by sharing some resources and by collaborating over this area. Klaus became enthusiastic about this idea, developing some work with a group of schools locally in Camden, and obtaining an ESRC grant to collaborate with colleagues on a research project to study clusters in relation to SEN. Two colleagues from this project, Brahm Norwich and Ingrid Lunt, have presented some of its findings and discuss issues of inter-school collaboration in Chapter 10.

In the mid-1980s, before the introduction of the National Curriculum, the DES was interested in the attainments of the 'lower 40 per cent' of pupils. Klaus took this opportunity to propose a project concerned with the curriculum for pupils with moderate learning difficulties. This led to the DES funding a major research project, directed by Klaus, looking at curriculum modification practices in special and ordinary schools. One outcome of this project was the production of an important training resource, *Pathways to Progress* (Evans et al., 1990). Two colleagues from the project, Judith Ireson and Peter Evans, present some aspects of this work in Chapter 6. This project reflects some shifts in Klaus's thinking. Although his model of 'compensatory interaction' (Wedell & Lindsay, 1980) has informed his work in the field over the past twenty years, there have been significant shifts in formulation and conceptualisation. His early concerns with more psychological aspects of individual children's needs and difficulties have made way for a greater focus, both on the interaction between factors in the child – initially through the applications of behavioural psychology – and more recently, a concern with the curriculum and ways in which this may be modified to meet needs. In Chapter 7, Harry Daniels presents some of the issues involved in individual teaching strategies.

Throughout his time in London, Klaus has been involved in overseas initiatives, many through academic and research contacts, and some through more formal channels. Work for UNESCO led to a study of approaches to teacher training for SEN in 14 countries (Bowman, 1986). He has acted as a consultant to the OECD since the mid-1980s, and was involved in the formation by the European Community of a European network on integration. Some of these aspects are covered in Chapter 11 by Peter Evans on international special education.

Over the past ten years, Klaus's interests in the political process and in lobbying have developed into a passion. He became tirelessly involved in the consultations in relation to the 1988 Education Reform Act, in particular on the National Curriculum and its impact on pupils with SEN, and was a key member of the Special Needs Consortium which lobbied successfully through the passage of the 1993 Education Act. Margaret Peter's Chapter 12 vividly captures some of the work of this group. The current difficulties in resourcing SENs, brought about by the legislative developments such as Local Management of Schools and by financial constraints at both local and national level in education, have meant more pressure from individual parents and schools and from national voluntary and lobby groups. Klaus has been active in attempting to coordinate some of these efforts through his involvement in lobbying and through his travels round the country giving keynote lectures and support to a range of groups.

Significance of his approach and interests

We have mentioned Klaus's many positive personal qualities, his encouraging and positive attitudes, his moral commitment and his energy. These all link with his considerable standing in the field and his impact on practice and on those who have worked with him and been his students. But a major aspect of his approach has been his commitment and interest in thorough conceptual analysis of the matters under consideration. This getting to the root of matters has been a hallmark of his intellectual approach to his original interests in educational psychology and to his more recent interests in special educational policy and curriculum matters.

Klaus's intellectual interests have been strongly influenced by his appreciation that practice depends critically on thorough conceptual understanding of the field under consideration. In this sense, he has been a living example of Kurt Lewin's principle that there is nothing so practical as a good theory. In this approach, theory – or 'conceptualisation', as he has often referred to it – acts as a tool with which to do a job, or a map to represent one's position and plan a journey. This is an instrumental view of concepts and theory, one associated in philosophy with pragmatic notions about the foundations of knowledge and its uses.

This interpretation of Klaus's intellectual approach can be supported by reference to changes in his theoretical orientation and focus from a cognitive information-processing model to a behavioural analysis one around the time of his moving to the Institute of Education. His earlier work on perceptuo-motor difficulties, as illustrated in his book on the field, assumed some of the basic concepts of an information-processing model as it was developing in the early 1970s. This is a model which deals with underlying and directly unobservable processes and stages. It is the model which has grown and developed into one of the major approaches to psychology in those areas relating to the field of education: areas such as perception, attention, memory, reasoning, and so on. It is therefore interesting that Klaus had a part in leading other professional psychologists away from an information-processing framework towards a behavioural functional analysis one towards the end of the 1970s. Here was a situation in which research-based theoretical psychology was moving away from behaviourist models towards embracing mental processing models, while applied or professional psychologists were moving in the opposite direction.

There are several possible ways of understanding these differences in theoretical shifts. One relates to the different occupational interests of research and professional psychologists. Research-based psychologists are more interested in building general models based on group averages which relate to the individual as an instance of a generalisation. Professional psychologists need to have knowledge about individual cases, which does not fit easily into general cases based on group averages. This differing interest in the general versus the individual case – the nomothetic and the idiographic approaches – connects to basic questions in psychology and education. These relate to how far general concepts and models are relevant and useful in the individual practical case. In his 1973 book, Klaus discusses these different perspectives in terms of problems of prediction from general kinds of deficiencies in sensory and motor functioning to subsequent educational attainment of individual children. In this discussion, he refers to the compensatory potential of the child's assets and environmental supports. The idea was that poor prediction may arise from other factors which operate at an individual level and so call into question the focus on predictive factors operating across different individuals. Yet despite this switch from a general to an individual focus of analysis, he did recognise that interacting factors were likely to alter the effect of functional deficiencies mostly for moderate to mild deficiencies. He did acknowledge that more severe functional deficiencies affected subsequent performance generally across individuals. This is a significant point in that it shows where there is some link between general patterns and relationships and individual cases.

At that time, Klaus and others, who are referred to in Chapter 2 by Geoff Lindsay and Chapter 7 by Harry Daniels, also concluded from the research findings that interventions focused on altering deficiencies had negligible impact on educational attainments. The implication drawn from these reviews was that intervention was better directed at the attainments themselves. Klaus's theoretical change in focus from general functional or processing deficiencies to specific attainment outcomes could also be associated with two other developments: one with the wider climate of beliefs and values in the education world, and the other with the idiographic and intervention stance of a professional psychologist. He can be seen to have responded to these two aspects in a characteristically creative way.

What is interesting about his version of compensatory interaction is that he gave an idiographic rather than a nomothetic version of it. In his idiographic interpretation, the interaction is seen as the outcome of individual assets and deficiencies in a way particular to the individual child. This version assumes that there are no general patterns of interaction which can be identified in advance and then used to predict outcomes. Predictive failure is sensibly regarded as a poor basis for interventions if it is focused on factors which are not known to have a causal relation to educational attainments. Although this is wise from a practical intervention position, a lack of knowledge does not have to lead to forgoing the continuing search for knowledge of general interactive factors, the nomothetic version of interaction and the predictive project. The current work by Fawcett and Nicholson (1994) to identify underlying functional deficiencies of specific learning difficulties, referred to by Geoff Lindsay in Chapter 2, can be seen to illustrate this point. So does the growth in information-processing accounts of learning difficulties and the use of more sophisticated research designs to investigate the causal relationship between functional factors and subsequent attainments. These studies use multiple control group designs in order to exclude other possible interpretations of the functional differences. They also use predictive longitudinal designs to show that the identified factors do predict future learning outcomes, and then supplement this with experimental training studies.

The fact that Klaus moved away from the nomothetic processing approach might also be understood in terms of the influence of the wider social context of beliefs and values in the educational world. The 1960s and 1970s were a time in which there were widespread concerns about social disadvantage and discrimination in educational provision. IQ testing and psychometrics came under scrutiny as falsely identifying and labelling children, and therefore denying them appropriate opportunities for learning and achievement. The placement of children from disadvantaged and minority backgrounds in special education and the unjustified use of intervention programmes to remediate dysfunction were then matters of much concern. Identifying functional difficulties or deficiencies fell into disrepute as discriminatory. Doubts and scruples were experienced about focusing on what came to be called 'within-child' factors. Environmental factors which constrain and which might be altered came into focus as an improved and more effective way of helping children with SENs. There was, he contended, no longer any practical value in focusing on general deficiencies in planning individual learning programmes. The poor predictive validity of functional deficiencies for many individual cases could be attributed to the compensatory interaction with other child and environmental factors. His interest in and promotion of the interactionist model of causation can be seen to derive from his interpretation of these matters in the then current social and educational context.

There was a need amongst teachers and psychologists for an alternative positive approach which was found in the functional behavioural approach associated with Skinner. This was a theoretical model which defined general deficiencies out of existence by directing analysis to the behavioural level and the particular functional relationships between behaviour, its setting and consequences. Klaus was impressed by the positive aspects of the behavioural analysis approach, and as previous chapters mention, was strongly influential in promoting it and its practical consequences to educational psychologists in the Midlands and to teachers in London. He was rigorous and consistent in his endeavour to carry through the implications of this model. This was evident in his approach to the tasks of modifying the curriculum for special needs and to the assessment needed for planning individual teaching programmes. But Klaus's individual strategy for investigating and intervention was always one step ahead of the pre-packaged behavioural objectives and task analysis approaches available more widely. In Chapter 7, Harry Daniels discusses in more detail some of the issues connected with such individual teaching or intervention strategies.

Much of Klaus's teaching at the Institute of Education in London was concerned with promoting and refining this approach. In time, he came to make significant changes to what he called the 'strategy'. He embedded it more into the general curriculum and class teaching context, and considered whether intervention should be focused on the pupil or on changing the general teaching. He also came to include child factors into the strategy in so far as this would inform decisions about what methods would best promote progress towards the objectives. Part of this change involved accepting objectives which were not strictly behavioural in nature. These changes are interesting, as they show how Klaus began to realise the rigidities of the behavioural objectives approach and moved more towards a cognitive-behavioural strategy, even if he did not conceptualise it exactly in these theoretical terms. This meant that teaching objectives could be directed to cognitive prerequisites of curricular objectives. These prerequisites needed to be identified from analyses which were assumed to have some general applicability. This linked the 'strategy' back to general models and patterns.

It is interesting that his 'strategy' began in this move to accommodate interventions not dissimilar from the deficiency-focused programmes he was avoiding in the 1970s. In fact, he was aware in the conclusion of his 1973 book (Wedell, 1973, p.114) that the direct objectives and indirect, deficiency-focused approaches had practical similarities. He realised that working back by task analysis from what a child can and cannot do may lead to focusing on deficiencies as sub-objectives. These sub-objectives may be similar to the ones found as part of general programmes focused on deficiencies. Yet he noted then that one difference between these approaches was that the focus on deficiencies in task analysis was more limited than in the general programmes. Another was that there would be more emphasis on training for transfer in the task analysis approach. But he also recognised that some of these general programmes also stressed the importance of transfer training, much as the current general deficiency-focused programmes, like Feuerstein's Instrumental Enrichment, do (Feuerstein et al., 1980).

Although there are these practical similarities between the deficit-focused approach and the task-analytic one, the theoretical differences are important because they incline the practical approaches either more towards a focus on difficulties or more towards the intended learning outcome. It is clear that Klaus was more inclined towards the latter, and, as mentioned above, not just on the technical grounds of whether the presumed functional difficulties were alterable and whether changing these would have positive consequences for attainment. Doubts about the validity of identifying difficulties, and concerns about false and wasteful labelling, were growing in the 1960s and 1970s. His views were in line with this scepticism about the relevance of general kinds of dysfunctions as a relevant basis for planning teaching.

His 'strategy' focused on the individual, and was influenced by a general functional behavioural analysis approach. It was an approach opposed in principle to the use of generalisations and general schemes about learning difficulties, the fitting of pupils to general patterns. However, in practice, the application of the behavioural approach led to the developments of general sequences of learning objectives based on general kinds of task analyses. Klaus, however, stuck firmly to the principle of analysing difficulties in learning in individual terms. What was generally applicable for him was the process of investigating and intervention. The starting points were the curricular goals, and the process was one of working back from these. The general working assumption that deficiencies relevant to the setting of tasks or goals and applicable to the individual in question could be known in advance of this working-backwards process was unacceptable to him. So part of his idiographic approach was the inductive principle of identifying difficulties in the individual case. Less considered were the practicalities of conducting such a process across the curriculum for each pupil and for many pupils. Nor did he place much weight on the difference between using generalities simply and rigidly when applied in advance to cases of individual teaching and using generalities as flexible guides in the general planning of teaching.

This sceptical attitude to generalities about difficulties and his inclination to an idiographic approach could, as mentioned before, be linked to both his personal and wider social concerns about false and discriminatory attributions of deficiencies. It also found expression in his interpretation of the 1981 Education Act as abandoning categories of difficulties or handicap in favour of the special educational needs of individuals. The SEN orientation was towards goals and means of progressing towards them, not on the difficulties. From this perspective, the necessary special provision could not be identified in terms of general categories of difficulty, as individuals do not simply follow general patterns, on account of the interaction of child and environmental factors. This perspective also connects with his promotion of the concept of SEN as relative. The 'relativity' of special needs can be understood partly in terms of how what is needed depends on the goals of provision. Therefore, changing the goal may mean altering or no longer having the SEN. In this sense, SEN is curriculum-specific or dependent. 'Relative' can also mean that the effect of a pupil's difficulties on his or her learning depended on the pupils' other learning characteristics and features of their learning environment. Knowledge about general difficulties therefore needed to be considered in the context of these other factors. In some situations, these factors could compensate interactively with the difficulties, thus his use of the concept of 'compensatory interaction'. But, as mentioned above, there is nothing about the interactionist concept which requires its exclusively idiographic-individualist use and interpretation. Nor are all interactions likely to be compensatory, as we know in practice of interactions between several difficulties which are aggravating, rather than compensatory. Therefore, what is not at issue is the critical role of child and environmental factors in the interactive origins of difficulties in learning, nor the significance of learning context and values. What *is* at issue is whether we can be justified in drawing out general features of similarity between individuals who experience difficulties in learning, and whether we can do this in a way which recognises and preserves the individuality of each learner.

Another significant change in Klaus's interests arose from his appointment as professor responsible for special educational needs at the Institute. As several chapters in this volume show, he became very involved and influential in policy and curriculum matters. This extension of his range of interests would be expected – some would say required – of someone interested in special needs education and not just educational psychology. This involved Klaus in mapping out with colleagues the range of topics which related to special needs education – topics concerned with curriculum modification and management, the organisation and development of services, inter-service and inter-professional collaboration, legislative and policy developments, the position of parents in services, and so on. Although Klaus continued to maintain his interest in and develop his individual teaching 'strategy', his interests moved substantively away from explicit developments of psychological thinking and practices. Of course, in this move he continued to draw on his extensive knowledge and understanding of psychological theoretical models, methods and practices.

This move is worthy of comment, as it illustrates the interesting relationship between psychology and special needs education. In higher education, there has been a tendency for psychologists – especially professional psychologists – to move into the special needs education field, and often, in the process, to leave behind significant aspects of their psychology. One possible explanation of this might be the relatively under-developed nature of special needs studies and courses in higher education until recently, and the gap in relevant experience of research and theory amongst special education teachers. Although this trend is less evident now than ten years ago, the effect was to leave professional psychology in education without a key leader like Klaus.

The role of professional educational psychologists like Klaus in special needs education raises long-standing and continuing questions about the relationship between psychology and special needs education. This is clearly part of the wider question of the inter-relationship between psychology and education. One way of considering this is in terms of the respective professional positions of psychologists and special needs teachers in their various specific roles, as trainers, advisers, interveners, researchers and theorisers. Another way is in terms of the relationships between the different kinds of psychology and special needs education. This is a complex two-way relationship which involves psychology as theory, knowledge and research skills and as an applied professional service, and special needs education as teaching practices at different levels and positions in the service and as practical knowledge and understanding. These relationships are changing, and continue to need to be clarified and further developed. It has been one of the main aims of this edited volume to bring together various contributions linked to Klaus Wedell's work in order to further our knowledge and understanding of special needs education and educational psychology, and their interdependent relationship. This seems to be a fitting way to honour the work of Klaus Wedell.

Postscript

Ingrid Lunt

My contacts with Klaus began when I moved to the Institute of Education in 1985 to take over as course tutor for the course of professional training for educational psychologists. Having held the same post in Birmingham for a number of years, Klaus was immensely supportive, encouraging and generous with his time and wise counsel when I was invited to restructure the course at the Institute. His sense of humour, integrity and humility and his clear thinking and ability to see through obstacles and get to the root of problems were of considerable help to me at the time. We worked together closely again, he as Chair and I as Deputy Chair of the Department of Educational Psychology and Special Educational Needs. It has been a great privilege to work closely with Klaus as colleague over the past ten years, and I am grateful to him for encouraging me in many opportunities and challenges which I am sure I would never have grasped without his support and inspiration.

Brahm Norwich

I first met Klaus when he had just started at the Institute and I was working as an educational psychologist in London. I came to work at the Institute with him in the early 1980s, at the time he started up the SEN Masters course at the Institute and when I became the course tutor to this course. I remember fondly how I considered myself fortunate to work with him: his thoughtful and analytic approach to matters, his encouragement, his vision and sense of importance about what he was doing. Like others, I learned much from him and am very grateful for that. I feel that he engendered a sense of intellectual and professional significance to the special needs educational field. For someone who works in higher education, this is a considerable achievement.

References

Bowman, I. (1986) 'Training and the integration of handicapped pupils: Some findings from a fourteen nation UNESCO study', *European Journal of Special Needs Education*, 1(1), pp.29–39.

Department of Education & Science (DES) (1978) *Special Educational Needs: Report of the Committee of Inquiry into the Education of Handicapped Children and Young People* (The Warnock Report), Cmnd 7212, London: HMSO.

Department of Education & Science (DES) (1983) *The Inservice Teacher Training Grants Scheme, Circular 3/83*, London: DES.

Evans, P., Ireson, J., Redmond, P. & Wedell, K. (1990) *Pathways to Progress: Developing an Approach to Teaching the National Curriculum to Children Experiencing Difficulties in Learning in the Primary School*, London: Institute of Education.

Evans, J., Everard, K., Friend, J., Glaser, A. & Norwich, B. (1989) *Decision-making for Special Needs: An Inter-service Resource Pack*, London: Institute of Education.

Fawcett, A. & Nicolson, R. (1994) 'Computer-based diagnosis of dyslexia', in C. Singleton (ed.) *Computers and Dyslexia*, Hull: Dyslexia Computer Resource Centre.

Feuerstein, R., Rand, Y. & Hoffman, M.B. (1980) *Instrumental Enrichment: An Intervention for Cognitive Modifiability*, Baltimore University Park Press.

Goacher, B., Evans, J., Welton, J. & Wedell, K. (1988) *Policy and Provision for Special Educational Needs*, London: Cassell.

Inner London Education Authority (ILEA) (1985) *Educational Opportunities for All?* (The Fish Report), London.

Wedell, K. (1973) *Learning and Perceptuo-motor Disabilities in Children*, London: John Wiley.

Wedell, K. & Lambourne, R. (1980) 'Psychological services for children in England and Wales', *DECP Occasional Papers*, 4(1) and (2), pp.1–84.

Wedell, K. & Lindsay, G. (1980) 'Early identification procedures: What have we learned?', *Remedial Education*, 15, pp.130–5.

Index

DEAFNESS, CHILDREN AND THE FAMILY

A GUIDE TO PROFESSIONAL PRACTICE
. . . .

Jennifer Densham

This is a research based book intended for professionals in medical, educational, health and social work fields who come into contact with deaf children and their families. Many of the issues raised also have implications for professionals working with parents of children with other forms of disability.

The book illustrates the need for change in some professional practice, and focuses attention on those areas where change may be effected. It covers the impact of deafness, parental reactions to diagnosis, attitudes of professionals and their affect on the communication, education and integration of deaf children, and emotional implications in terms of stigma, self-esteem and socialization.

Jennifer Densham is a freelance lecturer and consultant, and a research supervisor for the University of Hertfordshire, with a small private counselling practice.

1995   224 pages   Hbk   1 85742 221 X   £32.50
Price subject to change without notification

arena

The Children Act *1989* :
Putting it into Practice
Mary Ryan

This book provides a practical guide to those parts of the Children Act 1989 that relate to the provision of services by local authorities to children and families; the powers and duties of local authorities in such circumstances; care and supervision proceedings; and child protection issues.

The book is a unique combination of information on the legal framework contained in the Act, regulations and guidance and information on good social work and legal practice, relevant research and recent case law. It is grounded on the author's practical experience of providing an advice and advocacy service for families; providing training for social workers, lawyers and other child care professionals; being involved with the development of the legislation from the consultation period in the early 1980s, through the parliamentary process, and the subsequent consultation on regulations, guidance and court rules.

Mary Ryan, the Co-Director of the Family Rights Group, is a solicitor who after working in private practice as a family lawyer, was the Family Rights Group's legal advisor for 10 years.

1994   256 pages

Hbk   1 85742 192 2   **£30.00   Pbk   1 85742 193 0   £14.95**

Price subject to change without notification

arena

GOLDMINE

Finding free and low-cost resources for teaching

1995–1996

Compiled by David Brown

"It can be highly recommended because the choice of subjects, the organisation of the entries, and an index make a mass of information very easily accessible. Having used this directory to acquire resources for a couple of ad hoc topic areas, I can confidently state that it works - with ease and practicability. In the saving of teachers' time, let alone in access to materials, it really is a goldmine. I would advise any school to acquire this book. The title of the book is wholly accurate and the outlay is modest compared with the returns." **School Librarian**

David Brown has been teaching in primary, middle and secondary schools for 23 years. It was through David's need to find resources within a limited school budget that he began to uncover a wealth of low-cost, good quality material which was just what he was looking for.

Goldmine places these resources into topic areas, describes them and tells you where you can get them from. Since the first edition in 1985, **Goldmine** has developed into the country's leading directory of free and sponsored teaching resources, providing the wherewithal to obtain over 6000 resources from some 235 suppliers.

Budget-conscious schools will find it saves its purchase price many times over, and parents and teachers are safe in the knowledge that all the items described in here ar personally recommended by a teacher, the compiler himself.

1995   329 pages   1 85742 137 X   £15.00

Price subject to change without notification

arena

50 POPULAR TOPICS

A resources directory for schools

Compiled by David Brown

You are resourcing a topic, and you don't know who publishes what. The school doesn't have all the publishers catalogues you need, and you don't have addresses for those you haven't got.

THE RESOURCES DIRECTORY has been compiled to solve all these problems. The 50 most popular primary and secondary school topics are included with a huge range of books, videos, software, kits, packs, equipment and schemes for all ages between 5 and 13.

Over 2500 items from 50 suppliers are included, together with their addresses, all grouped in topics, cross-referenced in a comprehensive index and with an appendix of schemes in science, technology, geography and history.

David Brown is a schoolteacher with over 20 years teaching experience in primary, middle and secondary schools. He is also author of 'GOLDMINE', published by Arena.

1995   201 pages   1 85742 163 9   £15.00

arena